About this Book

This book is an up-to-date examination of recent experience in seeking to regulate large corporations. At a time when the gigantic transnationals have a huge impact on human health, the environment, working conditions and the economic prospects of nations, this book explores whether it is sufficient to continue relying only on industry self-regulation.

Keeping a focus on the general issues involved, the author examines the now famous case of the infant food industry. The WHO/Unicef Code of Marketing of Breastmilk Substitutes was introduced as long ago as 1981 to prevent socially irresponsible marketing. Yet still today an estimated one and a half million babies die unnecessarily as a result of mothers abandoning breastfeeding and using formula milk instead. How effective, therefore, has the Code been in changing industry behaviour?

The author argues that a key question now is how we can foster a political climate favourable to practical institutional arrangements for the better international regulation of TNCs. Recognizing the tension between global rule-setting on the one hand, and the globalized free market on the other, she urges that close attention be given to what corporations actually do and their compliance with what regulatory codes exist. She explores a range of relevant questions, including what constructive roles national governments, international agencies and citizen networks can play.

A host of public concerns – for example, job losses when industries migrate or the introduction of GM crops without public consultation – point to corporate regulation as a long-neglected political issue. This book contributes to the debate by questioning current over-reliance on promises of corporate responsibility and arguing instead for democratic control over corporations in order to make them socially accountable.

About the Author

Judith Richter was born in Germany. She is a sociologist specializing in international development and a registered pharmacist. She is also trained in ethics in the sciences and humanities. She has lived and worked in a number of countries. Her experiences with pharmaceutical TNCs as a staff member of a Thai consumer protection group in the late 1980s led her to write an MA in development studies on the use of corporate public relations as a tool of power. Since 1991 she has worked as a freelance researcher, writer and lecturer, and more recently as a consultant for UN agencies such as UNICEF and WHO. Much of her work over the last fifteen years has centred on the social, political and ethical aspects of communication and democratic decision-making, infant feeding, pharmaceutical policies and contraceptive research.

She is also actively involved in various social movements, including Health Action International (HAI) and the Women's Global Network for Reproductive Rights (WGNRR).

Her previous book was *Vaccination Against Pregnancy: Miracle or Menace?* (Zed Books, London and Spinifex Press, Melbourne, 1996).

Holding Corporations Accountable:
Corporate Conduct, International Codes
and Citizen Action

Judith Richter

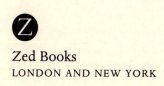

Zed Books
LONDON AND NEW YORK

Holding Corporations Accountable: Corporate Conduct, International Codes and Citizen Action was first published by Zed Books Ltd, 7 Cynthia Street, London N1 9JF, UK and Room 400, 175 Fifth Avenue, New York, NY 10010, USA in 2001.

Distributed in the USA exclusively by Palgrave, a division of St Martin's Press, LLC, 175 Fifth Avenue, New York, NY 10010, USA

The material in this book was commissioned by the United Nations Children's Fund (UNICEF) but does not necessarily reflect the policies and views of UNICEF.

Sales number E.01.XX.2

Cover designed by Andrew Corbett
Set in Monotype Dante by Ewan Smith, London
Printed and bound in the United Kingdom by Biddles Ltd,
Guildford and King's Lynn

A catalogue record for this book is available from the British Library.

Library of Congress Cataloging-in-Publication Data: applied for

ISBN 1 85649 983 9 cased
ISBN 1 85649 984 7 limp

Contents

Boxes and Table

Boxes

Table

Acknowledgements

Numerous people have contributed their thoughts, information and support to this book. I can name only a few, but others should feel included too.

My foremost thanks go to Eva Jespersen and David Clark, my project supervisors at UNICEF New York, for their support and guidance since 1998, when the idea of this study as part of the UNICEF project Children in a Globalizing World was born. Backed by their economic and legal expertise respectively, I felt safe in venturing into fresh pastures in the field of regulation of transnational corporations. It was a privilege and a pleasure working with them.

I am also grateful for the feedback and advice I received at the four UNICEF review meetings since the project's inception from staff from UNICEF headquarters and regional offices as well as the experts invited from various academic institutions and non-governmental and governmental organizations. Thanks go to the commentators, Roger Shrimpton, Harris Gleckman, Giovanni Andrea Cornia and Joanne Csete, for steering the project in exciting new directions.

Annelies Allain, Alison Linnecar, Jan Nederveen Pieterse, Nancy-Jo Peck, Peter Utting and David Westendorff greatly helped me by reading various versions or parts of the manuscript. Without the material collected over the years by UNICEF staff and members of the International Baby Food Action Network I could not have written this book. Special thanks go to Annelies Allain and Mike Brady for searching their files and patiently answering numerous questions.

Lída Lhotská and Helen Armstrong guided me through the intricacies of breast-feeding, Meri Koivusalo shared her knowledge on world trade issues, Sami Shubber answered my queries on the early Code debate and Paolo Giovine those on US politics, while Monika Bobbert, Uta Eser, Sigrid Grauman, Gotlind Ulshöfer, Micha Werner and Lars Thielman gave most helpful feedback on ethical issues pertinent to the topic of this study. Pascale Brudon, Peter Crawley, Nick Drager, Daphne Fresle, Harris Gleckman, Tony Hill, Gabriele Köhler,

Sandrine Monbaron, Ludger Odenthal, Jonathan Quick, Marta Santos Pais, Karl Sauvant, Myriam vander Stichele, Peter Utting, German Velasquez and Derek Yach granted me interviews on various aspects of corporate regulation. I thank them all for sharing their ideas. The responsibility for any shortcomings, however, is wholly mine.

Final thanks must go to Sarah Sexton. She not only transformed my German sentences into reasonably digestible pieces but, once again, greatly contributed to this book with her considerable editing skills and her thorough knowledge of development issues. Robert Molteno and the production team from Zed Books most patiently nursed the manuscript into book form. Patricia Lone and Jaclyn Tierney supported the process from UNICEF's side. My heartfelt thanks to them, and also to Willis Demas, Betsy Morriss and Susan Nurmi-Schomers for their support whenever it was needed.

Abbreviations and Acronyms

AIDS	acquired immune deficiency syndrome
BFHI	Baby-Friendly Hospital Initiative
BINGOs	business interest NGOs
CEDAW	UN Convention on the Elimination of All Forms of Discrimination Against Women
CI	Consumers International (formerly IOCU)
CRC	UN Convention on the Rights of the Child
CSO	civil society organization
ECOSOC	UN Economic and Social Council
FAO	UN Food and Agriculture Organization
GATT	General Agreement on Tariffs and Trade
GSP	generalized system of preferences
HAI	Health Action International
HIV	human immunodeficiency virus
IBFAN	International Baby Food Action Network
ICC	International Chamber of Commerce
ICCR	Interfaith Centre on Corporate Responsibility
ICDC	International Code Documentation Centre
ICIFI	International Council of Infant Food Industries
IFM	International Association of Infant Food Manufacturers
IFPMA	International Federation of Pharmaceutical Manufacturers Associations
IGBM	Interagency Group on Breastfeeding Monitoring
ILO	International Labour Organization
INBC	International Nestlé Boycott Coordinating Committee
INFACT	Infant Formula Action Coalition
IOCU	International Organization of Consumers Unions (now CI)
IOMS	International Organizations Monitoring Service
ISDI	International Society of Dietetic Food Industries
ISO	International Organization for Standardization Setting
MAI	Multilateral Agreement on Investment
NCCN	Nestlé Coordination Centre for Nutrition

NGO	non-governmental organization
NIEO	New International Economic Order
NIFAC	Nestlé Infant Formula Commission
OECD	Organisation for Economic Co-operation and Development
PAN	Pesticide Action Network
PHC	primary health care
PINGOs	public interest NGOs
PR	public relations
SAP	structural adjustment programme
SIDA	Swedish International Development Agency
SLAPPs	Strategic Lawsuits Against Public Participation
TNC	transnational corporation
UN	United Nations
UNAIDS	Joint United Nations Programme on HIV/AIDS
UNCED	UN Conference on Environment and Development
UNCTAD	UN Conference on Trade and Development
UNCTC	UN Centre on Transnational Corporations
UNDP	UN Development Programme
UNICEF	UN Children's Fund
UN PAG	UN Protein Advisory Group
UNRISD	UN Research Institute for Social Development
USAID	United States Agency for International Development
WABA	World Alliance for Breastfeeding Action
WBCSD	World Business Council for Sustainable Development
WEDO	Women's Environment and Development Organization
WHO	World Health Organization
WHA	World Health Assembly
WTO	World Trade Organization

TO NANCY-JO PECK
(1943–2001)
whose commitment, warmth and humour
helped make this world a better place

Globalization and Infant Feeding

> To protect and promote people's health in a global eco-
> nomy we need new rules, stronger regulatory frameworks,
> scientifically sound norms and standards. (Tomris Türmen,
> senior policy adviser to the director-general, WHO, 1999)[1]

§ 'Globalization' seems to be a concise term, but it is in fact a manifold and elusive concept for which there is no single definition. According to sociologist Anthony Giddens, 'there are few key terms as frequently used and as poorly conceptualized as globalization' (quoted in UNRISD 1997: 4). Giddens defines globalization as 'the intensification of world-wide social relations which link distant localities in such a way that local happenings are shaped by events many miles away and vice versa' (Giddens 1990: 64).

According to political sociologist David Held, who develops Giddens's definition, globalization processes have at least two distinct dimensions: a spatial one, suggesting that 'many chains of political, economic and social activity are becoming international and intercontinental in scope', and a time dimension, suggesting 'that there has been an intensification of levels of interaction and interconnectedness within and between states and societies' (Held 1998: 13).[2]

Despite the lack of agreement on a clear definition, several aspects of globalization can be considered: the internationalization of economy and finance; the expansion of technologies, particularly communication and information technologies; and the contraction of space for democratic decision-making and social welfare as the role and significance of the nation-state changes. A key question raised by all the economic and political changes over the past 30 years that come under the rubric of globalization is how to influence those practices of transnational corporations (TNCs) that conflict with societal well-being.

Globalization would seem to have little to do with infant and child nutrition. Infant feeding, especially in the first few months of a child's life, is by and large an extremely 'local' activity. Most mothers, wherever they are in the world, can provide their infants with the best possible nourishment: their breast-milk.

It is the replacement of breast-feeding by commercial infant foods, however, that is relevant to globalization and TNC practices. Long before the term globalization came into vogue, concern that the aggressive marketing of infant formula was undermining breast-feeding led to the first code of conduct aimed at regulating internationally the activities of a whole industry sector: the International Code of Marketing of Breast-milk Substitutes, which was adopted in 1981 by the World Health Assembly, the World Health Organization's governing body, and endorsed by the Executive Board of the United Nations Children's Fund a few months later. Efforts over more than two decades to rein in the marketing practices of infant food manufacturers worldwide represent one of the longest-standing attempts at international regulation of a particular industry practice.

The stakes are high: it is estimated that the lives of one and a half million infants could be saved each year if they were adequately breast-fed rather than artificially fed, while many poor households could save their scarce monetary resources for other essential needs. The stakes are also high for the infant food industry. The worldwide market for breast-milk substitutes is a huge and increasingly competitive one. In 1997, it was estimated to be worth at least US$6 billion.[3]

The process by which the 1981 International Code of Marketing of Breast-milk Substitutes was formulated, adopted and implemented is relevant to any study of global governance and TNC regulation. The Code is one of the few international codes adopted under the aegis of the United Nations at a time when the need for effective external regulation of TNCs was fully recognized. Twenty years after the adoption of the Code by the 1981 World Health Assembly and the UNICEF Executive Board as a minimum standard, 21 countries have enacted national laws based on the entirety of the Code. Many other countries still fall short on the commitments made by their representatives at the time.

Thus the effective regulation of the infant food industry, and of transnational corporations in general, remains a critical – and unfinished – task of global democratic governance. As a case study, it is relevant not only to the protection of infants from the potential harms caused by the inappropriate marketing of breast-milk sub-stitutes, bottles and teats. It also highlights important issues for current attempts to establish effective checks and balances on corporate activities that conflict with fundamental human rights and other social concerns in an increasingly globalizing world. Analysis of the roles that transnational corporations and civil society organizations have played in the international debate on the socially responsible marketing of breast-milk substitutes is also relevant to these attempts.

Chapter 1 provides a brief historical overview of efforts to hold corporations accountable to society by means of regulation. It describes how the approach of controlling the commercial sector by external, binding regulation has gradually been replaced by that of allowing the sector to regulate itself. The chapter outlines commonly accepted justifications of market regulation at the national level and contrasts them with current debates about the need and feasibility of establishing a coherent, international regulatory regime for trans-national corporations.

Chapter 2 looks at two common features of contemporary global governance discourse: the categorization of commercial actors as non-governmental or civil society organizations; and the perception that consensus-oriented 'dialogues' and 'cooperation' between 'partners' are the most appropriate way to set global rules. It argues for a clear distinction between citizen groups and alliances and business associ-ations, and for an analysis of international regulatory efforts as con-tested processes between specific actors with specific power resources.

Chapter 3 outlines how and why the marketing practices of the infant food industry came under a critical spotlight during the 1970s, and why various actors believed these practices had to be regulated at an international level. It describes how the issue was placed on the international policy agenda.

Chapter 4 describes the debates about how to develop a code of conduct to regulate the infant food industry's marketing practices and what form it should take. It details the political processes surrounding the formulation and adoption of the International Code of Marketing of Breast-milk Substitutes and illustrates how they led to the adoption of a Code with less precise wording and a weaker legal form than it could have had. The study continues with an analysis of developments since the Code's adoption in 1981 by the World Health Assembly.

Chapter 5 considers the Code's implementation in detail. It describes the challenges encountered in translating it into effective national measures and how they are being overcome. It suggests further exploration of the links between international regulation and human rights as a means of ensuring the social accountability of transnational corporations.

Chapter 6 analyses whether or not changes in the marketing practices of the infant food industry since 1981 demonstrate greater social responsibility on the part of industry. It questions the appropriateness of industry self-regulation in critical areas such as the health, growth and survival of infants. It also describes why the discovery in the late 1980s that the human immunodeficiency virus (HIV) can be transmitted via breast-milk has made the regulation of the marketing of breast-milk substitutes even more critical than ever.

Chapter 7 looks at the behaviour of the infant food industry in relation to efforts to establish national legislation based on the International Code and subsequent World Health Assembly resolutions. Both Chapters 6 and 7 reveal a great gap between industry statements of corporate responsibility and actual practices. The latter clarifies the responsibilities for Code implementation and monitoring and argues that 'freedom of commercial speech' is not an inalienable right. It concludes that overcoming industry opposition to Code implementation is possible as long as national authorities demonstrate sufficient political will and are supported by international agencies and civil society groups.

Chapter 8 takes a broader look at how transnational corporations influence world politics. It examines the development and use of corporate public relations – specifically international issues management or 'engineering of consent' – as a concealed instrument of corporate power that is used to influence legislation and political processes. The chapter points out how so-called dialogues and public–private partnerships are used to further corporate interests. If debates about the regulation of the infant food and other industries are to progress, it is argued, attention must be paid to regaining spaces for public, democratic decision-making in the face of the TNCs' increasingly influential corporate public relations and lobbying machinery.

Chapter 9 provides some insights into the involvement of international civil society organizations, in particular the International Baby Food Action Network (IBFAN), in the infant feeding debate over the past two decades. After some brief reflections on the civil society discourse in relation to citizen alliances, it explores the role of so-called single-issue networks in national and international regulatory efforts, and their impact in terms of public awareness-raising, agenda-setting and influencing corporate practices. It calls for increased efforts to create the institutional arrangements and political climate that would allow citizen groups, state authorities and UN agencies to deal more effectively with corporate malpractice and power.

Chapter 10 draws out some of the lessons learned by inter-governmental, governmental and civil society actors over the past two decades as they have attempted to regulate the marketing practices of the infant food industry effectively. These lessons are relevant to any effort to make transnational corporations more accountable to the citizens of the world. They include the following needs: to reassess the trend away from externally binding regulation; to explore how balances of power can and should be shifted back in favour of such regulation; to re-value the role of conflict in public policy-making; and to make a clear committment to democratic decision-making.

The most crucial ingredients in any attempt to curb corporate power, as evidenced by the struggle over the past two decades or so to rein in the infant food industry, are lucid analysis, principled and concerted action, and the courage and stamina to continue raising controversial issues if the public interest so requires.

Notes

1. Türmen 1999: 9.

2. Held stresses that 'globalization is neither a singular condition nor a linear process. Rather, it is best thought of as a multidimensional phenom-enon involving diverse domains of activity and interaction, including the economic, political, technological, military, legal, cultural and environmental' (Held 1998: 13). For an overview of 'globalizations in the plural' and various definitions of globalization from different academic disciplines, see Nederveen Pieterse 1994: 161–2.

3. Estimate by the *Financial Times*, 9 January 1997, quoted in Shubber 1998: 51. This may, however, be an underestimate. For the difficulties of calculating the value of the global infant food market, ses Chapter 6.

CHAPTER I

Regulation of Transnational Corporations: A Historical Perspective

Historically, progress associated with corporate social and environmental responsibility has been driven, to a large extent, by state regulation, collective bargaining and civil society activism. Increasing reliance on voluntary initiatives may be undermining these drivers of corporate responsibility. Such initiatives are often presented as effective alternatives to state regulation, when in fact their success in industrialized countries has often involved an important regulatory component. (Peter Utting, coordinator of UNRISD Project on Business Responsibility for Sustainable Development, 2000)

National Regulation of Corporations

Regulation – the establishment and implementation of rules-based regimes – has long been used to ensure that corporations are accountable to society at large. A historical overview of such regulation provides a useful background to this analysis of the regulation of the infant food industry. It illustrates the changing fortunes of, on the one hand, the strategy of influencing the commercial sector by means of external, binding regulation and, on the other, that of allowing the sector to regulate itself.

The notion that corporations should be subject to democratic control is not new. Early industrial enterprises in the USA, for example, were kept under close citizen and state control by means of corporate charters. These charters set out not only the privileges accorded to the corporations but also certain obligations. Charters often included revocation clauses giving state legislators the right to withdraw a charter if a corporation did not serve the public interest.

In the nineteenth century, however, corporations managed through various legal means to curtail or abolish the right of individual US states to amend or revoke their charters. The Supreme Court ruled in 1886 that corporations were 'natural persons' under the US Constitution and thereby 'entitled to the protections of the Bill of Rights, including the right to free speech and other constitutional protections extended to individuals'. This ruling overturned the concept that corporations were simply legal entities whose right to make profit was granted only on condition that they served the public interest. Instead 'corporations finally claimed full rights enjoyed by citizens while being exempted from many of the responsibilities and liabilities of citizenship' (Korten 1995: 59).

Other countries preferred the notion of an 'artificial person' to that of an anthropomorphized corporate citizen. In being accorded the status of 'legal personality', 'corporations are legally deemed to be single entities, distinct and separate from all the individuals who compose them. Legal personality means that corporations can sue and be sued, hold property and transact, and incur criminal liability in their own name and on their own account' (Wells 1998: 653).

Whatever their legal status, the question of how to ensure that corporations benefit society to the maximum – or at least that they do little or no harm – remains a key one all over the world. In most democratic countries today, a web of government regulations has evolved over the years to protect workers, consumers and society more generally and to guarantee their rights in law: for example, legislation on minimum wages and occupational health; on equal pay for women and on maternity leave; on product safety and advertising; and on environmental protection. More often than not, however, state authorities have been pressed into action by citizens:

> It should ... be noted that in none of these domains was national regulatory protection easily or completely achieved. The worker struggle was a century in the making in the developed world and continues in the less developed world. Women's rights and consumer rights, also the focus of decades-long struggle, are not yet secure. Environmental regulation, the newest 'global' social issue, has required decades of efforts by environmental organizations and activists. (Gleckman and Krut 1994: 20)[1]

The actual content and coverage of regulations, as well as measures to ensure that they are implemented effectively, may vary from country to country. But while national regulatory regimes are often anything but perfect, there is at least in most industrial countries a set of 'minimum standards which cannot be infringed upon without invoking substantial judicial response and public reaction' (Gleckman and Krut 1994: 20).

International Regulation of Transnational Corporations

As more and more corporations have expanded their operations over the past 30 years beyond national borders, the ability of an individual state to hold corporations accountable for their activities and to safeguard public interests through national regulation alone has substantially diminished. Recognizing this, developing countries and civil action groups have demanded a strong international regulatory regime to hold transnational corporations (TNCs) accountable to citizens wherever they operate in the world. But no effective and consistent web of binding laws and standards at the international level has emerged as yet, largely because of several changes over the past three decades in international economic and political spheres.

These changes took place in several phases.[2] During the 1970s, there were intense debates within various UN fora on the need to regulate corporations. Forceful opposition to binding industry regulation emerged in the 1980s as neoliberal economic theory and policies began to take hold. In the early 1990s, the impetus for industry regulation shifted from the UN to the business and NGO community. And finally, coming full circle, there was a resurgence at the end of the 1990s of calls from within the UN for universal standards governing corporate conduct – opinions differ, however, as to how these standards might best be implemented.

Moreover, a new global actor entered the regulatory stage in the 1990s: the World Trade Organization, whose activities may result in the de-regulation and down-regulation of existing internationally agreed standards in the name of 'free' trade.

The 1970s: Calls for a New International Economic Order

The current debate on the international regulation of transnational corporations dates back to the late 1960s and early 1970s, an era marked by calls from within the United Nations not only for comprehensive international regulatory regimes, but also for a radical restructuring of what was perceived as an unjust world economic order.

At this time, many former colonies had recently achieved independence and were deliberating how best to promote national economic development. The Group of 77 – a coalition of 77 developing countries – was formed at the 1964 United Nations Conference on Trade and Development (UNCTAD) to promote an international agenda and structure more responsive to their needs. Nationalization of TNC subsidiaries and plantations was part of this agenda.

A key year was 1972. In that year, Chile's President Salvador Allende alerted the General Assembly of the United Nations to plans of the International Telegraph and Telephone Company (ITT) and the Kenneth Copper Corporation to overthrow his government with the help of the US government.[3] In the same year, the first calls for international codes of conduct for TNCs were made at the UNCTAD Conference in Santiago (Hoogvelt with Puxty 1987: 42).

President Allende's violent death in a CIA-supported military coup a year later is rarely mentioned in histories of corporate regulation, yet it contributed significantly to the success of the lobby for UN codes of conduct as part of a programme for a New International Economic Order (NIEO) (Kline 2000: 43, 45).

The UN Economic and Social Council (ECOSOC) set up the UN Commission on Transnational Corporations, with the UN Centre on Transnational Corporations (UNCTC) as its special research and administrative body. This centre was entrusted with three basic tasks:

1. to monitor and provide reports on the activities of TNCs;
2. to strengthen the capacity of developing countries in dealing with TNCs; and
3. to draft proposals for normative frameworks for the activities of TNCs.[4]

In 1976, the UN Commission on Transnational Corporations made the formulation, adoption and implementation of a draft UN Code of Conduct on Transnational Corporations one of its top priorities. UNCTAD, meanwhile, began the coordination of negotiations for an International Code of Conduct on the Transfer of Technology. Discussions on both codes progressed slowly, however, partly because of the magnitude of the task and partly because of the widely diverging views of the different actors involved.[5]

The 1980s: Opposition to Regulation

By the early 1980s, the tide had started to turn against the regulation of TNCs. The election of influential conservative political leaders, particularly Ronald Reagan in the USA and Margaret Thatcher in the United Kingdom, introduced an era of international economic policy-making based on a neoliberal economic framework that continues today:

> As the world's largest source of Foreign Direct Investment, the United States became the leading opponent of efforts to control TNCs. In accordance with neoliberal textbook economic reasoning, the US position contended that outcomes of international trade and investment generally need to be market driven in order to maximise welfare and that interventionist policies in trade and investment would reduce global welfare. Consequently the very merit of an international code of conduct for TNCs was questioned. (Hansen 1999: 5)

The neoliberal credo of 'liberalization', de-regulation and privatization – in development circles known as the Washington Consensus – spread all over the world.[6] Proponents of the New International Economic Order, including various UN agencies, were sidelined. By the mid-1980s, efforts to draw up a UN Code of Conduct for TNCs had been more or less abandoned. The Code's official demise came in 1992, when the president of the UN General Assembly reported that 'no consensus was possible ... at present' and that 'delegations felt that the changed international environment and the importance attached to encouraging foreign investment required a fresh approach' (Samir Shihabi, quoted in *Transnationals* 1992: 1).[7] Negotiations on the International Code on Transfer of Technology had already been abandoned in 1985.

Indeed, few of the 30 or so international codes and guidelines envisioned during the 1970s were actually adopted. They include the 1981 International Code of Marketing of Breast-milk Substitutes; the 1985 UN Guidelines for Consumer Protection; the 1985 FAO International Code of Conduct on the Distribution and Use of Pesticides; and the 1988 WHO Ethical Criteria for Medicinal Drug Promotion. Even these frameworks would have been abandoned had it not been for continuous pressure from international citizen networks.[8]

The Early 1990s: Corporate Self-regulation and Co-regulation

One of the last attempts to introduce international corporate regulation via the UN was made at the 1992 UN Conference on Environment and Development (UNCED) – the 'Earth Summit' – held in Rio de Janeiro.

The UN Centre on Transnational Corporations drafted recommendations for environmental regulation of TNCs in the expectation that they would be included in UNCED's policy recommendations, or *Agenda 21*, as its global plan of action became known. But a coalition of Western industrial states and an organized industry lobby managed to get the UNCTC recommendations removed from the draft agenda. Instead, the UNCED secretary-general, Canadian businessman Maurice Strong, invited the newly formed Business Council for Sustainable Development to write the recommendations on industry and sustainable development. What remained of the coherent and comprehensive framework for TNC environmental regulation were a few ambiguous, non-binding recommendations scattered throughout the final 500-page document. The fact that the elimination of the UNCTC's draft chapter on the environmental responsibility of TNCs more or less coincided with the dismantling of the Centre by the United Nations secretary-general caused an uproar in the environmental NGO community, which regarded both as evidence of the capture of the UN by business interests (Greer and Bruno 1996: 24; Hansen 1999: 6, 7).

In 1995, one more attempt to advocate a coherent model of regulation for TNCs was made at the World Summit for Social Development held in Copenhagen. But just as at the Earth Summit, the idea of introducing binding externally defined norms for TNC conduct was abandoned in the face of industry pressure and assertions that business would behave in a more socially responsible manner in future and would regulate itself by means of guidelines, standards for good corporate practice and other so-called voluntary initiatives.

In hindsight, the 1992 Earth Summit can be seen as the beginning of what US consumer policy researcher Michael Hansen terms a 'regulatory vacuum' at the UN level. It marked a turning point in the emergence of other regulatory models. Industry bodies have repeatedly opposed external international regulation and have increasingly advocated industry self-regulation (or certification by private bodies), arguing that this is as effective as external regulation and significantly cheaper for society.

Nevertheless, some civil society organizations (CSOs) have continued to demand regulation that is independent of industry. Others have accepted and cooperated in industry self-regulation, or have initiated co-regulation between themselves and corporations in a variety of fields.[9] Those who support co-regulatory models tend to believe that corporations will keep their promises to behave in a more socially responsible manner, or that co-regulation is the most pragmatic approach at present.

Many governments, meanwhile, particularly those of poorer countries, have for various reasons given up their demands for international regulation. Numerous developing countries are deeply in debt and feel the need to attract foreign investment from transnational corporations, while others have developed sizeable industry sectors of their own that they do not want to be subject to international regulation.

The Mid-1990s: Enter the World Trade Organization

The establishment of the World Trade Organization (WTO) in 1995 to implement international rules on trade such as the General Agreement on Tariffs and Trade (GATT) introduced a new dimension to the international regulation of transnational corporations. One of the WTO's tasks is to 'harmonize' standards for products that are traded internationally; another is to resolve trade disputes between countries. The measuring-stick in this streamlining process is that national and international standards should present minimum barriers to trade. The WTO mechanisms intended to achieve these goals have elicited widespread concern about 'down-regulation' and 'de-regulation', not least the fear that accepted minimum standards in the fields of labour, health and environmental protection will be turned into maximum standards or be abolished altogether.

Moreover, both GATT and the WTO have been criticized for their undemocratic nature and for the excessive involvement and influence of transnational corporations in their decision-making processes. Unlike UN agencies responsible for other international agreements, the WTO can enforce its standards and decisions by means of trade or other sanctions (see e.g. Koivusalo 1999; UNDP 1999).

[The WTO has] at its disposal trade sanctions – among the most effective international weapons short of missiles. This means that the WTO, which is not even a UN organization, is probably the most powerful institution after the UN Security Council – and yet makes its rulings essentially in private and with limited participation of the poorest countries. (UNRISD 2000b: 109)[10]

The Floundering of the Multilateral Agreement on Investment

In the late 1990s, all these concerns prevented another trade agreement from being approved. The Organisation for Economic Co-operation and Development (OECD)[11] started to negotiate an agreement on investment from one country to another in relative secrecy. When details of the proposed agreement were leaked, however, widespread fears that this Multilateral Agreement on Investment (MAI) would give transnational corporations the right to file complaints against any state they believed was hindering their ability to trade in that country – effectively granting multinationals rights that had hitherto been regarded as the prerogatives of nation-states only – led to broad public mobilization against the agreement. This public opposition and concerns from some OECD states themselves led to the abandonment of the MAI in 1998 (UNRISD 2000b: 107–8). Critics were not opposed to bringing some order and coherence to the plethora of bilateral and multilateral trade and investment agreements. What they did object to were the profound shifts in the institutional arrangements for global economic decision-making that the MAI would have brought about.

The Late 1990s: The UN Re-enters the Debate

By the turn of the twentieth century, the UN and some of its agencies were once again becoming more vocal about the need for international business regulation.[12] Several draft measures proposed different arrangements to ensure the social accountability of TNCs, varying as to the extent to which standards should be legally binding.

The 1994 collapse of the Mexican economy and the 1997 financial crisis in a number of Asian countries[13] illustrated clearly that a wholly unregulated 'global' market was not good for the majority of the world's people or for transnational corporations.[14] Many TNCs began to worry about the impact of unstable financial and social environments on their operations. In 1997, the International Chamber of Commerce (ICC) – a business association of more than 7,000 transnational corporations from 130 countries – launched a major initiative towards 'dialogue' and 'partnership' with the UN (Maucher 1997). The ICC started to argue for better regulation in areas that would allow its member companies to operate in a more predictable business environment. But at the same time, it continued to advocate the de-regulation of national rules governing trade and other areas so as to minimize interference with companies' ability to maximize shareholder values. For example, at the 1998 World Economic Forum, an annual gathering of business and government leaders in Davos, Switzerland, top business people expressed their dismay at 'excessive government regulation', such as rules covering the workplace and the environment (Maak 1998: 25).

One year later, at the 1999 World Economic Forum, UN Secretary-General Kofi Annan proposed to the same business leaders a 'global compact of shared values and principles, which will give a human face to the global market'. The compact would comprise 'a set of core values in the areas of human rights, labour standards and environmental practices'. Annan explained: 'I choose these three areas because they are the ones where I fear that, if we do not act, there may be a threat to the open global market and especially to the multilateral trade regime.'[15] In exchange for UN support of free trade, Annan asked the ICC member companies to 'make sure that in your own corporate practices you uphold and respect human rights; and that you are not yourselves complicit in human rights abuses' (UN 1999b).

The UN–ICC Global Compact was launched on 5 July 1999 (UN/ ICC 1999). It relies on the ability and will of corporations to regulate themselves. Corporate compliance to the proposed standards is wholly voluntary. No mention is made of the need for effective procedures of monitoring and enforcement that are independent of industry.

Just one week later, on 12 July 1999, the United Nations Development Programme (UNDP) launched its annual *Human Development Report*. The report described in detail how 'profit-driven' economic globalization had resulted in the neglect of human rights and social justice for the vast majority of the world's people.[16] It proposed that corporations should be made more accountable to society:

> Multinational corporations are already a dominant part of the global economy – yet many of their actions go unrecorded and unaccounted … They need to be brought within a frame of global governance, not just a patchwork of national laws, rules and regulations (UNDP 1999: 100).

To achieve 'globalization with a human face', the UNDP report advocated the establishment of a 'more coherent and democratic architecture for global governance in the 21st century', which would include a binding code of conduct for multinational corporations:

> Today, they are held to codes of conduct only for what national legislation requires on the social and environmental impact of their operations. True, they have in recent years taken up voluntary codes of ethical conduct. But multinationals are too important for their conduct to be left to voluntary and self-generated standards (UNDP 1999: 12, 100).

As in the UN–ICC Global Compact, the UNDP report referred to human rights as a key source of universal ethical principles and norms for assessing the duties of transnational corporations towards society (see Box 1.1 for an overview of the standards proposed). Unlike the Global Compact, however, the UNDP report stressed the need to strengthen the current international human rights regime – for example, through a criminal court with a broader mandate – so that not only governments but also other important global players, such as TNCs and the World Trade Organization, could be held accountable to those affected by their actions (UNDP 1999: 9, 34–5, 111).[17]

ICC Secretary-General Maria Cattaui reacted promptly. In an open letter to the *Financial Times*, she claimed that the *Human Development Report* was 'on the wrong track in calling for a mandatory code of conduct for multinationals' and that binding rules 'would put the clock back to a bygone era' (Cattaui 1999).

De-regulation and Re-regulation Worldwide

Is a call for a binding international code of conduct for transnational corporations really putting the clock back? Does such a call not instead reflect people's needs in this era of 'globalization'?

When many countries lobbied some 25 years ago for a comprehensive system of international regulatory measures to hold multinational corporations accountable to the citizens of all the countries in which they operated, most of them believed that such regulation would be primarily a matter of 'international relations', of nation-states collaborating together under the aegis of the UN to develop international codes of conduct.

Since then, however, adherence to a neoliberal economic model

Box 1.1 Proposed Standards to Evaluate TNC Conduct

'A Compact for the New Century'

At the World Economic Forum in Davos, Switzerland on 31 January 1999, UN Secretary-General Kofi Annan challenged world business leaders to 'embrace and enact', both in their individual corporate practices and by supporting appropriate public policies, the following universally agreed values and principles:

The Universal Declaration of Human Rights

The secretary-general asked world business to:

a) support and respect the protection of international human rights within their sphere of influence; and

b) make sure their own corporations are not complicit in human right abuses.

The International Labour Organization's Declaration on Fundamental Principles and Rights at Work

The secretary-general asked world business to uphold:

a) freedom of association and the effective recognition of the right to collective bargaining;

b) the elimination of all forms of forced and compulsory labour;

c) the effective abolition of child labour; and

d) the elimination of discrimination in respect of employment and occupation.

The Rio Declaration of the 1992 UN Conference on Environment and Development

The secretary-general asked world business to:

a) support a precautionary approach to environmental challenges;

b) undertake initiatives to promote greater environmental responsibility; and

c) encourage the development and diffusion of environmentally friendly technologies.

The UNDP 1999 Human Development Report: Globalization with a Human Face

'Multinational corporations are too important and too dominant a part of the global economy for voluntary codes to be enough. Globally agreed upon principles of performance are needed for:

- Human concerns – to ensure compliance with labour standards and human rights
- Economic efficiency – to ensure fair trade and competitive markets
- Environmental sustainability – to avoid degradation and pollution.'

Sources: UN 1999a; UNDP 1999: 100–1.

has involved restructuring regulatory systems in the interest of large corporations and questioning the UN's legitimacy to establish international regulatory frameworks. At the same time, a variety of actors have established different codes of conduct and standards for industry practices, the majority of which are not legally binding on corporations.

The current discourse in policy-making arenas has also changed. Thirty years ago, most policy-makers considered regulation of corporate activities to be an issue of 'democratic control' over TNCs. At that time, it was understood that firm rules were needed to ensure both the optimal operation of markets and the prevention of so-called market failures, abuses of power and corporate neglect of responsibility. The archetype of the free market, the USA, had in fact one of the most developed regulatory systems in the world.

At the end of the 1970s the term 'de-regulation' spread from the USA as part of the neoliberal economic *laisser-faire* discourse, which also advocated privatization of state enterprises, downsizing of the state, reduced welfare entitlements, lower taxes and free trade. Since the demise of the communist bloc at the end of the 1980s, regulation and public ownership of specific sectors of the economy have often been confused with total state control over economies, and then completely dismissed.

All major industrial states have prospered throughout decades of regulated markets, and all reasonably well-functioning market economies continue to be partially regulated. These facts, however, do not figure in the free market discourse. Not mentioned either is the fact that 'liberalization' of markets under this paradigm has usually entailed not getting rid of regulations altogether but instead a selective de-regulation and re-regulation in favour of big business and finance (Hildyard 1998: 2, 3–6; UNDP 1999). The predominance of free market thinking stifles serious theoretical and policy inquiries about the merits and shortcomings of different types of regulatory arrangements as well as about which type of capitalist market system might best achieve the most socially just and environmentally friendly outcomes and under what circumstances.

The political debate about how to ensure democratic control over corporations that transcend national boundaries – corporations that in many instances have annual turnovers far exceeding the gross national products of many nation-states – has given way to debate about how best to attract corporate money, whether in the form of direct investment or via so-called public–private partnerships. More often than not, binding public regulation is traded away in return for promises of corporate responsibility and good governance. Both these concepts appeal to good intentions but overlook significant differential relationships of power.

Regulation in the USA

Regulation in the USA was instituted in three broad waves from the late nineteenth century through to the 1970s. The first wave began in 1887, when the US Congress set up the Interstate Commerce Commission to prevent railroad owners from abusing their monopoly position by charging small farmers higher rates than they could afford for transporting their goods. The subsequent 1890 Sherman Act dealt with the rampant problem of monopolies and price fixing. The 1906 Pure Food and Drug Act was enacted in response to public outrage at working and sanitary conditions in slaughterhouses. From 1907 onwards, public utility commissions regulated gas, electricity and telephone markets in which private companies were accorded a monopoly position if they agreed to charge publicly affordable prices. In the early twentieth century, labour laws were passed to limit employers' power to exploit both child and adult workers. This first wave of regulation – which began in the late nineteenth century and extended through the progressive era of Presidents Theodore Roosevelt and Woodrow Wilson – was primarily intended to prevent abuses of economic concentration and power of the newly emerging industries.

The second wave, known as New Deal regulation, came in response to the Great Depression in the 1930s. Under the leadership of US

President Franklin D. Roosevelt, an intricate regulatory system was set in place, the prime aim of which was to stabilize the economy so that people would not again be detrimentally affected by businesses' economic over-speculation. By the end of the 1960s, independent regulatory commissions were seen as a 'fourth branch of federal government' (Kuttner 1999: 231).

The third wave of regulation lasted from the mid-1960s to the end of the 1970s. It emerged in response to the emergence of a vocal consumer movement spearheaded by Ralph Nader and an environmental movement catalysed by Rachel Carson's 1962 book *Silent Spring*. Between 1965 and 1977, the US Congress enacted 20 new regulatory laws governing, for example, occupational health and safety, consumer product safety, clean air, clean water and toxic waste, and created an elaborate regime for assessing environmental impacts and regulating the financial system.

Kuttner pinpoints the reversal in public rule-setting activities to the late 1970s when the word 'de-regulation', which had entered public discourse in 1976, became a widely shared policy objective. What started in 1978 as 'regulatory reform' under President Jimmy Carter rapidly turned into a movement for complete de-regulation.

No societal group mobilized to defend this partially regulated mixed market system. Left-wing and centre movements were disillusioned with the machinery and politics of regulation because of 'regulatory capture', an idea introduced in 1955 by Marver Bernstein's influential book *Regulating Business by Independent Commission*. Bernstein exposed the subtle (and not so subtle) mechanisms by which corporations had gained influence over the content and execution of regulation. He also showed that the functioning of public regulation depended on the idealism and public-mindedness of the regulators. But instead of calls for an overhaul and revival of the regulatory system, what emerged were calls for the abolishment of the most criticized regulatory agencies.

Those who paved the way for a fundamental attack on the very idea of regulation, however, came from the new influential Chicago School of neoliberal economists, the most well-known of whom was Milton Friedman. By the end of the 1970s, their de-regulation ideology had been picked up by a revitalized conservative movement and by big business. Kuttner notes that big business was in fact one of the last to embrace the de-regulation ideology because most corporations had learned to live and manoeuvre within the system of regulation rather than attack it. Still today, most businesses prefer some sort of regulation, albeit in their favour, to no regulation at all.

In this discourse, the term 'polity failure' – failure of the political community or the political process – took the place of 'market failure'. The term 'polity failure' expresses a lack of confidence that a vibrant civic-minded society and its democratic state will set and enforce rules to the benefit of society. Instead, public regulation was invariably portrayed as an obstacle to the optimal functioning of a supposedly perfectly self-regulating market. If there was a need for regulation, it was argued, then regulation through market incentives was preferable.[18] Public, mandatory regulation was denigrated under the term 'command-and-control' regulation. From a public policy perspective, the introduction of such a negatively charged term was unfortunate:

> [A] fact is that any system of laws relies on commands. Thou shalt not run a red light, or cheat the IRS [tax-collecting Internal Revenue Service], or rob a bank. Thou shalt honor property rights in a variety of highly specified ways. *The issue is* not whether there are 'commands', but *whether the goals of public policies are sensible and attainable, and whether their means are appropriate to the specified goals*. (Kuttner 1999: 320, emphasis added)

Common Regulatory Regimes

Most other industrialized countries followed paths similar to that of the USA. Regulatory arrangements varied, depending on the function and type of state, the legislative and administrative system, the actions and reactions of the business sector, the aspirations and acts of labour and other social movements, media coverage, dominant personalities, balances of power, overall context and simple chance. Major common regulatory realms that temper the activities of corporations include:

- *Anti-trust*: to ensure economic competition and prevent abuses of monopoly power.
- *Anti-corruption*: to prevent corporations from using illicit payments to gain contracts or to influence law-making and enforcement.
- *Advertising and marketing*: to prevent harm from manipulation of customers.
- *Public relations*: to prevent manipulation of the media, legislators, policy-makers and the general public.

- *Corporate taxation*: to ensure corporations' contribution to public infrastructure and to set a disincentive for the production of negative externalities such as pollution.
- *Labour*: to protect and ensure the rights of the workforce.
- *Health and safety*: to ensure the safe operation of industrial plants.
- *Consumer protection*: to ensure safety and fair pricing of products and the right to full and unbiased information.
- *Anti-discrimination*: to prevent discrimination in the hiring, firing and treatment of employees on the basis of, for instance, race or sex.
- *Environmental protection*: to protect the natural environment. This is a most complex regulatory regime covering a range of issues such as whaling, toxic waste, air, water and soil pollution, acid rain, the ozone layer and biodiversity.[19]

In addition, a wide variety of regulatory regimes have been introduced for specific industry sectors. To ensure that industrially manufactured pharmaceuticals contribute to public health, for example, pharmaceutical companies are regulated in relation to their clinical trials, drug approval, manufacturing practices, product quality, post-marketing surveillance, marketing and advertising, and often drug pricing. In return, research-based pharmaceutical corporations have obtained a long duration of patents on their products, protection of their brand names and relatively low taxation. Other regulated industries include public utilities, mining, oil, food, garments and the financial sector.[20]

A Coherent Web of International Regulation

Despite the current free market discourse, most industrialized countries in fact accept that the state has a duty to provide for rules-based systems in the realms and industry sectors cited above. But this is not generally accepted for *international* regulation, even though numerous practices of transnational corporate and financial actors are beyond the control of any individual nation-state. A study by Harris Gleckman and Riva Krut, *The Social Benefits of Regulating International Business*, ponders this inconsistency:

It is as important to put regulations in place internationally as it is nationally. It is an accepted job of government to set domestic targets and standards for business that weigh the competing claims of economic and social development. On the international level this commonly accepted national assumption is not shared. (Gleckman and Krut 1994: 10)

Their study argues that 'a systematic method to regulate and set minimum standards for international business activity is crucial to the achievement of some critical elements of international social life and development' and that there is a need for an international structure to assist states in regulating international business on the basis of 'the fundamental rights of individual citizens, international society and the earth' (Gleckman and Krut 1994: 8). UNRISD shares the view that the 'invisible hands' of the market will not achieve optimal social outcomes. Its analysis of the outcomes of reliance for ten years on corporate self-regulation and 'voluntary initiatives' in the international policy arena concludes that:

> Left to their own devices, TNCs are likely to fulfil their responsibility in a minimalist and fragmented fashion. Their strategies may be conducive to economic growth and the stability of their operating environments, but not necessarily to sustainable human development. They still need strong and effective regulation and a coherent response from civil society. (UNRISD 2000a: 90)

Box 1.2 Why Regulate?

The Myth of the Perfectly Self-regulating Market

De-regulation has become a key word in current economic policy discourse. Many policy-makers today follow the neoliberal economic school of thought, which argues that unfettered markets deliver goods and services most efficiently and are therefore best left alone. It also argues that the 'invisible hand' of pricing mechanisms takes best care of societal welfare.

Regulations can certainly become inefficient, over-bureaucratic or redundant, and thus should be reviewed periodically. But such reviews are not the same as getting rid of regulations *per se* on the grounds that they are negative, rather than positive, policy measures. In fact, the 'free' market has never been wholly unregulated. Most industrial states have long relied upon an intricate rules-based system to create a stable business environment and to tackle the market's imperfections and abuses.

The collapse of the economies in the former communist countries of Eastern Europe is often cited as proof that *laisser-faire* economies work best. But centrally planned economies should not be confused with regulated markets. Since the Second World War, most Western European countries as well as the US economy have flourished under social welfare-oriented types of capitalism.

The market certainly does many things well. But until some 20 years ago, economists and policy-makers were well aware that there will always be goods that market mechanisms do not and cannot deliver, such as universal access to health care, or goods that they deliver but, in the interests of societal well-being, should not deliver, such as pollution and misleading or harmful statements about commercial products, including tobacco and pharmaceuticals. This is why regulation is often employed 'either to make the market work more efficiently or to solve problems that the market cannot fix' (Kuttner 1999: 329). Economist Robert Kuttner points out that:

> The system in which the private market operates is inevitably structured by law and by democratic choices. Those choices can contrive a relatively efficient, or inefficient, brand of mixed economy. But the quest for a perfectly pure free market, or an economy free of political influences, is an illusion. (Kuttner 1999: 327)

Over time, regulatory measures have been implemented for a variety of reasons. Classical economic theory makes a distinction between *economic* and *social* regulation. According to this theory, economic regulation is justified when markets fail to be effectively self-correcting. A classic example is the complex regulation of public utilities, such as water supply or electricity services, where entry, price, profits and terms of competition are heavily regulated to prevent unnecessary fragmentation of the market and to ensure that the company awarded the contract does not abuse its monopoly position. Social regulation, meanwhile, is justified because it corrects what economists call 'negative spillovers'. It encompasses regulation of pollution, advertising, and health and safety.[21] But as Kuttner points out:

> We should remember as a matter of economic and political

history that none of these regulatory systems resulted from bloodless expert analysis of externalities, information failures, natural monopolies, bargaining asymmetries, and the like. For the most part, they resulted from gross abuses of private economic power – followed by exposé, indignation, societal conflict, struggle, and ultimately political remediation. (Kuttner 1999: 230)

There has always been, and continues to be, a need to regulate the market. The key question is: what type of regulation allows differing markets to do their best while preventing undue harms to societies? In democratically minded societies, which in principle are based on the primacy of the needs and values of people over abstract economics, the answer to this question is a political one. From this perspective, the question becomes: for what reasons have societies decided to establish regulatory measures? What are the commonly accepted justifications for limiting market mechanisms?

Notes

1. Citizen action has often been prompted by industrial accidents. The death of over seventy children in the USA from a toxic solvent in a cough mixture in 1937, for example, marked the beginning of demands for industrially manufactured medicines to be tested for safety and resulted in legislation to this effect being introduced in 1938. Meaningful regulation to ensure the safety of pharmaceutical drugs emerged in many countries only after hundreds of children were born in the 1960s with stunted or no limbs because their mothers had taken thalidomide as a sleeping pill while pregnant. The drug had been advertised as being particularly mild. Concerns regarding health and environmental protection were raised by the 1976 dioxin spill at Seveso, Italy. They increased dramatically after the 1984 gas leak in Bhopal, India, when thousands of people living around the pesticide plant of the Indian subsidiary of the US company Union Carbide were poisoned, causing deaths and suffering for years to come. Such concern was kept in the public eye because of further industrial accidents – the 1986 Rhine spill of organophosphates produced by Swiss chemical firm Sandoz; the 1986 explosion of the Chernobyl nuclear reactor; the 1989 pollution of the Alaskan coast with oil from the wrecked *Exxon Valdez* tanker; and countless warnings about industry's contribution to holes in the ozone layer and to global warming

(Blum et al. 1981: 73–4; Reich 1991: 98–139; Greer and Bruno 1996: 15–16, 131; Krut and Gleckman 1998: 30–1).

2. Much of this section is based on Michael Hansen's (1999) summary of the historical evolution of the environmental regulation of TNCs. He distinguishes three phases in the debate on international economic regulation of TNCs: the 1970s – the advent of regulatory activism; the 1980s – the conservative backlash; and the 1990s – corporate self-regulation and NGO activism.

3. 'Last July, the world learned with amazement of different aspects of a new plan of action that ITT has presented to the US government in order to overthrow my government in a period of six months ... They wanted to strangle us economically, carry out political sabotage, create panic among the population and cause social disorder so that when the Government lost control, the armed forces would be driven to eliminate the democratic regime and impose a dictatorship ... Distinguished representatives, before the conscience of the World, I accuse ITT of trying to provoke a civil war in my country. This is what we call imperialist intervention' (Allende 1972).

4. For more details, see Hoogvelt with Puxty 1987: 41–3; 226–7.

5. For a description of the negotiations on the UN Code of Conduct on Transnational Corporations, see Hoogvelt with Puxty 1987: 43; Spröte 1993; for drafts of both codes, see UNCTAD 1996a: 161–201.

6. The commonly held view that 'liberalization' of markets has entailed getting rid of regulations altogether has been contested. Some analysts argue that the expansion of the neoliberal economic model has been a process of de-regulation with concomitant re-regulation in the interests of transnational corporations and financial industries. Hildyard, for example, argues that the nation-state's power has not necessarily been weakened, but has been re-directed. 'Far from doing away with state bureaucracy, the free market policies have in fact reorganised it. While the privatisation of state industries and assets has certainly cut down the direct involvement of the state in the production and distribution of many goods and services, the process has been accompanied by new state regulations, subsidies and institutions aimed at introducing and entrenching a "favourable environment" for the newly-privatised industries ... At issue, therefore, is not whether modern economies require any involvement from the state, but to what ends and in whose interests the state operates' (Hildyard, 1998: 3–6, 1).

7. This announcement was preceded by an official US Demarche Request sent on 26 March 1991 to all US foreign embassies asking them to lobby for the abolishment of the UN Code of Conduct negotiations: 'We believe that the Code is a relic of another era, when foreign direct investment was looked upon with considerable concern. The Code does not reflect the current investment policies of many developing countries ... In the light of the above, Washington agencies have decided to seek the support of host governments, officials responsible for foreign investment and quietly build a consensus against further negotiations ... We stress that the Demarche [mail] should be given to officials responsible for investment not those responsible for UN

affairs' (quoted in Braithwaite and Drahos 2000: 193; see also van Drimmelen 1998: 47–8).

8. Another international code was the OECD voluntary Guidelines for Multinational Enterprises, which was much less comprehensive than the envisioned UN Code of Conduct for TNCs, and which was not universally applicable. Hansen 1993: 3.

9. For a more detailed review of different types of co-regulatory, industry self-regulatory and other 'voluntary' initiatives, see Utting 2000: 3–9.

10. Another important economic player in global economics and politics, the World Bank, began to change its position in the mid-1990s on the regulation of markets. In the 1970s, when structural adjustment programmes (SAPs) began to be imposed on developing countries as a condition of further international loans, the Bank was a champion of minimal state intervention in the economic sphere. But after a decade of privatization of public services the world over, concern rose about poor people's lack of access to basic 'public goods' such as health care services and clean water. Moreover, when the Thai economy collapsed in 1997, largely as a result of unregulated international capital speculation, many feared an imminent world economic depression. Responding to these concerns, the World Bank's 1997 *World Development Report* called for the capacities of states to intervene in markets, either because of 'market failure' or out of a concern for 'equity', to be upgraded. Areas covered by the World Bank's proposals included utility regulation, anti-trust policies, financial regulation and consumer protection. But the report's recommendation that greater emphasis be given to 'personal responsibility' leaves considerable uncertainty as to the scope of government regulation in relation to industry 'freedom' of action and self-regulation and does not stress the need for international regulation. World Bank 1997: 26–7.

11. The Organisation for Economic Co-operation and Development was set up in 1960 to succeed the Organisation for European Economic Co-Operation of 1948, which had coordinated aid for economic recovery to Western Europe under the Marshall Plan after the Second World War. Today, the OECD brings together the governments of 29 major industrial countries.

12. One initiative outside the UN system was taken up by the OECD. In June 2000, the OECD adopted a revised set of its guidelines on TNCs, which set new standards on corporate governance, workplace conditions and environmental protection. These voluntary guidelines apply to TNCs based in the 29 OECD member countries and in four non-member countries: Argentina, Brazil, Chile and the Slovak Republic. OECD 2000a; UNRISD 2000b: 90.

13. Both were caused by the sudden massive flight of the largely unregulated international flow of private capital. See UNRISD 2000b: 7–8; see also Stiglitz 1998.

14. Except, perhaps, for those investors and speculators that have become transnational in their operations.

15. Annan reminded business leaders about the 'enormous pressure from various interest groups to load the trade regime and investment agreements

with restrictions aimed at reaching adequate standards in the three areas of human rights, labour and the environment'. But while the secretary-general saw these concerns as legitimate, he did not want them to be integrated into international trade and investment regimes. Some commentators have questioned the wisdom of proposing the Global Compact during the lead up to the new round of negotiations of international trade rules in Seattle at the end of 1999: in that year many civil society organizations and developing countries were calling for an impact assessment of the WTO's activities and rules, for the inclusion of social and environmental clauses in any new WTO agreements, or for the abolition of the WTO regime altogether. For details, see CEO 1999: 2–8.

16. UNDP 1999: 30.

17. The UNDP report recommends that this code of conduct should come under the jurisdiction of the WTO. It would be preferable, however, to put it under the more democratically accountable UN system and leave enforcement to the International Criminal Court with an expanded mandate to sue and sanction TNCs.

18. One much cited example is the creation of tradable pollution permits, the aim of which was to lower overall air pollution by inducing industries to adopt cleaner technologies. But as Kuttner points out, 'though marketlike, the resulting system was not free market'. Instead, it constituted 'the use of market incentives … within a highly contrived and regulated context'. The political process must still decide on the level of permissible pollution. Tradable permits, moreover, cannot deal with compensation of those harmed by pollution. See Kuttner 1999: 324–6.

19. A justification for regulation that has been used more in the international than the national arena is *human rights*: to ensure that people's human rights are not violated. The first time that corporations were tried for 'crimes against humanity' was during the Nuremberg trials after the end of the Second World War when German companies were indicted for various actions during the Nazi era. A call to link the human rights regime with the regulation of the conduct of transnational corporations re-emerged in the 1990s, particularly after environmental and human rights activists blamed the Shell oil company for complicity in the execution by the Nigerian state of Ken Saro-Wiwa and other Shell critics. See Meintjes 2000: 85, 97.

20. For details of these categories see Kuttner 1999: 227–31.

21. For details of these categories see Kuttner 1999: 227–31.

. . . .

CHAPTER 2

Democratic Global Governance: Regulation of the Corporate Sector

> Intergovernmental policy making in today's global economy is in the hands of the major industrial powers and the international institutions they control ... Their rule-making may create a secure environment for open markets, but there are no countervailing rules to protect human rights and promote human development. (UNDP, *Human Development Report 1999: Globalization with a Human Face*)

Governance and the 'Rule of Law'

Today, policy documents, academic papers and industry communications rarely address the question of industry regulation as an issue of 'democratic control' over the market and its institutions. Checks and balances on the market, if they are discussed at all, are explored as issues of 'good governance'.

Although it is an old concept, the term governance was not part of the political discourse in the 1970s. It derives from the Ancient Greek verb *kubernan*, meaning to take the helm and 'steer'. International relations theorist James A. Rosenau defines the process of governance as that 'whereby an organization or society steers itself' (Rosenau 1998: 30).

The World Bank reintroduced the term in international policy discourse in its 1989 report examining the roots of the sub-Saharan African economic crisis. This report queried why the Bank's structural adjustment policies had not yielded the promised benefits such as increased foreign investment. The World Bank is reported to have chosen the rather archaic term 'governance' rather than, for example, 'good government' because the Bank is not allowed, according to its founding principles, to intervene in national politics.

Thus the Bank's definition of governance in its April 1992 publication *Governance and Development* – 'the manner in which power is exercised in the management of a country's economic and social resources for the development' (World Bank 1992: 1) – sounds technocratic. This publication cited 'bad governance' on the part of recipients of World Bank funds as the reason why the World Bank's policy prescriptions had failed, and put in 'good governance' as a conditionality for future World Bank loans.[2]

Others who picked up on the term aimed to secure the 'peace dividend' anticipated after the demise of the communist bloc. A major actor in this respect was the Commission on Global Governance, which dates back to an initiative of Willy Brandt, the former German chancellor. Brandt had chaired the Independent Commission on International Development Issues (the North–South Commission) in the 1980s. In 1990, he invited individual members of that commission and other independent commissions – the Independent Commission on Disarmament and Security Issues (the Palme Commission), the World Commission on Environment and Development (the Brundtland Commission), and the South Commission (chaired by Julius Nyerere) – to Germany to discuss how to meet the challenges of the next decade.

Their meeting was followed by a gathering in April 1991 in Stockholm of some 30 public figures including Vaclav Havel, Gro Harlem Brundtland, Jimmy Carter, Robert McNamara and Maurice Strong. They discussed how to strengthen global cooperation to meet the challenge of securing peace, achieving sustainable development and universalizing democracy. In their 'Stockholm Initiative on Global Security and Governance', this group proposed the establishing of a commission to explore 'the opportunities created by the end of the cold war to build a more effective system of world security and governance' (CGG 1995: 359).[3]

Thus a 28-member Commission on Global Governance was set up, co-chaired by Ingvar Carlsson, a former prime minister of Sweden, and Shridath Ramphal, a former secretary-general of the British Commonwealth. With the release of its report in 1995, the term 'global governance' became firmly entrenched as a key concept in international policy discourse. The report stated that:

> Governance is the sum of the many ways in which individuals and institutions, public and private, manage their common affairs. It is a continuing process through which conflicting or diverse interests may be accommodated and co-operative action may be taken. It includes

formal institutions and regimes empowered to enforce compliance, as well as informal arrangements that people and institutions either have agreed to or perceive to be in their interest. (CGG 1995: 2)

According to the Commission, 'there is no single model or form of global governance, nor is there a single set of structures. It is a broad, dynamic, complex process of interactive decision-making that is constantly evolving and responding to changing circumstances' (CGG 1995: 4). Global governance arrangements to ensure that transnational corporations conduct themselves in a socially accountable way would differ, therefore, from governance arrangements to ensure world peace, for example.

The perception of which actors are involved in international decision-making processes has changed considerably as well:

At the global level, governance has been viewed primarily as inter-governmental relationships, but it must now be understood as also involving non-governmental organizations (NGOs), citizen movements, multinational corporations, and the global capital market. Interacting with these are global mass media of dramatically enlarged influence. (CGG 1995: 2–3)

The Commission realized that the creation of adequate global governance mechanisms would be difficult. It stressed that they needed to be 'more inclusive and more participatory – that is, more democratic than in the past' (CGG 1995: 5).

It recognized that key elements in establishing more democratic governance mechanisms included reforming and strengthening the existing system of intergovernmental institutions, improving their collaboration with other societal actors, and subjecting 'the rule of arbitrary power – economic, political, or military – to the rule of law within global society' (CGG 1995: 5).

Regulation of transnational corporations through 'the rule of law' by means of 'regimes empowered to enforce compliance' is thus anything but an outdated idea (CGG 1995: 2, 5). On the contrary, establishing binding international frameworks for corporate behaviour and practices is an acknowledged – and unfinished – task of global democratic decision-making.

Key Questions on Regulation

Key questions on appropriate regulatory regimes go well beyond simply asking whether international standards on corporations should be mandatory or not. Questions on democratic international rule-setting include:

- In which areas are binding laws needed? In which areas are other arrangements sufficient?
- Who sets the rules and on what basis?
- Who implements the rules and how?
- How can society ensure that any regulatory arrangement effectively prevents – or at least minimizes – potential harm from industry activities?

These questions may sound technocratic, but need to be raised and discussed in the context of changes in the international policy-making arena over the past 30 years and in the face of the increasing power of TNCs.

The trend towards industry self-regulation or co-regulation by industry and other societal actors has been supported by two beliefs. One is that the growing number of industry codes demonstrates an increased sense of corporate responsibility and that as a result society no longer needs to insist on externally defined binding international regulation. The other is that transnational corporations have gained so much power in recent decades (one means of exercising this power is to relocate manufacturing plants from country to country, or at least to threaten to do so) that it is now impossible to regulate TNCs by externally defined rules. Building on voluntary agreements with corporations is seen as more 'pragmatic' than antagonizing them with binding international regulation.[4]

These perceptions invoke further questions:

- Have TNCs shown a willingness and ability to regulate themselves effectively?
- Is there underexplored room to formulate and enforce externally defined international regulation?
- What is the appropriate role of each actor in the new structures of 'good global governance' (a term that is used in this publication to mean democratic decision-making about the most appropriate ways to ensure that TNCs are socially accountable by means of international regulation)?

Context and Relationships of Power in International Regulation

Answers to these questions require an assessment in context of the international regulation of TNCs, taking into account relationships of power between different actors. Several structural changes during the past three decades of increased economic and political globalization are relevant in this respect:

- Transnational corporations have gained a large amount of economic and political power.
- There is a void at the national level as nation-states have lost and have been giving away much of their sovereign decision-making powers to transnational corporations and other institutions.
- At the international level, decision-making powers have been shifting away from intergovernmental UN agencies towards the less democratically accountable World Bank, International Monetary Fund (IMF) and the World Trade Organization (WTO).
- Civil society organizations have become increasingly active in the international policy-making arena.[5]

Analyses of the dynamics of international regulation within the current global governance discourse meet with at least two problems: the first is the blurring of the distinction between commercial actors and civil society ones; the second is the frequent neglect of the different interests of the different actors involved in global rule-setting and the different relationships of power between them.

Business Actors and Civil Society Actors

Throughout the history of corporate regulation, transnational corporations have tended to disagree with citizen groups as to the best way to regulate corporate practices. Yet in many current analyses of global governance or international regulation, business and trade associations are subsumed under the categories of 'non-governmental organizations' (NGOs) or 'civil society organizations' (CSOs).[6] The Commission on Global Governance, for example, states:

> Among the important changes in the past half-century has been the emergence of a vigorous civil society ... This term covers a multitude of institutions, voluntary associations, and networks – women's groups, trade unions, *chambers of commerce* ... and so on. Such groups channel

the interests and energies of many communities outside government, from *business* and the professions to individuals working for the welfare of children and a healthier planet. (CGG 1995: 32, emphasis added)[7]

In addition, the terms NGO and CSO are often used interchangeably. Neither is clearly defined, but some general distinctions based on the respective histories of the terms in international policy fora may be useful.

Most people attach certain values to these terms. NGOs and CSOs are generally thought of as progressive groups or organizations working in fields such as Third World development, social justice, human rights or the environment. This is not necessarily the case. The term NGO is actually a 'non-definition', indicating organizations that are not part of the state machinery. It was first coined in 1945 to denote groups and organizations that had consultative status with the UN's main body, the Economic and Social Council (ECOSOC), and its subsidiary bodies (with the explicit exclusion of the UN General Assembly, the Security Council and the International Court of Justice) (Krut 1997: 9).

The ECOSOC statute defines the terms of acceptance of a group with consultative status, primarily that the aims and purposes of the group conform to those of the UN (Willets 1999: 251).[8] According to this definition, therefore, the term NGO can encompass a diverse range of groups and organizations.

There were three further conditions for acceptance: the group must not be profit-making; it must not be violent or criminal; and it must not be a political party. Corporations got around the first restriction by forming international business associations that, they argued, were non-profit-making (Willets 1999: 252).

There are no official statistics on the percentage of business interest organizations among the UN-accredited NGOs. International relations lecturer Peter Willets analysed the 1996 list of some 1,000 ECOSOC-accredited NGOs and found that nearly 15 per cent (155 of 1,058) NGOs represented solely commercial concerns (Willets 1998: 204). Business organizations such as the International Chamber of Commerce (ICC), sectoral trade organizations such as the International Federation of Pharmaceutical Manufacturers Associations (IFPMA), and issue-based corporate lobby organizations such as the World Business Council for Sustainable Development have all gained consultative NGO status with one UN agency or another.[9]

'The types of groups that are usually considered to be classic, idealistic, campaigning NGOs constitute just over half those at the UN,' says Willets (1998: 205), and this sub-grouping is anything but homogenous. It encompasses national organizations – including the National Rifle Association[10] – and international citizen networks such as Consumers International and the Worldwide Fund for Nature (WWF).

Attempts have been made to regain the distinction between 'associations of citizens' and 'organizations of capital' (Krut 1997: 8). Since the early 1990s, citizen groups have called for a distinction between PINGOs (public interest NGOs) and BINGOs (business interest NGOs). At the March 1995 preparatory meeting for NGOs for the Fourth World Conference on Women, for instance, women's health groups resolved to ban transnational corporations from their caucus meeting so as to ensure that public interest groups could discuss and make decisions without the presence and influence of organizations representing the infant food, pharmaceutical, pesticides, tobacco and other industries (WEDO 1995: 3).[11, 12]

At the same time, however, the term 'civil society organization' crept into UN policy documents as part of the governance discourse. Once again, this term rarely distinguished between citizen alliances and business organizations.[13]

But as use of this term spread, so calls were made to exclude the commercial sector from the category. A UN-sponsored seminar on the involvement of civil society in the follow-up to the 1995 Social Summit, for example, stated cautiously: 'Business enterprises should not be grouped together with volunteer or representative organizations, nor should they be considered a part of civil society, with the possible exemption of non-profit business organizations and cooperatives.' Participants at the seminar suggested that ultimately 'those organizations which represent businesses or are primarily concerned with promoting business should be accorded a different consultative status' (UN 1995: 4–5, 13). A 1996 discussion of the Organizing Committee of the UN Administrative Committee on Coordination (ACC) came up with a similar proposal (NGLS 1997: 3). Citizen groups lobbied the United Nations Secretary-General's Executive Office not to lump business together with civil society on its website listing of organizations that had official relationship status with the UN. The website now offers two separate links for 'civil society' and 'business'.[14] Civil society NGOs saw this as a victory:

UN officials have indicated that it is understood that NGOs and business have different structures, methods and objectives. While NGOs have many objectives, the common link among the private sector is the profit objective. (Foster and Anand 1999: 528)

Yet a recent publication from the UN Department of Public Information, *Basic Facts about the United Nations*, and many other UN publications continue to subsume business groups under the civil society heading:

An important new priority [of the 1997 UN reform package] is to strengthen outreach to civil society – NGOs, trade unions, business groups and others – to foster practical partnerships to further the goals and mandates of the Organization. These efforts have met with strong and positive response, including significant private [corporate] donations. (UN 1998: 18)

Until the question of definition is resolved satisfactorily, each group should be defined carefully and each term defined whenever it is used.

What is the relationship between the term NGO and the term CSO? Social scientist Riva Krut suggests the following in her study *Globalization and Civil Society*:

Non-governmental organizations, as a category of organizational entities, were created at the founding of the United Nations. The category was invented in order to describe a specific relationship between civil organizations and the intergovernmental process, and since then the term has been loosely applied to any organization that is not public. Outside of the United Nations process, these NGOs might be better called civil society organizations. (Krut 1997: 7)

Many citizen organizations, however, have become accustomed to calling themselves NGOs. In this book, the term non-governmental organization (NGO) and civil society organizations (CSO) will be used interchangeably in the understanding that the category of CSO encompasses a broader variety and number of groups and alliances than that of NGO.

Civil society organizations are regarded in this publication as 'groupings of individuals and associations formal and informal, that belong neither to government nor to the profit-making private sector' (UNRISD 2000b: 93).

Activities are considered to be part of civil society when they involve a deliberate attempt – from outside the state and the market, and in one or the other organized fashion – to shape policies, norms and/or deeper social structures. In a word, civil society exists when people make concerted efforts, through voluntary associations, to mould rules: both official, formal, legal arrangements and informal social constructs. (Scholte 1999: 4)

Business associations are not considered within the category of NGO or of CSO. This is categorically not to imply that corporations and business organizations are by definition 'bad' while CSOs or NGOs are by definition 'good'. It is simply an attempt to regain a lost distinction. In the 1970s, for instance, it was common to refer to government and public authorities as the First Sector, business and its organizations as the Second Sector, and people's organizations as the Third Sector, a categorization that several authors continue to use today (Foster and Anand 1999: 529; Giddens 2000: 674). In the USA, moreover, it is still customary to distinguish between business 'lobby groups' and 'public interest groups' (Willets 1998: 195).

Putting business associations back into the category of the market is an important precondition for a proper analysis of the forces and actors at work in the international regulatory arena. (For further exploration on the civil society category in relation to citizen alliances, see Chapter 9.)

Regulation of TNCs as Contested Processes

A second problem raised by the current global governance discourse is that the differential interests and power of the actors involved in the global arena are rarely taken sufficiently into account.[15]

In much of today's literature and policy statements on interactions with the corporate sector, a shift from 'confrontation' towards one of 'dialogues' and 'partnerships' is cited as a positive, socially desirable trend. For example, Gro Harlem Brundtland, the current WHO director-general and former chair of the Brundtland Commission, whose report *Our Common Future* initiated the 1992 Earth Summit process, said in 1990:

Partnership is what is needed in today's world, partnership between government and industry, between producers and consumers, between the present and the future ... We need to build new coalitions ... We must agree on a global agenda for the management of change ...

We must continue to move from confrontation, through dialogue to cooperation … Collective management of the global interdependence is … the only acceptable formula in the world of the 1990s. (quoted in Lohmann 1990: 82)

But do 'dialogues' and 'partnerships' really represent a more adequate political process of making TNCs accountable to society? What happens if a particular TNC or industry sector does not agree with regulation of a particular industry practice? Such a response can be anticipated wherever effective regulation conflicts with profit maximization. Regulation of the marketing of industrial products such as breast-milk substitutes, pharmaceuticals, tobacco, alcohol or pesticides fall clearly into this category.

Some authors and political actors think more broadly that regulation of transnational corporations cannot and should not be based on a preconceived idea of a harmonious political process. Sociologist Ulrich Beck, for example, believes that 'regulation battles' will be a major focus of international politics in future. He forecasts that, after the first wave of 'national de-regulations' under the neoliberal economic model, people's experience of the social and political consequences of the complete lack of control over transnational capital flows will spur a second wave of 'transnational re-regulations' (Beck 1998: 20, 62–3).

There are certainly areas where corporations envisage advantages to be gained from effective international regulation and where they may therefore cooperate in the regulatory endeavour – for example, regulations that help prevent conditions of 'ruinous competition' or which give them a local monopoly over utilities such as water or electricity services. But recent research suggests that 'win–win' situations that are being sold as opportunities for corporations to 'turn ethics into profit' are far less common in the area of environmental protection, for example, than is usually implied in the discourse on 'voluntary initiatives' (see e.g. Utting 2000: 21–2). Ultimately, there will always be areas and instances where there is a need for binding, industry-independent regulation in the public interest where confrontation cannot be avoided.

Given this research and historical evidence, the following analysis of the infant food debate conceptualizes the international regulation of transnational corporations as a *contested process* involving specific *actors* with differing *interests* and differing *power resources* in a precise *context*. This is a more fruitful framework within which to explore the opportunity for and limits to regulation of transnational corporations than an a-contextual framework based on a preconception of a harmonious process that disregards differences of power and interests.

Box 2.1 Regulation Versus Co-regulation Versus Self-regulation

Some Definitions

A crucial but difficult task of good governance is to establish limits for economic actors in areas where their commercial interests may conflict with public interests. For most people, the term regulation carries the connotation of public regulation whereby public authorities set rules and build the administrative and legal mechanisms to enforce them. This 'regulation by government authority' is known as command-and-control regulation (Buritt and McCreight 1998: 47).

Today, however, the term regulation has acquired a multitude of meanings. They range from straightforward legal definitions – 'the act or process of controlling by rule or restriction' (Garner 1999: 1289) – to the OECD's understanding of regulation as:

> the diverse set of instruments by which governments set requirements on enterprises and citizens. Regulations include laws, formal and informal orders and subordinate rules issued by all levels of government, and rules issues by non-governmental or self-regulatory bodies to whom governments have delegated regulatory powers.(OECD 2000b)[16]

The OECD definition thus encompasses 'non-governmental' and 'self-regulatory' bodies as regulatory protagonists but with the critical qualification that it is governments that have delegated the regulatory powers to them.

This book, which is concerned with regulations for big corporations, not citizens, uses a working definition of regulation as the 'establishment of rules and measures to influence effectively corporate practice in the public interest'. The term 'rules' is understood broadly as including legal, administrative and ethical principles, norms and rules as well as scientific standards.

This working definition thus encompasses current uses of the word 'regulation' that often go well beyond state-based rule-making, and explicitly expands the term 'rules' from the legal and administrative domain into the domain of ethics as well. (A topic for further discussion is the usefulness of a better distinction between state-sanctioned, legal and other types of rules-based regimes.)

Classification According to Rule-setters

'Rules require rule setters,' points out economist Robert Kuttner (1999). A distinction between 'public regulation', 'co-regulation' and 'industry self-regulation' draws attention to the major rule-setters operating today. It also helps point to some potential consequences for the quality of rules-based frameworks and the mechanisms to enforce these rules.

Public regulation refers to rules set by the parliament and/or government authorities. Public regulation, at least at national level, usually entails the establishment of measures to monitor and enforce the rules.

The primary role of corporations with respect to public regulation is to ensure their compliance with public laws and rules by devising company-internal guidelines and establishing effective auditing procedures, and to allow for public verification of their adherence to the regulatory measures.

At the international level, public regulatory frameworks are usually established through intergovernmental negotiations. As far as internationally agreed regulatory codes, guidelines, recommendations and laws for corporations are concerned, therefore, the duty of corporations is the same as that for national regulation. Depending on the type of international agreement, this duty may be a moral one or a moral *and* legal one. For example, since the 1992 UN Earth Summit agreed on 32 Principles for Multi-national Corporations as part of its international action programme, *Agenda 21*, these principles are being regarded as the minimum criteria for corporate behaviour towards achieving the international public aim of environmentally sound and socially just sustainable development (Krut and Gleckman 1998).[17]

Co-regulation refers to regulatory arrangements between business actors and one or more other parties. However, the term does not indicate who these co-regulatory parties are or should be. The term 'public and corporate co-regulation', referring to regulatory arrangements between industry and government authorities or UN agencies, is thus more specific.[18] Other parties to co-regulatory arrangements with economic actors can be labour, religious and/or civil society organizations.

The term co-regulation, moreover, does not indicate how many actors may be party to the rule-setting activity. It could refer to an arrangement between just one corporation and one NGO, or one between an international business association and a number of parties.

Furthermore, the term does not indicate who initiated the co-regulatory arrangement. Yet co-regulation initiated by government authorities is likely to differ significantly from arrangements initiated by civil society organizations and from arrangements initiated by corporations or business associations.[19]

A key feature of co-regulatory agreements as far as accountability is concerned is whether or not a government is one of the parties involved. Only public authorities can link voluntary co-regulation to legally binding enforcement measures should the industry fail to comply with the agreed rules-based framework.

This does not mean, however, that only the 'force of law' is effective in influencing corporate practices and conduct. Labour and civil society organizations, for example, have drafted model codes and pressured corporations publicly to adopt them as binding. Others have preferred to negotiate co-regulatory arrangements in tandem with industry. The primary means of making co-regulatory codes effective in practice is negative publicity – the 'naming and shaming' of those corporations that are found to violate the rules and standards which have been agreed.[20]

Self-regulation refers to arrangements where corporations or business associations establish their own rules in the form of codes of conduct, corporate guidelines or mission statements and pledge adherence to them.

'Self-regulation' may not, in fact, be the most appropriate term for arrangements in which the party to be regulated sets its own standards and whose effectiveness in protecting public interests depends entirely on a corporation's sense of moral obligation (see also Chapter 6).

Analyses of business codes, for example in relation to sustainable development, have concluded that industry codes omitted important *Agenda 21* standards and lacked effective enforcement mechanisms (UNCTAD 1996b).

Corporate Self-regulation: An Oxymoron?

Harris Gleckman and Riva Krut, who have investigated environmental regulation as an example of international social regulations, contend that:

> The campaign in favour of international environmental self-regulation by individual firms and industry trade associations has been energetic and has been supported by almost all the international trade associations. While not generally recognised as such, 'self-regulation' is really an oxymoron. Potential polluters cannot make 'laws' (i.e. regulate) and order 'sanctions' (i.e. authorise penalties and fines) that are against self-interest. Further, state regulation presumes that there is a political process that defines a level of pollution and regulations are issued to disperse this standard equitably over the generators of pollution. No individual 'self-regulator' can determine the publicly approved level of pollution or allocate itself the correct amount of pollution. (Gleckman and Krut 1994: 8–9)[21]

Gleckman and Krut postulate that public and corporate co-regulation and corporate self-regulation must be backed up by industry-independent measures if public interests are to be effectively protected. These include clear guidelines on how to ensure compliance to such codes; external third-party verification of the internal audit; and public reporting and public participation.[22]

Notes

1. UNDP 1999: 34.

2. See George and Sabelli 1994: 150, 154; Blundo 2000: 17; Archer 1994.

3. By the time the Commission released its report in 1995, however, political developments such as the 1992–95 war in Bosnia had made it clear that it would be much harder than originally envisioned to build such a system. For more information on the establishment and members of the Commission, see CGG 1995: 359–86.

4. Some commentators advise building on industry offers to behave in a more socially responsible manner but against a background of externally defined binding regulation should such co-regulatory arrangements fail.

5. See e.g. UNDP 1999; UNRISD 1999.

6. The term 'corporate citizen' adds further confusion. The 1999 UNCTAD *World Investment Report*, for example, regards the recent emergence of the notion of 'global corporate citizenship' as a positive development. It sees corporate citizenship as a broader concept than that of corporate responsibility and stresses that 'in the recent usage of corporate social responsibility … only the responsibilities or obligations of corporations to their host societies are discussed. Citizenship involves both rights *and* responsibilities. The "rights" involve the business community's concerns with standards of treatment in host countries for foreign investors.' Privileges granted to transnational corporations by host countries under the condition that they fulfil certain obligations are thus recast as unconditional rights, such as 'international investor rights'.

7. Elsewhere, however, the report does distinguish between civil society and the commercial sector, for instance, in its section on the unclear role of the 'private sector' in global governance (CGG, 1995: 25–6).

8. Each UN agency has its own criteria for acceptance.

9. Another 5 per cent were technical bodies, such as the International Organization for Standard Setting (ISO), while 22 per cent were professional, science or academic associations (Willets 1998: 204).

10. Some NGOs felt deeply uncomfortable when this influential US gun lobby gained NGO status in 1996 (Willets 1999: 259–60).

11. WEDO, the Women's Environment and Development Organization, produced two special education primers: *Transnational Corporations in the United Nations: Preventing Global Civil Governance* and *Transnational Corporations in the United Nations: Using or Abusing their Access?* The second quotes an NGO: 'It is unconscionable that people-centred groups should have to share their one channel to policy makers with profit-making concerns' (quoted in Krut 1997: 20).

12. Other acronyms include NGDO, non-governmental development organization; ENGO, environmental NGO; GRINGO, government-run NGO; GONGO, government-organized NGO; CBO, community-based organization;

GRO, grassroots organization; SMO, social movement organization (for further acronyms, see Krut 1997: 9).

13. Yet another UN classification, that of 'major groups', was created in 1992 within the environmental arena. The Earth Summit's *Agenda 21* contained a section on 'Strengthening the role of major groups'. The preamble to this section suggested that these groups were 'social groups' whose 'public participation in decision-making' was essential for the achievement of sustainable development. The nine major groups are: business and industry, NGOs, workers and their trade unions, local authorities, women, children and youth, indigenous peoples, farmers, the scientific and technical community. Willets 1999: 257.

14. See www.un.org/partners/

15. For example, the Commission on Global Governance report stressed that 'Governance would be strengthened through multilateral agreements that define minimum standards of corporate behaviour. It is in no one's interest that standards of safety are allowed to slide to a level that allowed the Bhopal disaster.' It is unclear, however, on what basis it concluded that while 'previous attempts to negotiate an overall UN code failed in more confrontational times … now there is a *high degree of convergence of attitude and common interest in creating a regime that* supports business but *outlaws abuses*' (CGG 1995: 173–4, emphasis added).

16. This definition guides the OECD's ongoing Regulatory Reform process in which existing regulations in OECD states are scrutinized with the primary aim of improving 'economic performance'.

17. Principles reproduced in Krut and Gleckman 1998: 132–4.

18. Term from Krut and Gleckman 1998: 92.

19. Co-regulatory and corporate self-regulatory arrangements are now often called 'voluntary initiatives', a term that creates much confusion. First, the term 'voluntary initiative' implicitly attributes the initiative to more socially responsible corporate conduct to the industry – even if a business association may have forcefully resisted a particular code of conduct at first and agreed to a co-regulatory arrangement only because of strong and persistent outside pressure. (The term 'voluntary' initiative is, in many ways, a misnomer, when, for instance, corporations put forward their own non-legally binding industry code to avoid tighter mandatory regulation or to defuse public pressure.) Second, the term does not distinguish between corporations' pledges of compliance to codes of conduct, corporate sponsorship, and a whole gamut of non-market-based corporate activities that are currently referred to as 'public–private partnerships'.

20. Murphy and Bendell (1999: 20) propose the term 'civil regulation' for efforts where civil society organizations are the prominent driver of a regulatory arrangement.

21. For other analyses of industry self-regulation from a societal perspective see also Greer and Bruno 1996: 33–7; Hansen 1999; UNSRID 2000a; Utting 2000.

22. For more details see Krut and Gleckman 1998: 92–108.

CHAPTER 3

'Commerciogenic Malnutrition':
The 'Bottle Baby Disease'

It is harsh, but correct, to consider some of these children
as suffering from 'commerciogenic malnutrition' – that is
caused by thoughtless promotion of these milks and infant
foods. (Derrick Jelliffe, Director of the Caribbean Food and
Nutrition Institute in Jamaica, 1971)[1]

If she continues to feed the baby with a dirty bottle and
dirty water, it can lead to the death of the child. We accept
no responsibility for hygienic conditions in the country
and for the lack of knowledge of writing and reading.
(Hans Rudolf Müller, vice-president, Nestlé, 1975)[2]

§ At the turn of the millennium, the World Health Organization
estimated that around 1.5 million infants die each year because they
are not breast-fed. This chapter outlines the origins and development
of the infant food industry, and illustrates how the industry's marketing practices, combined with the beliefs and practices of the Western-
trained medical community, contributed to the gradual replacement
of breast-feeding by commercial infant foods in industrialized and
developing countries.

It provides an overview of the marketing methods used by the
infant food industry in the 1960s and 1970s, when health professionals
and then citizen action groups began to raise the alarm about the
negative consequences of this trend in infant food marketing for infant
survival, health and growth, in particular in developing countries.

It describes how the regulation of the marketing practices of the
infant food industry became an international public issue. Dialogues
between health professionals, UN advisory groups and the industry
failed to persuade the industry to change its marketing practices. A

crucial turning point was when civil society actors brought the issue of harmful marketing practices onto the agenda of UN agencies.

Infant food manufacturers attempted to prevent the UN from taking up the issue by portraying external international regulation of industry practices as an interference in the free market. Nevertheless, in 1979 WHO and UNICEF called a Joint Meeting on Infant and Young Child Feeding to which, unusually, they decided to invite not only the industry but also its most outspoken critics from citizen action groups. The meeting was a milestone: it called for an international code of marketing practices; it catalysed the formation of an international issues network on infant feeding; and the network in turn catalysed the development of 'international issues management' – a corporate PR discipline that henceforth accompanied this and other regulatory debates.

The Birth of a Market[3]

In the middle of the nineteenth century, new techniques for processing milk were developed. Condensed tinned milk (1853), evaporated milk (1885), surpluses of whey in milk-producing countries, and new materials and production methods for feeding bottles and teats formed the basis of a new industry (Palmer 1993: 203).

German-born Henri Nestlé started his infant food business in 1867 by mixing toasted flour and condensed milk. As a chemist and merchant, he soon recognized the market opportunities for his *farine lactée*: 'My discovery will have a tremendous future because there is no food that might be compared to my flour mixture' (Buffle 1986).

By 1873, Nestlé's company was reporting sales of half a million boxes of 'Nestlé Milk Food' in Europe, America, Australia, Argentina, the Dutch East Indies and Mexico (Buffle 1986). Other baby food producers followed Nestlé's lead. By 1880, several brands of canned milk were advertised in Malaysia with statements such as 'Sweetened condensed milk is the food par excellence for delicate infants' (CAP 1981).

It was not until some 60 years later that the first criticisms of the gradual replacement of breast-milk with artificial baby milk were recorded. Paediatrician Dr Cicely Williams, subsequently the first director of the World Health Organization's Maternal and Child Health Programme, raised the alarm in her 1939 address to the Singapore Rotary Club entitled 'Milk and Murder':

If you are a legal purist, you may wish me to change the title of this address to Milk and Manslaughter. But if your lives were as embittered as mine is, by seeing day after day this massacre of the innocents by unsuitable feeding, then I believe you would feel as I do that misguided propaganda on infant feeding should be punished as the most criminal form of sedition, and that these deaths should be regarded as murder. (see Allain 1986)

Dr Williams did not single out infant food manufacturers as being responsible for these infant deaths. The gradual replacement of breast-feeding by artificial feeding was due to several synergistic factors. The Western medical community, caught in the prejudices of their time, believed that well-to-do upper-class women were too frail to breast-feed. Doctors experimented with 'infant formulas' – recipes that attempted to imitate human milk – so that these women would not have to use the services of wet-nurses. Mothers had to return to the doctor every few weeks to have the 'formula' adjusted to the individual digestion of their child. Thus when companies started marketing standard milk mixtures, mothers often found it more convenient and cheaper to purchase commercial formulas (Palmer 1993: 201–3).

Industry had decided to win over doctors as useful allies. Nestlé, for example, had been advertising directly to the public for decades with free samples and booklets. But when it launched Lactogen in 1924 in the USA, it specified that the product should be consumed 'only on the prescription or recommendation of a physician'. No feeding instructions appeared on the package label (Apple 1980). About the same time, infant food manufacturer Mead Johnson extolled the economic advantages of close cooperation between manufacturers and the medical profession:

> When mothers in America feed their babies by lay advice, the control of your paediatric cases passes out of your hands, Doctor. Our interest in this important phase of medical economics springs not from any motives of altruism, philanthropy or paternalism, but rather from a spirit of enlightened self-interest and co-operation because [our] infant diet materials are advertised only to you, never to the public. (Apple 1980)

After the Second World War, international trade opportunities began to expand. Nestlé and other companies, such as the British firm Cow & Gate, had already established their markets in countries under colonial rule. Later, when birth rates began to drop in industrialized countries, the newly independent countries became more significant as potential markets. In the early 1970s, for instance, a Nestlé publication stated of Thailand that 'the high birth rates permit a rapid expansion in the domain of infant nutrition' (Nestlé 1971).[4]

By the 1960s and 1970s, breast-feeding was in rapid decline in many parts of the world. In the USA, bottle feeding with commercial infant formula had become standard. The rate of breast-feeding newborns halved between 1946 and 1955; by 1967, only one-quarter of babies born in hospitals were breast-fed when their mothers took them home. Doctors who had little knowledge of breast-feeding, and who had been trained in clinical settings where mothers were routinely separated from their babies immediately after birth and given lactation suppressants, went out to developing countries as experts to help set up health care services (Palmer 1993: 220).

Marketing Methods

In the second half of the twentieth century, the infant food industry used a wide range of promotional methods to increase demand for commercially produced infant foods. Five of these methods are highlighted below.

Stressing equivalence or superiority to breast-feeding   Labels suggested that infant formula was as good as, if not better than, breast-feeding. For example, a label on a 1978 tin of Abbott-Ross's Similac proclaimed that 'there is no food equivalent that more closely resembles the milk of healthy well-fed mothers – SIMILAC with IRON – similar to mother's milk'. Wyeth stated on its S26 label: 'Nourishes the baby like mother's breast – S26 – a superior food for the infant' (quoted in Chetley 1979: 77).

Exploiting women's anxieties   Promotions played on women's fears of not producing enough milk. Nestlé stated that its products should be used 'When mother's milk fails' (poster for Lactogen formula from a clinic in Zimbabwe, quoted in Chetley 1986: 12). A radio jingle in the Belgian Congo crooned 'The child is going to die because the mother's breast has given out. Mama, O Mama, the child cries! If you want your child to get well, give it Klim milk' (*Printer's Ink* 1958).

Representing healthy, thriving babies   Images of chubby, healthy-looking babies in advertisements and on packaging suggested the promising outcome of feeding an infant with a particular brand. Such images were carefully chosen to appeal subconsciously to the promotional target: women with infants. Indeed, images in packaging, advertising or printed materials are often more important than the text in achieving a promotional goal.[5]

Disguising salespersons Free samples of breast-milk substitutes, literature and other gifts were distributed to mothers at a time when they were most vulnerable – just after they had given birth. Salespersons dressed as nurses ('milk nurses' or 'mothercraft nurses') would visit mothers of newborns in maternity wards or at home to promote bottle-feeding and to distribute samples. This particular marketing strategy reinforced product acceptance through association with an authoritative figure, albeit a bogus medical one. A Nigerian survey showed that 87 per cent of mothers using breast-milk substitutes did so in the belief that a health worker had recommended them (Baumslag 1995: 150).

Gaining medical endorsement Large amounts of free and 'low-cost' supplies were sent to maternity wards, creating a genuine medical seal of approval for early infant feeding with commercial foods. Gifts and sponsorships were given to health professionals. Infant food companies continued to find it effective to work through the medical profession. In 1970, *American Drug* magazine touted: 'Baby formula ... a high-volume item that is practically pre-sold to new mothers via physician/hospital endorsement.' Wyeth's 1975 *Infant Formula Sales Manual* stated that 'maternity services should be given primary allocation of free samples, geared to producing potential sales' (Borgholtz 1982: 186). Cow & Gate's 1976 annual report highlighted its highest-ever exports, thanks to 'wide contacts with the medical profession' (Borgholtz 1982: 177).

The success of these promotional techniques also depended on effective media strategies. In the 1970s, Nestlé prided itself on its imaginative reach into the poorest households:

> The advent of television as a universal means of communication with the shack as well as the mansion permits the standardisation to an increasing extent of advertising and promotion. Nestlé uses the medium extensively wherever it can. Where it still can't, the company relies on newspapers, colour magazines, billboards and other outdoor displays.

In less developed countries, the best form of promoting baby food formulas may well be the clinics which the company sponsors, at which nurses and doctors in its employ offer child-care guidance service.

In the less developed countries, effective distribution may call for unusual, imaginative techniques. (Willat 1970)

By means of all these promotional methods, powdered baby milk (which can be a useful feeding alternative for orphaned infants and in cases when a mother truly cannot breast-feed) 'was transformed into a consumer item to be pushed as suitable for every baby' (Allain 1991: 2).

While this trend towards artificial feeding benefited the manufacturers of infant formula, the promotion and indiscriminate use of breast-milk substitutes did little to benefit infants. Feeding with formula interferes with women's milk production. In addition, a mother's insecurity about her ability to breast-feed can reduce the flow of her milk. The use of bottles and teats, moreover, interferes with babies' ability to suckle. When infant formulas began to be promoted widely, both mothers and health personnel were quick to call these effects 'insufficient milk' and to believe that they indicated a permanent 'inability to breast-feed'. In the 1970s, it was not widely known among medical professionals that difficulties in breast-feeding could be reversed through encouragement, more frequent feeding and skilled help with positioning the baby at the breast.

It was widely known, however, that the use of artificial baby milk deprived babies not only of the best possible nutrition, but also of the immunological protection provided by antibodies in their mothers' milk. Moreover, at the end of the 1970s, no large infant food manufacturer could claim to be unaware that preparing baby milk in poor socio-economic and hygiene conditions might be detrimental to the health and lives of the 'end-consumers' of their product.

'Dialogues' with no Effects

The relationship between artificial feeding and increased child death and disease rates had been brought to the attention of infant food manufacturers in the early twentieth century. A 1910 study carried out in Boston had shown that bottle-fed babies were six times more likely to die than breast-fed ones. Another study on infant mortality, carried out in eight US cities between 1911 and 1916, had demonstrated the same six-fold increase in risk for babies from low-income families and a four-fold increased risk for babies in higher-income families (quoted in Palmer 1993: 207, 210).[6]

Yet it was nearly fifty years before concerns raised by health professionals working in developing countries about the potential fatal consequences of the inappropriate marketing of breast-milk substitutes began to be heard. These doctors and nurses began to issue warnings about the 'bottle baby disease', as they called the vicious cycle of artificial feeding, diarrhoea and malnutrition they observed in areas with poor access to safe water. Moreover, because commercial baby foods were expensive, families often did not have the resources to purchase the amount of infant formula needed to feed an infant adequately. Instead, they over-diluted the powder.

In 1968, Dr Derrick Jelliffe, director of the Caribbean Food and Nutrition Institute in Jamaica, indicted the infant food industry for causing 'commerciogenic malnutrition' (Jelliffe 1971: 55). One year later, Dutch paediatrician Dr Catherine Wennen described the marketing practices she had witnessed while working in Nigeria in the journal *Tropical and Geographical Medicine* (Wennen-van der May 1969).

Both these doctors initially believed that a dialogue between health professionals and industry representatives would solve the problem. Dr Wennen, for instance, had been shocked by the slogan broadcast regularly over Nigerian radio, 'Mother believe in Lactogen ... All things in mother's milk are also present in Lactogen. Mother watch the health of your baby, and give him the best, give Lactogen' (quoted in SAFEP 1975: 8). When she approached the Nestlé manager in Lagos 'to point out the sad consequences of their indiscriminate sales promotion', she found that 'he did not like to enter into dialogue' (quoted in SAFEP 1975: 10).

Jelliffe and another eminent paediatrician, Dr Bo Vahlquist, concluded that a higher-level discussion with as many companies as possible was necessary to make any impact and persuaded the UN Protein Advisory Group (PAG) *ad hoc* Working Group on Feeding the Pre-School Child to organize such a meeting. Twelve paediatricians, twelve industry representatives, and representatives from several UN agencies including UNICEF and the Food and Agriculture Organization (FAO) met in November 1970 in Bogotà, Colombia. The discussions took place behind closed doors to ensure full industry participation. A comprehensive report of this meeting was never published. Yet it is known that the industry disputed any relationship between the availability and promotion of infant formula and the decline in breast-feeding.

Several other meetings followed before the UN Protein Advisory Group decided to make a statement on the issue. Published in November 1973, the final PAG statement was, however, ambiguous. Although it referred to the advantages of breast-feeding, it paradoxically advocated a closer collaboration between governments and industry to widen the use of commercial infant foods still further: 'In any country lacking breastmilk substitutes, it is urgent that infant formulas be developed and introduced.' The statement asked governments to provide fiscal and financial incentives to encourage industrial investment and to consider subsidizing the distribution and promotion of such products (PAG 1973: 18). According to the author of *The Politics of Baby Foods*, Andrew Chetley, the statement gave an official stamp of approval for both the industry's products and marketing practices with its dual message: 'Breast milk is best, infant formula is virtually the same' (Chetley 1986: 41).[7]

Not much headway was made in another part of the UN system. The International Organization of Consumers Unions (IOCU) submitted a draft Code of Practice for Advertising of Infant Foods to the FAO/WHO Codex Alimentarius Commission in early 1972. This UN food safety and quality standards body paid little attention to the issue, which it felt was outside its area of competence (Chetley 1986: 42).

The Industry Under Public Scrutiny

If the expression of these concerns had been limited to these relatively secluded meetings, the infant food industry would probably have seen little need to change its marketing approaches. But other events intervened. The year 1974 is regarded by many analysts as a critical turning point in raising public awareness of the infant food issue and bringing it on to the agenda of policy-makers.

The build-up started in August 1973, when the UK-based magazine *New Internationalist* ran a cover story on 'The baby food tragedy'. Two child health specialists, Dr R. G. Hendrickes and Dr David Morley, accused the baby food industry of creating malnutrition through irresponsible marketing methods.

In 1974, the London-based War on Want organization published *The Baby Killer*, a devastating report on infant food promotion and its consequences based on evidence collected primarily in Africa (Muller

1974). The graphic pictures and plain language raised public awareness of the sometimes fatal effects of bottle-feeding. Twenty thousand copies were sold, and the booklet was widely translated.

In Switzerland, Arbeitsgruppe Dritte Welt (Third World Action Group) wrote a new foreword to its translation and changed the title to 'Nestlé tötet Babys' ('Nestlé kills babies') (Arbeitsgruppe Dritte Welt 1974). Published in May 1974, the book received wide coverage in the Swiss press. Two months later, Nestlé sued the group on four counts of libel: the title; that the company's practices were unethical; that the company was responsible for the death of and damage to thousands of babies; and that in developing countries baby food sales representatives dressed as nurses. Arbeitsgruppe Dritte Welt refused subsequent offers from Nestlé to settle out of court, stating that 'the trial about the consequences of processed baby foods in developing countries will be of public interest' (quoted in Chetley 1986: 44).

The infant food industry realized that controversy about its marketing practices was not going to go away and thus changed its tactics. Two days before the first of three hearings in the libel case, eight infant food companies – Cow & Gate, Dumex, Meiji, Morinaga, Nestlé, Snow Brand, Wakado and Wyeth – announced the formation of an International Council of Infant Food Industries (ICIFI).[8] One of the first acts of this business association was to draft a code of ethics, which was released with much press fanfare two days after the end of the first court hearing (ICIFI 1975, amended 1976).

Many people saw the ICIFI code as a positive step, an indication that the industry had voluntarily adopted controls on itself and that it had the ability to enforce them internationally. Closer examination of this voluntary code, however, revealed that it would have allowed most promotional practices to continue. Given the timing of the formation of the business association and the release of the code, several NGOs felt that the ICIFI code was 'little more than a public relations exercise designed to stave off critics and deep public concern over their marketing methods'. What was needed, in their view, was 'a legal obligation on the companies, enforced by government and monitored by UN agencies' (War on Want 1975).[9]

Just before the last of the three hearings in July 1976, Nestlé dropped three of the four libel charges, leaving just the complaint about the title of the Swiss booklet. The judge fined members of the group a symbolic 300 Swiss francs each because Nestlé 'in terms of criminal law' could not be held responsible for the infant deaths. The judge nevertheless emphasized that the company's advertising practices in developing countries 'went considerably further' than those in industrialized countries:

> The need ensues for the Nestlé company to fundamentally rethink its advertising practices in developing countries concerning bottle feeding, for its advertising practice up to now can transform a life-saving product into one that is dangerous and life-destroying. If the complainant in future wants to be spared the accusation of immoral and unethical conduct, it will have to change advertising practices. (quoted in Chetley 1986: 45)

The libel case generated not only broad public recognition but also much documentation on Nestlé's promotional practices. It also prompted the formation of a network of citizens from eight countries committed to collecting and exchanging information on the issue (Clement 1988: 352).

Nestlé responded by citing prevailing standards of practice. A few days after the judge's verdict, the company's managing director Arthur Furer told his staff that he had personally investigated the marketing practices of the company:

> I was able to see that they were normal and usual advertising methods, used by manufacturers of such products all over the world ... [therefore] we must affirm that we have full confidence in the ethical basis of our action. (quoted in SAFEP 1976: B3)

Shareholder Resolutions, a Consumer Boycott and a US Senate Hearing

It was also in 1974 that the issue of artificial infant feeding crossed the Atlantic from Europe to the USA. Media coverage had stimulated wider interest in the issue. Peter Krieg's half-hour film *Bottle Babies*, documenting the conditions and consequences of the use of infant formulas in Kenya, helped to build a campaign in the USA where infant food corporations had not yet come under scrutiny.

During 1974, the US National Council of Churches, concerned about a wide range of TNC practices, founded the Interfaith Centre on Corporate Responsibility (ICCR). Its aim was to monitor those TNCs in which churches had invested money. If any particular industry practice was deemed to be against social interests, shareholder power could be used to bring about change.

At the end of 1974, the ICCR helped to prepare shareholder resolutions seeking disclosure of information about the marketing strategies of US-based infant food companies. When one of these, Bristol Myers, made misleading statements to its shareholders – it claimed that it did not market its products in places where chronic poverty could lead to harmful effects – an order of Catholic nuns, the Sisters of the Precious Blood, filed a lawsuit. The case dragged on for almost two years, from spring 1976 until January 1978, when the company offered to settle out of court. It agreed to send a report to the shareholders, including all the evidence collected by the Sisters and the ICCR that countered Bristol Myers's claims. It also agreed to halt all direct advertising and the use of 'mothercraft' nurses (Chetley 1986: 50–2).

Yet many ordinary people felt that more had to be done than filing shareholder resolutions or getting involved in difficult legal cases. Many of them were moved by disquieting scenes in the *Bottle Babies* film, such as that of a severely malnourished baby screaming as a drip was placed into a vein in her head (Palmer 1993: 239). Thus on 4 July 1977, the Minneapolis-based Infant Formula Action Coalition (INFACT) launched a consumer boycott of Nestlé.

INFACT chose Nestlé for three reasons. Because the company had nearly half the world's market share of infant food, any change in its marketing practices would have a major positive impact on the health and well-being of children, and other companies could be expected to follow suit. Moreover, of all the infant food companies, Nestlé most consistently denied having anything to do with the deaths of bottle-fed babies, questioning instead the motives of those involved in the campaign to change corporate promotional practices. Finally, at the time, as Nestlé was Swiss-based, US citizens could not exert pressure via shareholder resolutions (Chetley 1986: 52).[10]

Nestlé's immediate reaction to the consumer boycott was to contact church leaders across the USA. One of the world's largest public relations firms, Hill and Knowlton, mailed 300,000 copies of a 24-page glossy publication to clergy and religious organizations across the country, stating that Nestlé's marketing practices were ethical and asking them not to participate in the boycott. Ironically, many church members heard about the boycott for the first time through this publication. Nestlé's newly founded Office of Corporate Responsibility also implied in a two-page leaflet that the World Council of Churches intended to overthrow capitalism (Nestlé 1977). Yet by the end of 1978, the boycott had spread across the USA and beyond to Canada,

New Zealand and Australia. Church groups, student groups, trade unions, women's organizations, health workers, public figures and some prominent politicians had all become part of it (Chetley 1986: 53; Palmer 1993: 247).

US citizens wrote to their congressional representatives and other politicians asking them to take a stand. US Senator Edward Kennedy, chair of the Senate Sub-Committee on Health and Scientific Research, held a public hearing in May 1978 on the promotion of infant formula in developing countries. In his testimony, Nestlé Brazil's president, Oswaldo Ballarin, stated:

> The US Nestlé Co has advised me that their research indicates that this [boycott] is actually an indirect attack on the free world's economic system. A world-wide church organization, with the stated purpose of undermining the free enterprise system, is in the forefront of this activity. (Ballarin 1978)

Senator Kennedy dismissed Nestlé's interpretation by stating that 'a boycott is a recognised tool in a free economic democratic system … and it is not recognised as being a part of an international kind of conspiracy to bring the free world's economic system down' (quoted in Sethi 1994: 77).[11]

WHO and UNICEF Become Involved

The US Senate hearing brought the issue of harmful marketing practices onto the international policy agenda. Concerned about the infant food manufacturers' disavowal of responsibility for the consequences of their practices, Kennedy went on to organize a meeting with industry representatives to discuss the issue further. Afterwards, he concluded that unilateral regulation of US-based companies 'might not be appropriate'. Instead, he felt an international solution to an international problem was required (quoted in Chetley 1986: 57).

In July 1978, Kennedy wrote to the director-general of the World Health Organization, Halfdan Mahler, to inform him that the industry representatives had requested:

> that the World Health Organization convene a conference of industry representatives, industry critics, nutrition experts, and appropriate government officials and health professionals from developing nations to address the problem [of the promotion and marketing of infant formula] on a global basis.

He added, 'the conference may consider, among other things, the adoption of a meaningful, uniform code of ethics acceptable to all infant formula manufacturers' (Kennedy 1978).

WHO and UNICEF set October 1979 as the date for a meeting on the broad question of infant and young child feeding. The industry's business association, the International Council of Infant Food Industries, immediately notified WHO of its willingness to participate in such a meeting, hoping that the UN agencies would moderate the dispute and 'depoliticise the controversy' (McComas et al. 1983: 14). In the 15 months before the meeting, the industry emphasized that there was no need for public debate or a boycott because the issues would soon be resolved in the 'proper forum for discussion of all questions related to these problems'.[12]

Intense struggles between all the players took place before and during the 1979 meeting, a meeting in which the involvement of civil action groups was key and one that was considered 'a major departure from the traditional relationship between the United Nations and non-governmental organisations. For the first time, the public itself was recognised through several constituency-based organizations from both industrialised and Third World countries' (Lemaresquier 1980: 120).[13]

The composition of the participants was unprecedented: representatives of 23 governments, 14 officials of the UN and other specialized agencies; 19 delegates from NGOs, 26 representatives from industry; and 22 experts on nutrition, paediatrics, sociology, public health and marketing (Sokol 1997: 8).

When the infant food industry realized that it could not control the process of the WHO/UNICEF meeting and that the other participants might recommend that limits be put on its marketing practices, it protested about 'an abandonment of free enterprise' and began to describe the development of an international code of conduct governing its actions as an infringement of states' national sovereignty. ICIFI President Ian Barter explained: 'We welcome codes of conduct. We want to see as many codes as possible. The idea of a generalised code is one we do not find helpful' (quoted in Chetley 1986: 67–8).[14] Yet the unanimous consensus of the WHO/UNICEF meeting was that:

> There should be no marketing or availability of infant formula or weaning foods in a country unless marketing practices are in accord with the national code or legislation if they exist, or, in their absence, with the spirit of this meeting and the recommendations contained in this report or with any agreed international code. (WHO 1979: 29)

WHO and UNICEF were requested to begin the process of preparing an international code of marketing of breast-milk substitutes.

Citizen Networks and Corporate Counter-actions

The 1979 Joint WHO/UNICEF Meeting was a watershed because it put the formulation of an international code on marketing practices firmly on the agenda of two major UN agencies. It was also a landmark in the broader history of international regulation.

Towards the end of the meeting, representatives from six NGOs – Arbeitsgruppe Dritte Welt, ICCR, INFACT, IOCU, Oxfam and War on Want – decided to form a dispersed multinational network to work on the issue of artificial feeding. Its first aim was to monitor corporate activity throughout the world relating to infant food and to share this information as widely as possible. This network, the International Baby Food Action Network (IBFAN), subsequently became a model for a number of issue-based international networks, such as Health Action International (HAI), formed in 1981 to follow consumer issues related to the pharmaceutical industry, and the Pesticide Action Network (PAN), which has been monitoring the chemical industry since 1982 (for more details see Chapter 9).

The industry perceived the formation of the IBFAN network and its effectiveness in influencing the debate as a threat. As proposals for an international code on the marketing of breast-milk substitutes became more concrete, ICIFI's newly elected president, Nestlé's vice-president, Ernest Saunders, wrote:

> In view of the overall propaganda campaign now being mounted through IBFAN and the professionalism of the forces involved, it is always possible that we could even win a battle in the US and lose the war as a result of the determined pressure on Third World governments and medical authorities. It is clear that we have an urgent need to develop an effective counter-propaganda operation, with a network of appropriate consultants in key centres, knowledgeable in the technicalities of infant nutrition in developing countries, and with the appropriate contacts to get articles placed. (Saunders 1980b)[15]

As shown in Chapter 8, the Code became a key factor not only in the evolution of international citizen networks, but also in the development and spread of 'international issues management' – one of the most strategic public relations disciplines designed to help industry

'shape rather than to react to public discourse and decision making'
(Baskin et al. 1997: 80–2).

Notes

1. Jelliffe 1971.

2. Müller 1975.

3. Chapters 2 and 3 draw extensively on Chetley 1986 and Palmer 1993.
Other sources include Sethi 1994; Shubber 1998: 2–45; Sokol 1997: 1–36.

4. Commercial distribution of breast-milk substitutes was also helped by
the widespread establishment of milk depots in health care centres where
cows' milk was distributed free to child-bearing and -rearing women in the
mistaken belief that it was the food *par excellence* to guard against malnutrition. Charities, including UNICEF, participated. For details, see Palmer
1993: 193–4, 221–7).

5. A former director of an international marketing firm in South-East
Asia described the marketing strategy at the end of the 1970s: 'It was the
Western way of doing things and this had enormous appeal to these people
[in developing countries] … It's such a huge market … [I]f we could get these
people to use these products, it's a vast amount of money involved … We
were discussing the marketing strategy behind these products … Mothers are
very emotional about their children … for visual imagery, large-scale posters,
and so on, we wanted the youngest possible babies … The information about
the terrible dangers inherent … the multinationals did nothing about it, as far
as I can see … Nobody talked about boiling water, nobody told us about the
advantages of breast-feeding.' This marketing professional turned whistleblower on Nestlé after he saw a film documentary in which a Filipina mother
quoted the slogan of his marketing firm. Her baby had died not because she
had not cared but because she had wanted to give her child the 'next best
thing' (Gravet 1989).

6. Even these early studies showed that higher mortality rates were caused
not only by diarrhoea, a disease often associated with poor hygiene, but also
by pneumonia, measles, whooping cough and other communicable diseases.
These results suggested that bottle-feeding put children's health at risk not
only if contaminated bottles and water were used but also by depriving
children of the immunological protection of breast-milk, rendering them
more susceptible to infectious diseases (Palmer 1993: 210).

7. The statement referred in just two places to the promotion of breast-
milk substitutes: anything that 'could discourage appropriate breastfeeding'
should be avoided; and promotion to mothers in maternity wards was inappropriate (quoted in Chetley 1986: 42).

8. US company Abbott-Ross decided not to join the ICIFI because the
business association's code did not specifically rule out mass media advertising
of infant food, a practice Abbott-Ross found 'inappropriate in Third World
settings' (quoted in Chetley 1986: 48).

9. For more details, see Chetley 1986: 48–50.

10. In 1999, *The Independent* stated: 'until ten years ago, non-Swiss were not even allowed to own the company's registered shares' (Koenig 1999). And in 1996, it was reported that Nestlé shareholders had to hold a market value of 140 million Swiss francs' worth of shares to bring any item onto the official agenda of the company's shareholder meeting (INBC 1996).

11. For more information about boycotts as a democratic means to influence corporate practices, see Chapter 9.

12. Nestlé chief executive officer Arthur Furer, personal correspondence, 14 August 1979, quoted in Chetley 1986: 57.

13. For a detailed description of the dynamics of the meeting, see Chetley 1986: 57, 61–74.

14. Chetley points to the contradiction between the ICIFI's most vocal objections to a universal UN-brokered code of marketing and its concomitant promotion of the ICIFI's own industry code as international and all-embracing (Chetley 1986: 68).

15. For a description of the context of the letter, see Chetley 1986: 55–6.

CHAPTER 4

. . . .

Formulation and Adoption of the International Code of Marketing of Breast-milk Substitutes

> We are not today dealing with an economic issue of particular importance only to one or a few Member States. We are dealing with a health issue of essential importance to all Member States, and particularly to developing nations, and of importance to the children of the world and thus to all future generations. (Statement of WHO Executive Board member Torbjørn Mork to the World Health Assembly 1981)[1]

§ Any international regulatory code should ideally be as clearly and unambiguously worded as possible. It should be adopted in such a way as to facilitate its swift translation into national legislation and other measures so that its aim can be achieved most effectively.

In the real world, however, setting rules to govern the activities of TNCs is an extraordinarily difficult exercise. The different opinions of various actors involved in code formulation and adoption and the balance of power between them may adversely influence both the content and the legal standing of a code.

This chapter describes how the political processes surrounding the formulation and adoption of the International Code of Marketing of Breast-milk Substitutes, in particular the pressure exerted by the infant food industry and the US government, resulted in the Code being watered down and adopted as the weakest of the WHO's three possible forms of legal instruments.

A Breakthrough in the Debate

The World Health Assembly (WHA), the decision-making body of the WHO, which comprises the Ministers of Health of all member states, had twice adopted resolutions expressing their concern about 'the general decline in breast-feeding, related to socio-cultural and environmental factors, including the mistaken idea caused by misleading sales promotion that breast-feeding is inferior to feeding with manufactured breast-milk substitutes' (Resolution WHA 31.47, 1974).[2]

The 1974 Resolution urged member states 'to review sales promotion activities on baby foods and to introduce appropriate remedial measures, including advertisement codes and legislation where necessary'. The 1978 WHA Resolution went further and recommended 'supporting and promoting breast-feeding by educational activities among the general public; legislative and social action to facilitate breast-feeding by working mothers ... and regulating inappropriate sales promotion of infant foods that can be used to replace breast-milk'.[3]

Implementation of both Resolutions was at the discretion of member states, however, and few had done so. The 1979 Joint WHO/UNICEF Meeting took things further. Sami Shubber, a former WHO senior legal officer responsible for Code matters, regards this meeting and its unambiguous consensus as 'the breakthrough, insofar as the development of an *international* code is concerned' (Shubber 1998: 5, emphasis added). At this meeting, the WHO and UNICEF were requested to prepare an international code of marketing:

> There should be an international code of marketing of infant formula and other products used as breast-milk substitutes. This should be supported by both exporting and importing countries and observed by all manufacturers. WHO/UNICEF are requested to organize the process for its preparation, with the involvement of all concerned parties, in order to reach a conclusion as soon as possible. (WHO 1979: 29)

Conflicts in Developing the Code

The formulation of the International Code of Marketing of Breast-milk Substitutes was without precedent. It involved an extraordinary process of consultation with constituencies ranging from member states and UN organizations to consumer action and development NGOs, professional associations and industry. Between January and December 1980, four drafts were produced and discussed under difficult circumstances.[4]

Two major controversies arose about the way in which the Code should be developed and the legal form it should take.

Process of Code Drafting

The 1979 Joint WHO/UNICEF Meeting request to involve 'all concerned parties' in the Code drafting process was not easy to carry out in practice. UNICEF and the WHO pointed out to civil society organizations and to industry that they were being invited to 'consultations', not 'negotiations'.[5]

NGO representatives questioned the involvement of industry in the consultations as one of the 'concerned parties'. They cautioned that there were potential adverse consequences stemming from a lack of distinction between the party to be regulated (the infant food industry) and the parties involved in the consultations about appropriate regulatory measures (also the infant food industry). They warned that there were insufficient precautions to prevent the infant food industry having undue influence on the process:

> If the code development process is one of political negotiations and compromise rather than adherence to a set of principles based on notions of 'equity', 'social justice' and 'what is best for infants', then … the code may serve the interests of the industry more than the populations in whose interest the code development process was undertaken. (Post and Baer 1980: 57–8)[6]

The NGOs wanted the Code to spell out clearly its overarching ethical principles and to contain unambiguous and tightly worded sections detailing which marketing practices were inadmissible. Without these, they argued, the Code might not fulfil its aim effectively; indeed, it might even legitimize certain sales practices because it would leave too much room for industry 'interpretations of convenience'.[7]

During this process, the industry association's statements fluctuated from expressing its total opposition to any external international regulation to requesting an international Code – on condition that it was as loosely worded as possible and that its interpretation was left to national governments (in cooperation with industry). The infant food manufacturers' most powerful ally was the US government.

Several industry statements give some impression of the pressure the UN agencies and WHA member states were under as they drafted the marketing code. For instance, while a New York-based professor, David Kadane, was preparing a first draft for WHO and UNICEF, Nestlé wrote to the director of WHO's Family Health Division, Dr Angèle Petros-Barvazian, with its suggestion for a first draft – the ICIFI

International Code of Marketing in Developing Countries (Fookes 1980). When WHO came to circulate its own draft, ICIFI protested that it was 'unacceptable' and suggested that 'the draft code which ICIFI submitted informally ... is a far more realistic basis for discussion' (Barter 1980).

In March 1980, ICIFI urged that 'an attempt to develop <u>one</u> detailed international code is unrealistic in practical terms'. Instead it suggested that parties should work 'on a draft code of <u>general principles</u> ... leaving *detailed codes to be worked out between governments and industry* as required'. ICIFI went on to remind WHO of the 'the essential importance of working <u>with</u> industry as opposed to being in competition with us' (Saunders 1980a; underlining in original, emphasis added).

US-based companies, meanwhile, lobbied their government to support their position. As a result, the US government sent a letter to WHO calling for a general voluntary code for recommendations which was categorically *not 'mandatory on governments or corporations'*. The USA also asked that 'the contents of the documents must be subject to full *intergovernmental negotiations'* (both quotes in Bryant 1980; emphases added). Investigative health researcher Andrew Chetley explains why industry favoured intergovernmental negotiations:

> It would mean a much slower process: the UN had been negotiating a code of conduct for TNCs for over five years, and major stumbling-blocks still remained in it. In addition, as negotiations drag on, the provisions of any such code are more likely to become more generalised, weaker and ineffective. From the perspective of the TNCs this would be helpful, for while negotiations were in progress, TNCs could argue that it would be improper to implement any of the proposed provisions until *all* the provisions had been agreed. (Chetley 1986: 77; original emphasis)

WHO's Sami Shubber makes a similar assessment:

> Had the [intergovernmental negotiations] been accepted, it would be reasonable to suggest that the International Code could not have been completed in time for submission to the [WHO] Executive Board in January 1981 ... [Moreover] a group of states could have been subjected to more pressure from the infant food industry than that brought to bear against the secretariats of WHO and UNICEF. (Shubber 1998: 21)

WHO's members settled the issue at the 1980 World Health Assembly.

In a resolution, they endorsed the statement and recommendations made by the 1979 Joint WHO/UNICEF Meeting 'in their entirety' and reconfirmed the mandate of WHO:

> to prepare an international code of marketing of breast-milk substitutes ... [and to] submit the code ... together with proposals regarding its promotion and implementation, either as a regulation ... or as a recommendation ... outlining the legal and other consequences of each choice. (Resolution WHA 33.32, 1980)

Although the USA voted for this resolution, it insisted that:

> [The US] government does not want this decision to be considered as a precedent for the drafting of codes in other UN agencies. The US delegation believes that agreements of this nature between governments should be negotiated between governments. That is the practice regarding preparation of codes in ECOSOC, UNCTAD, the ILO and other parts of the UN system. (quoted in Chetley 1986: 79–80)[8]

Regulation or Recommendation?

The legal form of the International Code became the next contested issue. Which of the three legal forms allowed under WHO's constitution would it take: a Convention, a Regulation or a Recommendation?[9]

A Convention, which has the strongest legal status, requires a two-thirds majority of the WHA for adoption. In the case of the marketing of breast-milk substitutes, the WHO Secretariat and the 1980 WHA felt that the time needed to agree a Convention combined with the political manoeuvring to achieve two-thirds of the votes would delay Code adoption (Chetley 1986: 80; Post and Baer 1980: 57–8; Shubber 1998: 28).

A Regulation requires a simple majority of the WHA. It automatically comes into force in all member countries within a stated period of time, except in those that specifically reject it or attach reservations to it.[10]

WHO Recommendations may also be adopted by a simple majority of the World Health Assembly. They are not binding on member states in a strict legal sense, but they do 'carry some moral and political weight, as they constitute the judgement of the collective membership of the Organisation' (Shubber 1998: 30).[11]

In the early 1980s, most WHA members favoured a Regulation. The infant food industry, however, lobbied governments to ensure that any code drawn up and accepted by the WHA was in the weaker form of a Recommendation.

In theory, decisions at the World Health Assembly are taken according to the 'one country one vote' principle. But the comments made in 1981 by the chairperson of a major US pharmaceutical company, Robert Dee of Smith Kline, illustrate that in practice the votes of some countries carry more weight than others because of their influence in other spheres:[12]

> My … recommendation is that we put intense pressure on the UN – and on its health agencies … For this year and next, 70% of WHO's budget will be paid by 13 industrialised countries – 13 out of 156 WHO member countries. Certainly this entitles the industrialised world to stand up to WHO. We must have the will to do so. (Dee 1981)

In considering the legal form of the Code, WHO staff were well aware that the USA was contributing 25 per cent of the agency's budget. A US official reported:

> The [WHO] Secretariat left no doubt that it is under pressure from both sides, but it wants to find a *formula acceptable to the US*. (quoted in Chetley 1986: 83; emphasis added)

It was WHO's understanding that, if the Secretariat advocated that the Code be a Recommendation, the USA would help to get an unanimous vote from WHA members. In November 1980, WHO Assistant Director-General David Tejada explained to a meeting of IBFAN representatives that WHO would press for a consensus Recommendation because it was more likely to be accepted and implemented than a controversial Regulation.

As soon as the infant food manufacturers heard about this shift, they intensified their efforts to prevent WHO acceptance of the Code at all or at least to weaken its content still further (Chetley 1986: 85, 90–2).[13] At each revision of the fourth (and final) draft, the text became 'more unclear on the essential elements of the code and an increasing amount of industry wording, and industrialised country wording found its way into the code' (War on Want 1980).

At the WHO Executive Board's deliberation on the Code in early 1981, several government delegates expressed concern about this broad wording. The Samoan delegate, Dr Ridings, noted that 'the code is far too loose from the point of view of a developing country. In fact, it's got so many holes in it that an unscrupulous manufacturer could drive a herd of milk cows through it' (Chetley 1986: 90). Other Board members considered the text a 'bare minimum of measures' and a 'minimum requirement'.[14]

Yet ICIFI's Ernest Saunders wrote in a letter to the WHO Executive Board on the final draft:

> The world industry has found this present draft code unacceptable ... highly restrictive ... irrelevant and unworkable ... The various provisions, if applied, could have a negative effect on child health by restricting the flow of factual information, both to the medical profession and the mothers in need. (Saunders 1981)

The industry pursued other avenues as well to express its opposition to the Code. For example, it circulated newspaper articles to Executive Board members calling the process of drawing up the Code an 'unprecedented attempt at international legislation by ideological intimidation'[15] (Lefever 1981) and describing church support for the Nestlé boycott as 'Marxists marching under the banner of Christ' (Nickel 1980).

In March 1981, the *Washington Post* reported that:

> three American manufacturers of infant formula publicly launched a joint campaign yesterday to defeat a proposed international marketing code for breastmilk substitutes. Executives of Bristol-Myers Co., Abbott Laboratories and American Home Products Corp. began a two-week series of visits to officials of all affected federal agencies and to key legislators to urge that the United States oppose adoption of the draft code ... The [World Health] Assembly's more than 150 other member governments are being pressed by foreign formula-makers to reject the draft. (Mintz 1981)

As the 1981 World Health Assembly opened, Stanislas Flache of ICIFI reiterated in an interview with the *International Herald Tribune*: 'We oppose the universal code and some believe that it is a sign that the UN system is moving to control multinationals' (quoted in Krause 1981).

The USA's Volte-face

When a WHO Executive Board representative introduced the Code to the 1981 World Health Assembly, he explained that the Board's decision to suggest adoption of the weaker legal form of the Code was based on:

which alternative had the better chance of fulfilling the purpose of the code – that is to contribute to improved infant and child nutrition and health. The Board agreed that the moral force of an unanimous recommendation could be such that it would be more persuasive than a regulation that had gained less than unanimous support from Member States.

The introductory speech ended with a 'plea for consensus' and a reminder of what was at stake:

> We are not today dealing with an economic issue of particular importance only to one or a few Member States. We are dealing with a health issue of essential importance to all Member States, and particularly to developing nations, and of importance to the children of the world and thus to all future generations. (both quotes Mork, WHO 1981a: 35–6)

Despite expectations of an unanimous vote, however, the US delegation suddenly announced that it could not support the Code, even as a Recommendation. Thus 118 states voted in favour of the Code, one against, while three countries (Argentina, Japan and the Republic of Korea) abstained (Shubber 1998: 43).[16, 17]

This sudden change in the US position generated much debate during and after the 1981 World Health Assembly, not least because the wish to avoid controversy had significantly shaped the choice of the legal form of the Code. But, taken by surprise, the WHA member states did not insist on discussing whether a Regulation was preferable to a Recommendation, as had been originally called for in the 1980 Resolution. Given the prevalent mood at the time, however, the WHA might well have voted for the Code's adoption as a Regulation.[18]

Today's Question About Yesterday's Trade-offs

It is still a pertinent question today: was it wise to trade the stronger legal form of a Regulation for the anticipated moral force of a consensus Recommendation? A decision to opt for a Regulation could have had adverse financial consequences for WHO in terms of withheld US contributions.[19] But on the other hand, as the next chapter suggests, the fact that the Code was passed as a broadly worded Recommendation, not a Regulation, has had significant implications as far as its implementation is concerned – and as a result for the well-being of millions of children the world over.

Notes

1. Torbjørn Mork, director-general of health services, Norway.

2. The Pan American Health Organization (PAHO), a regional arm of the WHO, had adopted guidelines in 1970 to prevent advertising of 'commercial milk', access of 'mothercraft nurses' and acceptance of 'free' milk samples.

3. Resolutions WHA 27.43 and WHA 31.47. Quoted in the introduction to WHO 1981b: 5 and Shubber 1998: 5.

4. For details of the process, see Chetley 1986: 75–100; Shubber 1998: 6–45.

5. See Chetley 1986: 81 and Shubber 1998: 43, fn. 50.

6. Leah Margulies from the ICCR argued: 'We feel the code should clearly state what are the best kind of practices to ensure infant health and it should not be arrived at through a negotiation where the companies say, all right, we will stop such and such practice if you will take out of the code another kind of restriction. We feel that it is the job of the international health agencies to articulate the finest possible code of conduct to protect infant lives' (quoted in Chetley 1986: 76).

7. As summarized by James Post, professor of management and public policy at Boston University, and James Baer, associate director of the Infant Formula Program of the Interfaith Centre on Corporate Responsibility (ICCR). They captured the dilemma facing WHO and UNICEF secretariats by posing the question: 'How strict can the code's provisions be and still retain the participation and commitment of the industry?' In Post and Baer's view, both agencies seem to have believed that 'more progress can be achieved by gathering industry support, even if it means weakening the code, than by adopting a code that would be "ideal" but unacceptable to the industry' (Post and Baer 1980: 57–8).

8. Canada had similar reservations put on record (Chetley 1986: 80).

9. Constitution of the World Health Organization, Articles 19, 21 and 23.

10. A Regulation as a concrete legal form under the WHO Constitution should not be confused with regulation in general, which is understood in this publication as a rules-based regime to ensure that industry practices conform to public interests. Regulation under the WHO Constitution is therefore distinguished from more general rules-based regimes by using a capital letter.

11. For more details about the standing of the different forms of legal instruments, see Shubber 1998: 28–30 and Del Ponte 1982. In fact, non-binding resolutions of UN agencies can subsequently gain the weight of international customary law. The most important example can be found in the United Nations Universal Declaration of Human Rights, which was adopted in 1948 as a 'common standard of achievements for all peoples'. Even before the Declaration was specified further in the form of two Covenants, many of its provisions had made their way into national constitutions (UN 1998: 18).

12. This practice continues today; see Bienen et al.: 298–9 and Foster 1999.

13. Sami Shubber refers to a 'hostile campaign carried against WHO, UNICEF and the International Code, carried out, basically by the infant food industry' at the time of discussion of the fourth draft by the WHO's Executive Board (Shubber 1998: 39).

14. See e.g. Shubber 1998: 44, 203–4.

15. For detailed quotation, see Shubber 1998: 35, fn. 19.

16. For further details about the confusion surrounding the vote, see Sokol 1997: 12–13 and Shubber 1998: 42–3.

17. The US delegation itself seems not to have known until the very last minute whether or not it could support the Code. In 1980, the US delegation had supported the WHA Resolution requesting the Code. Apparently, the replacement of US President Jimmy Carter by Ronald Reagan that same year prompted a hard-line decision. As the *Financial Times* stated, 'the decision to vote against the World Health Organization's Code was taken by the White House ... after direct representation by industry and over the more cautious advice of lower level bureaucrats in both the State and Health and Human Services Departments that the US simply abstain' (see Chetley 1986: 95 and Shubber 1998: 16, 49).

18. A similar observation applies to the UN Code of Conduct on Transnational Corporations discussed in Chapter 1. The former executive director of the UN Centre on Transnational Corporations, Sidney Dell, saw it as 'highly probable' that the draft Code would have gained approval of the majority of states had it been put to vote in 1985.

19. For industry and US predictions of adverse consequences if the Code were passed as a Regulation, see Chetley 1986: 93 and Shubber 1998: 41.

CHAPTER 5

· · · · · · · · · · · · · · · ·

Implementing the Code

> Governments should take action to give effect to the prin-
> ciples and aim of this Code, as appropriate to their social
> and legislative framework, including the adoption of
> national legislation, regulations or other suitable measures.
> For this purpose, governments should seek, when neces-
> sary, the cooperation of WHO, UNICEF and other agencies
> of the United Nations system. (Article 11.1, International
> Code of Marketing of Breast-milk Substitutes)

§ The International Code of Marketing of Breast-milk Substitutes
applies to infant formula and other products marketed or represented
as replacements for breast-milk, as well as feeding-bottles and teats.
The Code prohibits promotion of breast-milk substitutes to the general public, and direct or indirect contact between marketing personnel
and pregnant women or mothers of infants and young children. It
sets standards for pictures and information on labels, information and
educational material on infant feeding, provision of samples and free
supplies, and interactions between companies and the health care
system. (For more details, see Chapter 6.)

Adopting an international code is just one step in the process of
making transnational corporations more socially accountable by means
of international regulation. It is up to national governments to render
such codes effective by implementing them via national legislation, or
equivalent measures such as decrees, and by providing for effective
mechanisms of monitoring and enforcement.

This chapter demonstrates that the translation of the International
Code into effective national legislation and other regulatory measures
has been uneven. A majority of countries have adopted regulatory
measures, but they fall short of expectations at the time of the Code's
adoption. Others have yet to implement the Code in any form.

This chapter points to various factors that might have adversely affected the pace and extent of national implementation. While there is a lack of systematic case study research into the complications encountered during Code implementation at the *national* level, the origins of three major obstacles at the *international* level can be identified:

- legacies of the process of Code formulation and adoption;
- industry dissemination of its own interpretations of the Code; and
- a change in the international political climate concerning TNC regulation under the aegis of the UN, which dampened WHO's support for national Code implementation.

Nevertheless, UN agencies, the World Health Assembly, national authorities and civil society organizations have endeavoured to overcome these obstacles in various ways. The chapter concludes by linking the International Code to the human rights framework, a link that could present a major avenue in the future to make infant food manufacturers (and other industries) accountable to the societies in which they operate.

Obstacle 1: Legacies of the Process of Code Formulation and Adoption

As described in Chapter 4, a crucial moment in the Code debate was the 1981 WHO Executive Board's decision to follow the WHO Secretariat's advice to press for a Recommendation rather than a Regulation so as to gain US acceptance of the proposed international regulation of an industry.[1] Many members of the Board were apprehensive that the Code might be too loosely worded to be of use and that the weaker legal status might be interpreted by member states as an indication that implementing the Code at national level could be considered a low priority.

Nevertheless, the Board members decided to press for the Code's adoption, imperfect as it was, because of the urgency of protecting infants from the inappropriate marketing of breast-milk substitutes, and because of apprehension that tightening the Code and insistence on a strong legal status might delay its adoption. Thus, as stated in the previous chapter, the legal force (and other advantages) of a WHO Regulation was traded at the 1981 World Health Assembly for the anticipated 'moral force' of a 'minimum compromise', a 'minimum standard' approved by consensus.[2]

When the Executive Board proposed the adoption of the Code as a Recommendation, it also made it clear to the World Health Assembly that the Code might require subsequent revisions and potentially even upgrading to a Regulation. To make up for its foreseeable short-comings, the Board suggested that the Code's adoption should be accompanied by a strongly worded Resolution urging member states to translate the Code into effective legal and other measures.[3]

The World Health Assembly followed the Executive Board's advice. It adopted the Code and a strong Resolution, which recognized that the 'adoption of and adherence to the International Code of Breast-milk Substitutes is a *minimum requirement* … in order to protect healthy practices in respect of infant and young child feeding'. The Resolution also urged all member states 'to give *full and unanimous support* to the implementation … of the International Code in its *entirety*' and 'to translate the International Code into national legislation, regulation and other suitable measures' [Resolution WHA 34.22, 1981; emphasis added].

This Resolution also proposed that the process of Code compliance and implementation should be assessed two years later at the 1983 World Health Assembly so as to decide whether Code revisions or other measures were needed to assist member states (and other con-cerned parties) in ensuring that the Code effectively prevented the harmful marketing of breast-milk substitutes.[4]

Given that the International Code of Marketing of Breast-milk Substitutes and the accompanying Resolution had been passed by such a broad majority of the World Health Assembly – 118 member states in favour, three abstentions and just the USA against – and was en-dorsed by UNICEF's Executive Board a few months later, it seemed reasonable to expect that most of these countries would introduce legislation and other measures within a few years to tackle the un-ethical marketing of breast-milk substitutes.

By October 2000, however, nearly two decades later, just 21 WHA member states had adopted comprehensive legislation based on the International Code 'in its entirety'. Many other countries have opted for weaker regulatory arrangements: while 26 countries do have many provisions in law, others have legislation covering just a few of the pro-visions, or have adopted non-legally binding, voluntary agreements with industry that leave adherence to the discretion of infant food manufacturers (see Table 5.1).

Is this tally to be rated a success or a failure? The answer is not

Table 5.1 National implementation of the International Code of Marketing of Breast-milk Substitutes

Code provision in law (21)	Many Code provisions in law (26)	A few Code provisions in law (19)
Bahrain	Austria	Algeria
Benin	Bangladesh	Armenia
Brazil	Belgium	Canada
Burkina Faso	China	Chile
Cameroon	Colombia	Cuba
Costa Rica	Denmark	Estonia
Dominican Republic	Finland	Ethiopia
Ghana	France	Guinea
Guatemala	Germany	Guinea-Bissau
India	Greece	Hungary
Iran	Indonesia	Israel
Lebanon	Ireland	Japan
Madagascar	Italy	Mongolia
Nepal	Lao (PDR)	Mozambique
Panama	Mexico	Saudi Arabia
Peru	Netherlands	Turkey
Philippines	Nigeria	United Arab Emirates
Sri Lanka	Norway	Yemen
Tanzania	Oman	Zaire
Uruguay	Papua New Guinea	
Zimbabwe	Portugal	
	Senegal	
	Spain	
	Tunisia	
	United Kingdom	
	Viet Nam	

Voluntary Code (12)	Some voluntary provisions (8)	Action to end free supplies only (2)
Australia		
Bolivia	Bhutan	Libyan Arab Republic
Ecuador	Hong Kong	Sudan
Kenya	Jamaica	
Kuwait	Korea (Republic)	
Malawi	Singapore	
Malaysia	Switzerland	
New Zealand	Uruguay	
South Africa	Venezuela	
Thailand		
Trinidad & Tobago		
Zambia		

Table 5.1 National implementation of the International Code of Marketing of Breast-milk Substitutes (continued)

Draft measures awaiting final approval (19)	Code being studied (27)	No action (7)
Albania	Angola	Central African Rep.
Botswana	Argentina	Chad
Burundi	Belarus	Somalia
Cape Verde	Cambodia	United States
Congo	Croatia	Iceland
Côte d'Ivoire	Czech Republic	Kazakhastan
El Salvador	Egypt	Moldova
Gabon	Eritrea	
Georgia	Gambia	
Haiti	Honduras	
Iraq	Latvia	
Jordan	Lesotho	
Morocco	Lithuania	
Namibia	Macedonia	
Nicaragua	Mali	
Pakistan	Mauritania	
Sierra Leone	Mauritius	
Sweden	Myanmar (Union of)	
Uganda	Niger	
	Paraguay	
	Poland	
	Romania	
	Russian Federation	
	Rwanda	
	Slovakia	
	Syrian Arab Republic	
	Togo	

Source: Nutrition Section, UNICEF New York, October 2000. This table was prepared with the assistance of the International Code Documentation Centre (ICDC), Penang

Key to Categories

Code provision in law: These countries have enacted legislation or other legal measures encompassing all, or substantially all, the provisions of the International Code.

Many Code provisions in law: These countries have enacted legislation or other legal measures encompassing many of the provisions of the International Code.

A few Code provisions in law: These countries have enacted legislation or other legal measures encompassing a few provisions of the International Code.

Voluntary Code: These countries have adopted all, or nearly all, the provisions of the International Code through non-binding measures.

Some voluntary provisions: These countries have adopted some of, but not all, the provisions of the International Code through non-binding measures.

Draft measures awaiting final approval: A final draft of a law or other measure to implement all or many of the provisions of the International Code is pending final approval in these countries.

Code being studied: These countries are still studying how to implement the International Code.

Action to end free supplies only: These countries have taken some action to end free and low-cost supplies of breast-milk substitutes to health care facilities but have not implemented other parts of the International Code.

No action: These countries have taken no steps to implement the International Code.

No information was available for the remaining 49 WHA member states

simple. Code implementation has to be evaluated in context. Moreover, these figures do not present a qualitative picture of a dynamic situation. First, coverage by the Code is not just a matter of the number of countries that have implemented it. The fact that India opted for strong national legislation based on the Code, for instance, may protect nearly one-fifth of the world's newborns from inappropriate marketing practices. Second, many of the countries that initially adopted weak measures subsequently decided to strengthen their framework. In contrast, some major Western countries, in particular the USA and Canada, have not implemented the Code, and about half the members of the European Union have implemented measures weaker than the Code (IBFAN/ICDC 1998).

A crucial question remains: what lies behind the discrepancy between the overwhelming commitment of government delegates at the international level in 1981 and the actual pace and extent of Code implementation?

One reason for the relatively slow pace of Code implementation is that the Code, and the appropriateness of the implementation measures, were never thoroughly revised at the 1983 World Health Assembly, as originally suggested. In just two years, the political climate for industry regulation had changed to such a degree that it was decided to keep the Code, imperfect as it was, rather than to open it up for discussion and risk a further weakening of its content.[5]

When the 1983 WHA did not press for changes to the content or legal status of the International Code, many governments and baby food activists realized that the 1981 version was likely to be the final version, at least for the time being, and felt that further clarification or strengthening of the Code would have to take place primarily in other fora (Chetley 1986: 122). National delegates were thus left with the task of implementing a Code that was ambiguously worded and adopted under the weakest of the three possible legal forms of WHO instruments.

To assess the gap between support for the Code at the various World Health Assemblies and the pace and extent of Code implementation at national level, it is important to think of Code implementation as a contested process between a variety of actors at the national level. Delegates at the WHA, for example, tend to come from national ministries of health. Their power to translate the International Code into effective regulatory measures depends significantly on differing opinions and balances of power back home between various other actors, such as ministries of finance and industry, health professional associations, civil society groups, infant food manufacturers and chambers of commerce. It also depends on the power of a country in relation to pressures exercised and support received at the international level. Nationally and internationally, decisions over the past two decades on health and other social issues have tended to be overruled by policy decisions in support of a 'free' market.

There is a lack of systematic comprehensive qualitative studies of the various factors that facilitated or hampered Code implementation. But the fact that it was adopted and remained in the weaker legal form of a Recommendation has had important implications for the pace and modalities of its implementation.

A WHO Recommendation leaves implementation entirely up to the individual member state. A Regulatory Code, however, would have had to be introduced into national legislation by member states within a specified period of time (except by those that had explicitly notified WHO of their rejection of it or attached reservations to it).[6] Had member states committed themselves in 1981 to a period of implementation of, for example, two years, more countries might have adopted the Code sooner and in a stronger legal form, because during the early 1980s the international political climate had not yet turned completely against industry regulation (see Chapter 1 and below). Moreover, a Regulation would probably have included some kind of mechanism for the settlement of potential disputes about Code interpretation, which might have helped to clarify some of the ambiguities and gaps in the Code text (Shubber 1998: 29–30).

In fact, the first draft of the International Code anticipated the establishment of a 'Central Office' by WHO and UNICEF. Its task would have been to review the advertisements, training and educational material of infant food companies, to interpret the Code, and to prepare regular reports on Code compliance for the World Health Assembly. But the provisions for a Central Office were removed from the draft after the first round of consultations because of 'administrative and political problems' (Post and Baer 1980: 59; Shubber 1998: 13).

The abandoning of a Central Office (or similar institutional arrangement at the international level) initially deprived member states of valuable UN support for the development of legislation based on the Code and for the task of setting up the most appropriate monitoring and enforcement arrangements.[7]

Obstacle 2: Industry Interpretations of the Code

The loose wording of the Code has created difficulties in translating it into unambiguous legal language. But clarity of the Code's wording has not been the only problem. Several companies disseminated their own interpretations of the Code and its provisions, and these were at variance with its letter and spirit.

For example, in March 1982, just a few months after the WHA's adoption of the Code, Rafael Pagan Jr., president of the newly founded Nestlé Coordination Centre for Nutrition (NCCN), unveiled at a large press conference 'Comprehensive policy guidelines to be applied in countries which have not yet taken measures to implement the WHO Code of Marketing of Breast-milk Substitutes'. Journalists were handed a press release, 'Nestlé completes WHO code implementation process', together with a 32-page document instructing all Nestlé companies in the Code. The core of this document was the text of the International Code, accompanied by 'itemised implementation instructions' for each provision. The underlying message of the PR media package was that the company had changed its practices and thus the ongoing Nestlé boycott could be called off. Numerous articles in the USA and elsewhere carried a similar message (Nestlé 1982).

Those who actually knew the Code had a different opinion. The reputable British medical journal *The Lancet*, for example, stated that Nestlé's instructions:

raise some doubts about the purity of Nestlé's intentions ... Analysis of Nestlé's guidelines discloses ways in which they might be used to circumvent various parts of the International Code, such as the Code's stipulations on free samples to health workers and free supplies to institutions. (*The Lancet* 1982)

At the 1982 World Health Assembly, delegates from several developing countries voiced their concerns about the Nestlé instructions. Dr G. Ondaye from the Congo warned that, without good national legislation, 'we may fall into the trap of the large multinational companies which are proposing various "interpretations" of the International Code to be applied in our countries but which may, in fact, take into account more the commercial interests than those of health'. Dr A. Tarutia from Papua New Guinea said that 'the Nestlé document is a serious distortion of the World Health Organization Code. Marketing practices prohibited by the Code are approved of and encouraged by the Nestlé document. My delegation is convinced, no private sector has the right to amend the WHO/UNICEF Code' (quoted in Chetley 1986: 118).

Independent legal experts invited a month later to a WHO meeting to develop legislation based on the Code cited eight major points of variance between the Nestle instructions and the International Code.[8] UNICEF, too, felt compelled to voice 'serious misgivings on Nestlé's interpretation of significant aspects of the Code and on the possible harmful effects of its instructions in the implementation of the true spirit and intent of the Code' (Grant 1982). UNICEF and WHO issued a joint set of notes in which they tried to clarify the Code's intent and spirit (WHO/UNICEF 1982).

In the light of these criticisms, Nestlé issued a second set of revised instructions in October 1982 that came closer to the International Code. Yet, in a memo to field staff, UNICEF drew attention to the fact that there were still 'notable differences ... the most important one [being] that Nestlé does not follow a universal policy as regards implementation of the Code' (UNICEF 1983). Nestlé's instructions referred to Code compliance only in developing countries, whereas the International Code is intended to cover all countries without distinction.[9]

Little could UNICEF and others have anticipated that issues of 'universality' and of the Code's scope and specific provision concerning free supplies to institutions were to remain the main points of contention right up to the present day, or that nearly two decades later Nestlé would represent the agencies' criticisms of Nestlé's internal instructions as a legitimizing 'review' from WHO, UNICEF and governments.[10]

It is not known to what extent this and other misleading industry interpretations hampered the process of national Code implementation. What is certain, however, is that they did not facilitate Code interpretation for non-experts and the general public.

Obstacle 3: Changes in Political Climate

Whether or not the pace and extent of national implementation of an international code can be considered a success depends on the context of implementation. As shown in Chapter 1, significant changes in the international political climate took place between the 1970s and the 1990s.

The public debate about infant feeding started at a time when developing countries were demanding a New International Economic Order (NIEO):

> based on equity, sovereign equality, interdependence, common interest and cooperation of all States [to] correct inequalities and redress existing injustices, make it possible to eliminate the widening gap between the developed and developing countries and ensure steadily accelerating economic and social development and peace and justice for present and future generations.[11]

Action programmes and codes of TNC conduct were believed to be important tools in achieving these aims. While the UN Economic and Social Council (ECOSOC) embarked on its New International Economic Order Action Programme, other UN agencies embarked on their own 'new order' declarations and programmes. UNESCO started to work for a New World Information and Communication Order, while the International Labour Organization (ILO) updated its World Employment Programme and called for 'Basic Needs' policies. In 1978, WHO together with UNICEF launched Primary Health Care as the major strategy to reach 'Health for All by the Year 2000' in their Declaration of Alma Ata.[12]

Jeffrey Harrod, an expert in the politics of international economics, commented that:

> The 'new order' programmes not only spawned anti-hegemonic

publications and research but also the only real form of action any international organisation could take in support of proposed changes in the processes by which the world is governed – the formulation, promulgation and monitoring of codes of practice and conduct. 'Codes' then proliferated in the same manner as 'new orders'. (Harrod 1988: 140)

By the mid-1980s, more than thirty codes of conduct for various industries or covering various corporate sectors and practices were reportedly under consideration by various UN bodies (Clement 1988: 354; Pagan Jr. 1985: 376). Few of them, however, saw the light of day. The tide had started turning against such codes after the election of conservative governments in the USA and UK in 1980 and after neo-liberal economic policies began to be implemented more widely but without any meaningful countervailing powers:

By the end of the 1970s and the early 1980s ... the ability of developing countries to determine the agenda of international economic relations decreased considerably. Their bargaining position weakened, in part because of the slackening and eventual termination of the Cold War and partly under the impact of excessive indebtedness. (UNCTAD 1996a: xxii)

While the end of the Cold War was a positive development, the consequences in terms of power balances and ideological shifts have not been in favour of regulation of big business. The UN Code of Conduct of Transnational Corporations was abandoned in 1992, even though the focus had shifted during the 15-year negotiations from one of regulation of corporate practices in the interest of the host countries to that of rights and obligations of both TNCs and governments (Dell 1986).

Changes in senior management of WHO also had an impact on Code implementation. In 1988, WHO's director-general, Halfdan Mahler, who had been a major supporter of primary health care, left after 15 years in office. His successor, Hiroshi Nakajima, was not so supportive of WHO's programme on infant feeding and other primary health care policies.

According to Annelies Allain, director of IBFAN's International Code Documentation Centre, just one year after Nakajima took the helm of WHO, the agency seemed reluctant to back the Code and to stress that it had been adopted as a 'minimum requirement' for all countries and that member states could clarify the Code through WHA Resolutions:

> In less than a decade, one single country – the US – succeeded in setting the stage for a complete switch from WHO's commitment to PHC [Primary Health Care] to a much more 'high-tech' policy which accommodates and possibly even welcomes the transnational pharmaceutical and milk companies ... Eight years after its adoption, the scene for further implementation looked bleak. The WHO Secretariat made no efforts to push for legislation at the national level or to clear up some of the Code's loopholes. (Allain 1991: 25)

Moving Code Implementation Forward

It had become clear by 1983 that WHO support for implementation of the Code at national level was going to be less than optimal. But this did not mean that progress towards implementation came to a halt. Other avenues had to be explored instead. Some of the most important international measures which evolved were as follows.

World Health Assembly Resolutions   As the envisioned 1983 thorough review of the Code never took place, the Code-mandated[13] biannual reviews of the state of Code implementation became a major means of strengthening and updating the Code. Member states adopted additional World Health Assembly Resolutions to clarify still further its meaning, close some of its loopholes, take into account new marketing techniques that might be harmful to infant health, and keep up to date with new scientific knowledge in the field of infant and young child feeding.

Code monitoring   The publication of Code violations, in particular IBFAN's regular Code monitoring reports, often served as the basis for debates at World Health Assemblies and in other important policy arenas at regional and national levels about the extent and nature of manufacturers' compliance with the International Code.[14]

Code training   The Penang-based International Code Documentation Centre (ICDC), which had been set up by IBFAN in 1986 to monitor the Code, developed regional and interregional seminars to train lawyers and policy-makers in how to develop national legislation and to share experiences on how to overcome potential obstacles at the national level. Between 1992 and 1998, the ICDC (often with support from UNICEF and sometimes from WHO) held 14 training courses in Code implementation for more than 350 government policy-makers and other officials from nearly one hundred countries.[15] WHO later followed IBFAN's lead and organized three additional Code training courses, while UNICEF also developed training support.

Model law The IBFAN legal adviser at the Code Documentation Centre, Ellen Sokol, translated the International Code into legal language. The text was published in 1997 as part of *The Code Handbook: A Guide to Implementing the International Code of Marketing of Breast-milk Substitutes*, a book based on ICDC's training experiences that now serves as a central tool in its Code training courses (Sokol 1997).[16] UNICEF cooperated in the formulation of this model law and makes frequent reference to it when asked for legal advice on national Code implementation.[17]

A Multi-Pronged Approach

Clarifying, updating and monitoring the Code, training lawyers to draft national legislation, and keeping up public pressure were not the only ways of moving Code implementation forward. Another important strategy to achieve the Code's aims to protect society from the harms caused by the inappropriate marketing of breast-milk substitutes was to pursue a concerted multi-pronged international programme to protect, promote and support breast-feeding more generally.

The 1979 WHO/UNICEF Meeting had stressed that an international code would be just one measure to ensure optimal infant feeding. The 1981 Resolution of the World Health Assembly reiterated this point, stressing that 'adoption of and adherence to the International Code is a minimum requirement and *only one of several important actions* to protect healthy practices in respect to infant and child feeding' (WHA 34.22, emphasis added).

While implementation of the Code might help to protect mothers from manipulative promotion of commercial infant foods, more was needed to create a favourable environment in which women could breast-feed and to undo the 'bottle-feeding culture' created by decades of advertising and promotion as well as by sub-optimal practices within health care systems.

In the 1980s, many health workers recommended formula milks to mothers of newborns soon after they had given birth. 'Decades of misinformation have led health workers to witness more breastfeeding failure (including their own) and many believe that the problems caused by damaging medical practices are actually faults of nature' (CIIR 1993: 11). Mothers who had reared their children during the heyday of infant food advertising often urged their breast-feeding daughters to give supplement feeds of infant formula.

Moreover, workplace arrangements and labour laws were not usually structured to enable women to breast-feed their infants once they returned to work.

Since the late 1980s, broader policy approaches and actions to limit and prevent the inappropriate marketing of breast-milk substitutes have included the following:

- 'Ten Steps to Successful Breastfeeding';
- the *Innocenti Declaration*;
- a new citizen alliance for breastfeeding action;
- the UNICEF/WHO Baby-Friendly Hospital Initiative; and
- UN Convention on the Rights of the Child.

'Ten Steps to Successful Breastfeeding', the Innocenti Declaration, and a new citizen alliance

At the end of the 1980s, policy-makers finally started to tackle the broader issue of creating an environment that would enable women to breast-feed and to guarantee that they would get accurate, comprehensive information on the best way of feeding their infants.

In 1989, UNICEF and WHO published a *Joint Statement Protecting, Promoting and Supporting Breastfeeding: The Special Role of Maternity Services*. The statement lists 'Ten Steps to Successful Breastfeeding' (see Box 5.1) and includes training staff in how to give advice on breast-feeding and how to help women overcome any potential difficulties, and redesigning the medical system so as to facilitate breast-feeding. The steps also aim to protect breast-feeding from commercial pressures by demanding that 'newborn infants are given no other food or drink unless *medically* indicated' and by advising against teats or dummies for breast-feeding infants – new research showed that infants might reject the breast once they had sucked on teats or dummies, a phenomenon now called 'nipple confusion'.

In August 1990, UNICEF, WHO, the United States Agency for International Development (USAID) and the Swedish International

Development Agency (SIDA) jointly sponsored a meeting at which high-level policy-makers from 32 countries and ten United Nations agencies adopted the *Innocenti Declaration*. This called on governments to take concrete action to protect, promote and support breast-feeding by 1995, including implementing the 'Ten Steps' in maternity services, enacting legislation to enable women in paid employment to breast-feed, and translating the International Code and subsequent World Health Assembly Resolutions into meaningful national regulatory measures. The *Innocenti Declaration* was endorsed by heads of states attending the World Summit for Children in September 1990, by the UNICEF Executive Board in May 1991, and by the World Health Assembly in May 1992 – and committed governments to the deadline of 1995 for national Code implementation.[18]

Box 5.1 'Ten Steps to Successful Breastfeeding'

Every facility providing maternity services and care for newborn infants should:

1. Have a written breastfeeding policy that is routinely communicated to all health care staff.
2. Train all health care staff in skills necessary to implement this policy.
3. Inform all pregnant women about the benefits and management of breastfeeding.
4. Help mothers initiate breastfeeding within half an hour of birth.
5. Show mothers how to breastfeed, and how to maintain lactation even if they should be separated from their infants.
6. Give newborn infants no food or drink other than breast-milk, unless medically indicated.
7. Practise rooming-in – that is, allow mothers and infants to remain together – 24 hours a day.
8. Encourage breastfeeding on demand.
9. Give no artificial teats or pacifiers (also called dummies or soothers) to breastfeeding infants.
10. Foster the establishment of breastfeeding support groups and refer mothers to them on discharge from the hospital or clinic.

Meanwhile, with the encouragement and initial funding of UNICEF, several individuals, civil action groups and international networks striving for national implementation of the International Code and for policies that would support women who wished to breast-feed formed a new umbrella coalition, the World Alliance for Breastfeeding Action (WABA). A major focus of the international network was to persuade governments to take up the four operational targets of the *Innocenti Declaration*.

WABA's key contribution to the multi-pronged approach has been awareness-raising through World Breastfeeding Week, organized for the first week of August each year.[19] In 1994, WABA chose 'Protect Breastfeeding: Making the Code Work' as the theme for its World Breastfeeding Week. The aim was to remind governments of their commitment to reaching the *Innocenti Declaration*'s goals by 1995 and to stimulate greater awareness of the importance of the Code as an instrument to protect women's right to make informed choices about infant feeding (BFHI News 1998b).[20]

The Baby-Friendly Hospital Initiative

In June 1991, UNICEF and WHO launched the Baby-Friendly Hospital Initiative (BFHI), aimed at getting health services worldwide to put into practice the 'Ten Steps to Successful Breastfeeding'. This Initiative is regarded as an important policy measure in tackling the marketing ties between health professionals and the infant food industry and the lack of knowledge about breast-feeding among health professionals. Hospitals joining this programme promise not to accept 'free' or low-cost supplies of breast-milk substitutes from infant food manufacturers and distributors and pledge to redesign their services so as to create a supportive environment in which mothers who choose to do so can breast-feed. 'In Baby-Friendly settings, where breastfeeding is the norm, alternative feeds are rightly seen as a special intervention requiring specific decisions' (UNICEF 1997a: 47).[21]

The UN Convention on the Rights of the Child

Code implementation gained a wholly new dimension in September 1990 when the United Nations Convention on the Rights of the Child (CRC) entered into force. This Convention calls on states, UN agencies and other societal actors to act always in the 'best interest of the child' and obliges state parties to respect, protect and fulfil the 'the right of the child to survival, protection, development and participation'.

It also enshrines the 'right of the child to the enjoyment of the highest attainable standard of health' and the obligation to 'ensure that all segments in society, in particular parents ... are informed, have access to education and are supported in use of basic knowledge of child health and nutrition, [and] the advantages of breastfeeding' – UNICEF 1989: Art. 24.1 and Art. 24.2(e).

The adoption of the Convention on the Rights of the Child was a decisive moment in linking the International Code to human rights. Although the prevention of harm from inappropriate marketing of breast-milk substitutes can be linked to several other human rights instruments, starting from the 1948 Universal Declaration of Human Rights' obligation to protect every human being's 'right to life', commitments under the Convention on the Rights of the Child are of particular importance.[22]

The CRC is a legally binding human rights agreement. It is the most widely ratified human rights instrument: all UN member states except two – the United States and Somalia – have ratified it and are therefore bound by it. Moreover, the institutional body backing up the Convention, the Committee on the Rights of the Child, has recognised the implementation of the International Code of Marketing of Breast-milk Substitutes as a practical 'appropriate measure' to fulfil states' obligations to protect breast-feeding under the Convention on the Rights of the Child.

Thus every government that has ratified the CRC must report regularly to the Committee on its progress towards implementing the Code. The Committee has recommended that countries that have not enacted the Code do so, and that other states strengthen and enforce their existing measures. The Netherlands, for example, has been encouraged 'to undertake breastfeeding promotion campaigns, stressing its advantages and the negative impact of substitutes' (BFHI News 2000).

Since the mid-1990s, UN agencies have further strengthened their commitment to implement human rights. In 1996, for instance, UNICEF put the realization of the Convention on the Rights of the Child (and of the Convention on the Elimination of All Forms of Discrimination Against Women, CEDAW) at the heart of its mandate (Lewis 1999: 2). In 1997, UN Secretary-General Kofi Annan declared human rights to be the cross-cutting theme of the multifaceted work of the United Nations as a whole. He called upon all UN agencies to 'mainstream' human rights in their policy and programme work. WHO embarked on the process at the end of 1999 (WHO 2000a).

Human Rights: The Avenue of the Future?

Whether or not the human rights approach will help to prevent the harmful marketing practices of infant food manufacturers depends not only on whether and to what degree the world's nations and UN agencies take their obligations seriously. It also depends on their power in relation to that of large corporations. One shortcoming of the current human rights regime is that only states, not transnational corporations, can be held accountable to it (UNDP 1999: 35). In the words of the *1996 Report of the Secretary-General on the Impact of the Activities and Working Methods of Transnational Corporations on the Full Enjoyment of All Human Rights*:

> even though each TNC subsidiary is, in principle, subject to its host country's regulations, the TNC as a whole is not fully accountable to any single country. The same is true for responsibilities they fail to assume for activities or their subsidiaries and affiliates. The global reach of TNCs is not matched by a coherent global system of accountability. (Commission on Human Rights 1996)

Indeed, human rights instruments have until now referred primarily to the relationship between individuals and the state. Only more recently have transnational corporations been considered as societal actors that may profoundly limit people's realization of their human rights and there has been recognition that TNCs are often beyond the reach of those states that wish to ensure the fulfilment of their citizens' human rights.

It has been pointed out that the 'Everyone has duties to the community' principle contained in Article 29 of the 1948 Universal Declaration of Human Rights also applies to 'non-state actors'. However, the only human rights instrument that explicitly addresses TNCs is the Convention on the Elimination of All Forms of Discrimination Against Women (CEDAW). Article 2(e) calls on signatories 'to take all appropriate measures to eliminate discrimination against women by any person, organization or *enterprise*' [emphasis added].[23]

How can this vacuum be addressed in international law? One important step in this direction was a Resolution adopted in 1998 by the

United Nations Sub-Commission on the Prevention of Discrimination and Protection of Minorities. This Sub-Commission called for the establishment of a sessional Working Group on the Working Methods and Activities of Transnational Corporations under the auspices of the United Nations Sub-Commission on the Protection and Promotion of Human Rights. Referring, among others, to the Working Group on the Right to Development's recommendation to adopt 'new international legislation and creat[e] effective international institutions to regulate the activities of transnational corporations and banks', the Resolution set out the following mandate:

1. To identify and examine the effects of the working methods and activities of transnational corporations on the enjoyment of economic, social and cultural rights and the right to development, as well as civil and political rights;

2. To examine, receive and gather information … on the effects of the working methods and activities of transnational corporations on the enjoyment of economic, social and cultural rights and the right to development, as well as of civil and political rights;

3. To analyse the compatibility of the various international human rights instruments with the various investment agreements, regional as well as international, including, in particular, the Multilateral Agreement on Investment;

4. To make recommendations and proposals relating to the methods of work and activities of transnational corporations in order to ensure that such methods and activities are in keeping with the economic and social objectives in the countries in which they operate, and to promote the enjoyment of economic, social and cultural rights and the right to development, as well as of civil and political rights;

5. To prepare each year a list of countries and transnational corporations, indicating, in United States dollars, their gross national product and financial turnover, respectively;

6. To consider the scope of the obligations of States to regulate the activities of transnational corporations, where their activities have or are likely to have a significant impact on the enjoyment of economic, social and cultural rights and the right to development, as well as of civil and political rights of all persons within their jurisdiction. (Commission on Human Rights 1998)

This three-year sessional working group seems to offer a unique chance for states and social justice groups to place the regulation of the inappropriate marketing of breast-milk substitutes, and other harmful corporate practices, firmly on the world's public law and policy agenda. Whether this will actually happen will depend, among other factors, on the way the group sets its priorities.

Some NGOs expressed concern at the working group's first session in 1999 that changes made to the initial six-point mandate might lead in the wrong direction. For example, the Centre Europe-Tiers Monde, the Association of American Jurists and Pax Romana protested that the provisional agenda for the three-year work suggested, in an extension to point four, that the Working Group consider voluntary industry codes of conduct as an important option to ensure TNCs' respect for human rights (Commission on Human Rights 2000b: 2).[24]

The organizations pointed out that corporate statements of support for codes of conduct do not necessarily mean that they will adhere to them in practice, as the infant food and many other industries illustrate. Pax Romana said that it could be 'expected that companies meet core [human rights] standards ... since these obligations apply to all international agents', be they states, human beings or artificial legal entities.[25]

A number of human rights organizations therefore urged the Working Group to focus on exploring legally binding measures and institutional arrangements that would make it possible to address more effectively corporate malpractice and crimes. Suggestions included the elaboration of 'one or more compulsory codes of conduct for transnational corporations, which could take the form of international conventions' (Commission on Human Rights 2000b: 4).

Yet much of the August 2000 meeting of the Working Group was devoted to the discussion of a *Draft Human Rights Code of Conduct for Companies*, which highlighted respect of human rights as an issue of 'corporate responsibility' (Weissbrodt 2000). Working Group members and other experts of the UN Sub-Commission on Human Rights argued that such guidelines might simultaneously 'encourage' companies to implement the draft principles, help governments to identify the types of legislation to enact, and lay the groundwork for binding international laws (Commission on Human Rights 2000b: 7–8).

At the same time, the Working Group and other human rights experts deplored the fact that 'states might lack a legal, regulatory, investigatory infrastructure to take effective action', and suggested that 'the international community should develop a system to assist development of such an infrastructure' (Commission on Human Rights 2000a: 9). And indeed, TNC promises to take moral obligations seriously do not discharge states and the UN system from their duty to establish a functioning legal system to protect, respect, facilitate and fulfil people's human rights worldwide, including protection from potential human rights violations by transnational corporations.

It can only be hoped that the UN Working Group on the Working Methods and Activities of Transnational Corporations will contribute to this task of the international community by helping to codify the human rights obligations of corporations – in the form of duties and prohibitions – as well as by drawing up some suggestions as to the possible enforcement machinery. It is also hoped that the end of the Working Group's three-year mandate in August 2001 will not mean the end of international efforts to deal with this long-neglected task in international law-making.

Overcoming Obstacles to Code Implementation

This chapter has provided some insights into the difficulties of translating the International Code of Marketing of Breast-milk Substitutes into effective national regulatory measures.

In 1991, ten years after the International Code's adoption, only nine countries had passed legislation based on the Code in its entirety; eight had approved legislation encompassing many of the Code's provisions; and 29 had drafts awaiting further action.[26]

Because of the compromised wording of the Code, its relatively weak legal status, the confusion created by industry interpretations of the Code, and the political climate steadily going against regulation of TNC practices, the gap between the commitments made by national delegates at the 1981 World Health Assembly and national implementation is not surprising. Indeed, given the obstacles at the international level, the implementation of the International Code of Marketing of Breast-milk Substitutes in a substantial number of countries can be regarded as a significant move against the tide. According to UNICEF's legal officer on Code implementation, David Clark, national Code implementation can be seen as a continuous 'uphill struggle' in which still too many governments have done less than they could have done but others have implemented strong measures in the face of considerable resistance[27] (for some more obstacles at the national level, see Chapter 6).[28]

By 2000, however, national implementation figures had risen: 21 countries had implemented legislation encompassing all or substantially all provisions of the International Code of Marketing of Breast-milk substitutes; 26 countries had introduced many, and another 19 a few, of the Code's provisions into their law; 20 countries had adopted voluntary measures; 19 had drafted measures awaiting adoption and another 27 – among them many Central and Eastern European countries – were studying Code implementation. (The USA is one of the seven countries that reportedly took no action with respect to national Code implementation)[29] (see Table 5.1).

This progress can be attributed to a variety of strategies to move Code implementation forward. Measures to clarify, update and monitor the Code have been important, as has training lawyers in drafting national legislation. Also key has been the inclusion of the Code in a multi-pronged strategy that insists that promotion and support of breast-feeding, and the creation of environments enabling women to take a genuinely free and informed decision as to how to feed their children, cannot be separated from the protection of breast-feeding from commercial pressures.

The *Innocenti Declaration*'s date of 1995 for Code implementation set a new target to which IBFAN and WABA groups could hold governments accountable. IBFAN and over 1,000 European development and consumer groups referred to this date when lobbying the European Commission to adopt a Directive on Infant Formulae and Follow-on Formulae in 1991, an infant food export Directive in 1992, and a European Council Resolution calling for monitoring of the marketing practices of European Union-based baby food companies operating outside the EU (CIIR, 1993: 7).[30]

A major new development over the past decade has been to link the regulation of the inappropriate marketing of breast-milk substitutes to human rights. Human rights considerations can strengthen the framework under which such marketing is addressed, and may also change perspectives profoundly. In the words of UNICEF's former deputy executive director, Stephen Lewis:

> Those who make claims about infant formula that intentionally undermine women's confidence in breastfeeding are not to be regarded as clever entrepreneurs just doing their job but as human rights violators of the worst kind. (Lewis 1999: 4)

Box 5.2 The Pharmaceutical Industry and WHO

A 1978 World Health Assembly resolution requested a code for the pharmaceutical industry similar to that called for in 1974 to regulate the promotion of breast-milk substitutes. Subsequent deliberations greatly influenced WHO support for the International Code of Marketing of Breast-milk Substitutes after it was adopted in 1981. The two regulatory debates were intimately intertwined.[31]

The pharmaceutical industry learned from the experiences of the infant food industry and was determined that a code governing the marketing of pharmaceutical drugs would not be passed. When the International Code was adopted by the World Health Assembly in 1981, the former executive vice-president of the pharmaceutical business organization, the International Federation of Pharmaceutical Manufacturers Associations (IFPMA), commented: 'Nestlé and the other companies made a lot of mistakes to get to the point they did. We won't ever get to that stage if we can help it' (Peretz 1981).

The IFPMA was a force to be reckoned with. It represented member associations in 47 countries and an industry with an annual turnover of US$100,000 million.[32] The IFPMA had had 'official relations' with WHO since 1971, unlike the infant food association ICIFI, which was still struggling to obtain this status.[33]

Following ICIFI's example, the IFPMA launched its own Code of Pharmaceutical Marketing Practices in March 1981. It argued that the pharmaceutical industry should be given time to implement its voluntary code and claimed that WHO insistence on the formulation, implementation and monitoring of an international regulatory code would waste precious public resources unnecessarily.

Others were of a different opinion. Immediately following the 1981 World Health Assembly, and encouraged by its adoption of the International Code of Marketing of Breast-milk Substitutes, some 50 consumer, health and development activists from 27 countries decided to form Health Action International (HAI), a coalition loosely modelled on IBFAN (Chetley 1990: 71; Reich 1991: 24).

Just one year later, at the 1982 World Health Assembly, the HAI presented a *Draft Proposal for an International Code on Pharmaceuticals* – a comprehensive model regulatory framework covering not only marketing practices but also other problematic pharmaceutical practices such as drug trials and registration, research and development, transfer of technology, and patents (Patel 1983: 268).[34]

As with the baby food issue, WHO found itself at the centre of intense lobbying from industry, a citizen action network, and governments with different interests. Discussions about a pharmaceutical code dragged on without any decision being made until delegates at the 1986 WHA reiterated their demand that WHO at least draw up ethical criteria for drug promotion. The president of the IFPMA tried once again to prevent such an action:

> [The IFPMA] fully accepts the adoption of international ethical standards although we seriously question whether ... [such standards] will do much to improve drug supply and use in the developing countries ... I would remind delegates that our code requires neither national regulation nor government administrative or financial resources for its operations. (quoted in Kanji et al. 1992: 59)

Several pharmaceutical producing countries reiterated their position that WHO should not act as a 'supranational regulatory body'. Neil Boyer from the US State Department reaffirmed the strong position of the USA:

> that the World Health Organization should not be involved in efforts to regulate or control the commercial practices of private industry, even when the products may relate to concerns about health. This is our view regarding infant foods products, and pharmaceuticals and tobacco and alcohol. (quoted in Chetley 1990: 92)

The International Organizations Monitoring Service (IOMS), an information service for business, commented in its 1986 WHA intelligence report on the paradox between staunch US resistance to international regulation by WHO and its domestic policies: '[The USA] finds defence of industry interests difficult because those very industries are heavily regulated within the US for the same reasons now being used by advocates of international regulations at the World Health Assemblies' (IOMS 1986: 13).

In 1986 and 1987, the USA finally carried out its threat to withhold large portions of its contributions to WHO.[35] But its actions did not deter WHO's director-general, Halfdan Mahler, from pursuing his mandate, and a WHO expert meeting was called to produce 'Ethical Criteria for the Promotion of Drugs'.

The 1988 World Health Assembly adopted the relatively weak and non-committal *Ethical Criteria for Medicinal Drug Promotion*. When Mahler was replaced in 1988 after 15 years in office by Hiroshi Nakajima, who had once been an R&D director with the Japanese subsidiary of Hoffmann-La Roche, WHO lost a major supporter of primary health care. In January 1989, a few months after Nakajima had taken office, the director of WHO's Action Programme on Essential Drugs, Ernest Lauridsen, resigned in protest at the way the aims of WHO's drug strategy were being 'watered down' and at how bureaucratic 'harassment' hindered his work (quoted in Chetley 1990: 121–2, 125).[36]

Notes

1. The fourth draft of the International Code was in fact presented to WHO's Executive Board in January 1981 in two forms: a Regulation and a Recommendation, as requested by the 1980 WHA Resolution (Shubber 1998: 27). The 1980 Resolution also requested that 'the legal and other consequences of each choice' be outlined (Resolution WHA 33.32, 1980). One consequence of the Board's decision to present the Code to the WHA in the form of a Recommendation only was that details of the potential consequences of both legal forms were omitted and consequently a discussion on the respective merits of the two regulatory forms was precluded.

2. Shubber 1998: 44, 73, 203.

3. See Shubber 1998: 33. Dr Torbjørn Mork, representative of the Executive Board to the 1981 World Health Assembly, presented the draft resolution with the words: 'The Executive Board examined the draft code very carefully. Several Board members indicated that they considered amendments in order to strengthen it and make it still more precise. The Board considered, however, that the adoption of the code by the thirty-fourth World Health Assembly is a great urgency in view of the serious situation prevailing, particularly in developing countries, and that the amendments introduced at the present stage might lead to postponement of the adoption of the code. The Board therefore unanimously recommended to this thirty-fourth World Health Assembly the

adoption of the code as presently drafted, realizing that it might be desirable or even necessary to revise the code at an early date in the light of the experience obtained in the implementation of the various provisions ... It was considered, however, that the implementation of the code should be closely monitored ... that future Assemblies should assess the situation in the light of the reports from Member States; and that the Assembly should take any measures it judges necessary for its effective application' (WHO 1981a: 34–5).

4. Resolution WHA 34.22, 5.(3) and 5.(4) in WHO 1981b: 26.

5. For details on how this decision came about, see Chetley 1986: 122.

6. Moreover, a Regulation would have contained 'specific rules intended to impose specific obligations' and would have been worded in 'mandatory language' (Shubber 1998: 29–30).

7. James Post and James Baer predicted that abolishing the idea of a Central Monitoring and Advisory Office would have important implications for the capacity of WHO and UNICEF to provide expert advice to member states wishing to act on the Code: 'Given that there are relatively few experts in the world on infant formula practices and strategies, and still less on regulatory actions that have successfully affected the behaviour of trans-national firms in the food and pharmaceutical industries, a need exists for organising this expertise in a technical assistance office of WHO/UNICEF. The failure to do so will leave government officials at the mercy of industry executives, lawyers, and lobbyists, all of whom have a pecuniary interest in seeing the weakest form of enforcement adopted at the national levels' (Post and Baer 1980: 59).

8. Letter from a group of lawyers to Edmund Muskie, chair of the Nestlé Infant Formula Audit Commission (NIFAC), 30 June 1982, quoted in Chetley 1986: 118.

9. For details of INFACT's criticisms, see Chetley 1986: 119.

10. The 1999 PR magazine *Nestlé International (WHO) Code Action Report* cites as proof of the company's long-standing Code implementation efforts 'the original Nestlé Instructions (1982) [which] were reviewed by WHO and UNICEF as well as by national governments' (Nestlé 1999c: 1); see also Chapter 8.

11. Preamble of the Declaration on the Establishment of a New International Economic Order reproduced in UNCTAD 1996c: 48) .

12. For more details, see Harrod 1988: 137–42.

13. Code Art. 11.7.

14. IBFAN publishes regular *Breaking the Rules* reports in time for the bi-annual WHA meetings, as well as two types of charts: *The State of the Code by Country* and *The State of the Code by Company*. For Code monitoring reports by national IBFAN members and other organizations, such as the Interagency Group on Breastfeeding Monitoring (IGBM), see Chapter 6. For more details on the general activities of IBFAN, see Chapter 9.

15. One significant result of an ICDC Regional Training Workshop in Nepal was the adoption of a draft model code in 1996 by over one hundred

delegates at the 3rd SAARC Ministerial Conference on Children of South Asia, which took place in Rawalpindi, Pakistan, as the *SAARC Model Code for the Protection of Breastfeeding and Young Child Nutrition*. SAARC, the South Asian Association for Regional Cooperation area, includes Nepal, India, Bhutan, Bangladesh, Sri Lanka, Maldives and Pakistan.

16. The model law defines the aim of legislation based on the Code as: 'An Act to ensure safe and adequate nutrition for infants and young children by promoting and protecting breastfeeding and by regulation of the marketing of certain foods and of feeding bottles, teats and pacifiers' (in Sokol 1997: 134).

17. The *Code Handbook* also contains a summary of the infant feeding issue, overviews of how to interpret the various provisions of the International Code, and examples of different national legislation (Sokol 1997).

18. For more information, see e.g. Sokol 1997: 20–1. For a reproduction of the *Innocenti Declaration* see Sokol 1997: 351–3.

19. Some WABA members have chosen the fortieth week of each year as World Breastfeeding Week as a way of linking the event with the average length of a pregnancy.

20. For more information on WABA, see www.elogica.com.br.waba

21. By December 2000, 15,044 hospitals in 136 countries had implemented the 'Ten Steps', eliminated free and 'low-cost' supplies of breast-milk substitutes, and been awarded 'Baby-Friendly' status (UNICEF 2000).

22. For more information on the links between various human rights treaties and the issue of regulation of marketing of breast-milk substitutes, see e.g. BFHI News January/February 2000; Clark 1998; Margulies 1994; Skogly 1996.

23. For more information on TNCs and human rights, see e.g. the background reader by the Centre Europe-Tiers Monde, American Association of Jurists and the FICAT Foundation. These organizations call for a change of the 1998 Statute of the International Criminal Court, which does not include TNCs within its jurisdiction and does not allow the Court to hear cases involving crimes against economic, social and cultural rights (CETIM/ AAJ/FICAT 2000: 169). The UNDP's 1999 *Human Development Report* called for a 'broader mandate for human rights' for the International Criminal Court (UNDP 1999: 12, 35). For a update on the current situation of human rights from a human development perspective, see UNDP 2000.

24. For details on the changes proposed in the provisional agenda see Commission on Human Rights 2000b: 2. The Working Group itself put some of these tasks back onto its mandate and expanded the rights list to include also the 'right to a healthy environment and the right to peace'. For the final agenda for the three-year mandate of the Working Group, see Commission on Human Rights 1999: 2–3.

25. Statement made by Pax Romana at the Working Group on the Working Methods and Activities of Transnational Corporations of the United Nations Sub-Commission on Human Rights, 1 August 2000.

26. Figure based on ICDC data bank, quoted in Sokol 1997: 23.

27. Personal communication, David Clark, legal officer, Nutrition Section, UNICEF, New York, March 2000

28. Whether countries used all their room for manoeuvre to implement the Code in national legislation remains an open question. A good qualitative analysis of a representative sample of states may indicate which factors facilitated or hampered national Code implementation. There are indications that a commitment to legislation achieved better results than voluntary arrangements. The 1997 monitoring report *Cracking the Code* found that Code violations were less frequent in a country with laws governing the marketing of breast-milk substitutes (Bangladesh) and more frequent where there was no legal regulation governing any aspect of marketing (Poland). There are also indications that the support of citizen action and health professional groups moved Code implementation forward. Giovanni Andrea Cornia, Senior Research Fellow at the UNICEF Innocenti Research Centre, considers Code implementation a 'success in terms of social mobilization' (personal communication by Giovanni Andrea Cornia, senior research fellow UNICEF Innocenti Research Centre, March 2000). For more information on this aspect, see also Chapter 10.

29. The others are: Central African Republic, Chad, Iceland, Kazakhstan, Moldova and Iceland.

30. The European Directive still falls short of the Code and several countries did not meet the 1995 deadline.

31. Several pharmaceutical companies were, and still are, infant food companies as well.

32. For more information on IFPMA at that time, see Kanji et al. 1992: 31.

33. See Chapter 9 on the efforts of infant food manufacturers to gain NGO status for their business association.

34. The pharmaceutical code was meant to be an international policy instrument to ensure that people everywhere had access to 'essential drugs', one of the eight basic components of primary health care. In fact, the essential drugs concept encompasses wider provisions than simply access. It also includes the removal of harmful or inappropriate drugs from the market. In addition, it aims to eliminate those marketing practices that promote the consumption of unnecessary drugs and that overstate the benefits of pharmaceuticals and/or omit information on adverse effects, including potentially fatal ones. For a reproduction of the HAI model international code on pharmaceuticals, see Patel 1983: 317–28.

35. The USA started paying back some of the arrears when an editorial in *Science* in 1988 pointed out the unfairness of withholding $118 million when one of WHO's achievements – the eradication of smallpox – saved the USA $100 million in vaccination costs per year (Chetley 1990: 120–1).

36. The *Ethical Criteria for Medicinal Drug Promotion* were weaker than the originally envisaged code and were never advocated for incorporation into national legislation in the same way that the International Code was.

CHAPTER 6

. . . .

Corporate Conduct: Socially Responsible Marketing?

> In view of the vulnerability of infants in the early months of life and the risks involved in inappropriate feeding practices, including the unnecessary and improper use of breast-milk substitutes, the marketing of breast-milk substitutes requires special treatment, which makes usual marketing practices unsuitable for these products. (Preamble, International Code of Marketing of Breast-milk Substitutes, 1981)

> Marketing is *not advertising* … Marketing is not even a combination of advertising and a whole bunch of other stuff added in, such as packaging, and promotions, and market research, and new-product development … Those are marketing tools … Marketing is a strategic activity and a *discipline focused on the endgame of getting more consumers to buy your product more often so that your company makes more money* … That's what it's all about, what it has always been about, and what it will always be about. (Sergio Zyman, former chief marketing officer of the Coca-Cola company, 1999)[1]

§ Much of the international trend over the past 20 years or so away from the notion of external, binding regulation of TNCs towards industry self-regulation or co-regulation is based on an assumption that transnational corporations are now behaving in more socially responsible ways. The multitude of corporate codes of conduct and statements of commitment that TNCs will in future be good corporate citizens is often taken as an indication of such responsibility.

But do the actions of TNCs support their words? Are they practising what they preach? From a policy perspective, what matters is not the number of industry codes or statements of intent but whether and to what degree industry has reduced or stopped its potentially harmful practices, and whether any changes in a criticized industry practice, considered in context, reflect a greater willingness and ability on the part of industry to regulate itself.

Without an evaluation of these two aspects, a policy shift away from international and national regulation in favour of industry codes of conduct may be harmful to society. As a 1998 *Encyclopedia of Applied Ethics* points out, codes of conduct such as codes of practice, corporate charters and mission statements can have various functions, ranging 'from quasi-legal requirements through moral prescriptions to mere advertising puffery' (Pritchard 1998: 538).[2] They are useful to society if they act as a 'warranty ... of how business will conduct itself in regard to certain moral principles' such as respect for human rights and dignity. The *Encyclopedia* explicitly warns, however, against assuming that all functions of codes are positive:

> One of the negative functions of codes is that, rather than improving standards of practice, they may actually serve to reduce them ... [A] code may be put in place to avoid statutory regulations being imposed on a business or industry. Thus by pretending to have moral standards, legal constraints are sought to be avoided. The code, by misleading people about managers' intentions, makes the situation worse than had it never been adopted at all. (Pritchard 1998: 530)

Statements and Questions

The International Code of Marketing of Breast-milk Substitutes is a mix of external regulation and co-regulation. As stated in Chapter 4, the infant food industry was officially invited as one of the 'concerned parties' to participate in both the 1979 Joint WHO/UNICEF Meeting on Infant and Young Child Feeding and the consultations on drafting the Code. The UN agencies deliberately took the risk of ending up with a less than ideal Code in the hope of garnering industry support for some regulation of its marketing practices. Yet the president of the International Council of Infant Food Industries (ICIFI), Ernest Saunders, who was also Nestlé vice-president, still called the Code 'unacceptable' (Saunders 1981).

Today, industry statements suggest a significant change in attitude from that of 1981. For instance, ICIFI's successor, the International Association of Infant Food Manufacturers (IFM), now states on its website: 'In October 1989, IFM reaffirmed to the WHO Director General the commitment of its members to support the principles and aim of the WHO Code' (IFM 1999). And Nestlé, an IFM founding member, asserts in its widely distributed corporate charter that it complies 'with both the letter and the spirit of the World Health Organization's International Code of Marketing of Breast-milk Substitutes' (Nestlé 1996).

Does the conduct of the infant food industry back up its proclamations of support for the International Code? Does its conduct reflect a greater commitment to corporate social responsibility? An answer requires investigation of two further issues:

1. Have the industry's marketing practices changed since the adoption in 1981 of the International Code? If so, do these changes suggest a greater willingness and ability on the part of the infant food industry to regulate itself?
2. Does the infant food industry now accept the principle of outside regulation?

This chapter explores the first question of changes in marketing practices.

Summary of the Code's Provisions

The aim of the International Code of Marketing of Breast-milk Substitutes is to 'contribute to the provision of safe and adequate nutrition for infants, by the protection and promotion of breast-feeding and by ensuring the proper use of breast-milk substitutes, when these are necessary, on the basis of adequate information and through appropriate marketing and distribution' (WHO 1981b: 13).

The Code (Article 3) defines breast-milk substitutes as 'any food being marketed or otherwise represented as partial or total replacement for breast-milk, whether or not suitable for that purpose'. The Code (Article 2) also covers the marketing of feeding-bottles and teats because their use has been shown to interfere with breast-feeding.[3]

The Code's specific provisions, as clarified by subsequent relevant WHA Resolutions, can be summarized as follows:

1. No advertising or other form of promotion of breast-milk substitutes, feeding-bottles or teats to the general public.
2. No pictures of infants or other pictures or text on labels idealizing the consumption of infant formula. Labels must state clearly the

superiority of breast-feeding and must include preparation instructions and a warning about the health hazards of inappropriate preparation.

3. Information and educational material on infant feeding must explain the benefits and superiority of breast-feeding, the health hazards associated with artificial feeding, and the difficulty of reversing the decision not to breast-feed. Information about the use of infant formula must include details of the social and financial implications of its use. The materials may not contain pictures or text that idealize the use of infant formula, nor may they refer to a product brand name.

4. No free samples, direct or indirect, to mothers.

5. No contact between marketing personnel and pregnant women or mothers of infants and young children.

6. No promotion of products within the health care system, including no free or 'low-cost' formula, other breast-milk substitutes or feeding-bottles and teats.

7. Product information for health professionals must be limited to scientific and factual matters.

8. No gifts to health workers; samples may be given under very limited circumstances only.

9. Manufacturers should disclose any contribution made to health workers for fellowships, study tours, research grants, attendance at professional conferences and the like; as should the recipients.

10. Unsuitable products should not be promoted for babies.[4]

The International Code recognizes the role and importance of corporate responsibility by specifying that:

> independently of any other measure taken for implementation of this Code, manufacturers and distributors of products should regard themselves as responsible for monitoring their marketing practices according to the principles and aim of this Code, and for taking steps to ensure that their conduct at every level conforms to them. (WHO 1981b, Article 11.1.3)

Box 6.1 The Benefits of Breast-feeding

There is increasing evidence that exclusive breast-feeding for the first six months provides all the nutrients an infant requires for his or her healthy growth and development. Breast-milk continues to play an important role in the child's diet until at least two years of age. Between the ages of 6 and 12 months, breast-milk can provide up to half or more, and between 12 and 24 months up to one-third, of necessary nutrients. Nutrients in breast-milk that may not be otherwise available include:

- suitable proteins in an easily digestible form for infants;
- micronutrients, including iron and vitamins, in a form that is well absorbed; and
- long-chain polyunsaturated fatty acids, important to the development of the infant's brain.

However, the value of breast-feeding goes far beyond its nutritional value. Breast-milk protects infants from diarrhoea and acute respiratory infections, two leading causes of infant death. It contains hundreds of health-enhancing antibodies and enzymes, as well as growth factors that stimulate the development of the infant's digestive system. No substitutes contain these important elements. Breast-milk requires no mixing, sterilization or equipment. It is always the right temperature.

Breast-feeding also provides an important opportunity for the baby and his or her mother to develop a close and trusting emotional relationship. An artificially fed infant may have fewer opportunities to receive full attention and stimulation from his or her mother.

Exclusive breast-feeding also contributes to women's possibilities of child spacing as it delays the return of fertility after birth. Unlike many other child-spacing options, it carries no risk of adverse effects for the mother. Moreover, the lives of many children have been saved as a result because those born too soon after a previous birth are at greater risk of dying before the age of five.

Corporate Practice
Monitoring Reports

The President of the International Association of Infant Food Manufacturers (IFM) claims that:

> IFM member companies are committed to putting the health and well-being of infants and young children first at all times. We share with WHO the strong belief that breastfeeding is the best way to feed infants, and we have expressed this in many, many messages designed to promote nursing as the best feeding choice. (Borasio 1998)

In many developing countries today, there is certainly less blatant advertising of infant formula to the general public compared to 20 years ago. Most labels on infant formula assert the superiority of breast-feeding and no longer depict chubby, smiling infants. The practice of disguising sales personnel as 'mothercraft nurses' has almost disappeared. But there is still plenty of advertising to pregnant women and mothers – now often through parent clubs or telephone help lines – while advertising through the media and the provision of free supplies to hospitals and maternity wards continues in some major industrialized countries.

These positive changes are welcome but are not necessarily evidence of a greater commitment on the part of manufacturers to the Code. Any change in practice and any statement about a change of attitude or practice has to be assessed in the specific socio-political context.

In the case of infant food, this means taking into account the fact that the infant food industry has been closely watched for its adherence to the International Code by civil society groups, in particular the International Baby Food Action Network (IBFAN). Changes in marketing methods could be ascribed to clear international standards set by the Code for inappropriate marketing practices and to the negative publicity companies attracted when their Code violations were exposed by national governments, UN agencies, civil society organizations or the media.

International and national monitoring reports of corporate behaviour in fact reveal continued widespread violations of the provisions and spirit of the Code (IBFAN 1998a; IGBM 1997a; TheNetwork 1998). The results of a six-month study to monitor industry practices in Poland, Bangladesh, Thailand and South Africa, carried out in 1996 by the Interagency Group on Breastfeeding Monitoring (a group of British-based NGOs, academic institutions and churches), are illustrative. Published as *Cracking the Code*, the study:

> found evidence of violations of the International Code of Marketing of Breast-milk Substitutes in all four countries studied ... The research shows that many companies are taking action which violates the Code, and *in a systematic rather than a one-off manner*. It therefore highlights the need for on-going monitoring which is independent of manufacturers and distributors of breast-milk substitutes. (IGBM 1997b: 1; emphasis added)

IBFAN concluded from its monitoring in 31 countries in 1997 that the infant food industry not only continues to 'break' the Code, but is finding new ways of 'stretching' it (IBFAN 1998a).[5] Its most significant finding was that the industry continued to 'focus on the health care system', and that its promotional messages threatened the beneficial practices of exclusive breast-feeding for the first six months and continued breast-feeding (with adequate complementary foods) for two years or beyond:

> On the surface, it would appear that companies have jumped on the bandwagon to promote breastfeeding by diligently including a 'breast is best' message on nearly all their materials. The underlying messages, however, are that breast-milk needs to be supplemented, i.e. while it is good for newborns, it will not be enough on its own for very long; that follow-up formulas are necessary at four to six months, implying that breastfeeding should stop; that working mothers need substitutes; that fathers need to take part in feeding; that babies need herbal drinks, special water and early complementary foods. (IBFAN 1998a: iii)

The IBFAN report also documented the promotion of a whole range of new products that have been introduced or are marketed more widely since the Code was adopted by the 1981 World Health Assembly. The most striking of these is the introduction of 'follow-on formula' or 'follow-on milk'. As these products were introduced in more and more countries, the World Health Assembly specified in a 1986 Resolution that 'follow-on formula' is not necessary to provide infants with good nutrition (1986 WHA 39.28). Companies, however, claim that commercial milk products for infants older than six months are not 'replacing' but 'supplementing' breast-milk, and are not therefore covered by the Code. But since UNICEF and WHO now recommend breast-feeding for up to two years and beyond, any promotion of other milks does potentially replace breast-milk. Such milks are therefore covered by national legislation in a number of countries (see also also Chapter 7).[6]

More recently, special nutritional products for pregnant and nursing women have been introduced on the market, and complementary foods – commercial, processed foods such as cereals and infant meals – are promoted more intensely, including providing women with free supplies just after their delivery.[7] All these products are used to gain direct marketing access to mothers of babies and young children.

Evidence of marketing that undermines breast-feeding also comes from recent media reports about the use of innovative advertising techniques to gain access to pregnant women and mothers of infants. In summer 1999, Nestlé received the 'Best of Europe Award for Big Brand Direct Marketing' for its successful campaign in Denmark, which targeted mothers with children aged two months to one year.[8] In autumn of the same year, advertising company OgilvyOne was awarded the Asian Direct Marketing 'Best of the Year' Award for a 'well thought-out and proven effective loyalty campaign designed for its client Nestlé Philippines', a campaign that aimed to build a relationship between women and Nestlé infant food brands through direct mail packs (*Business World* 1999).[9] Today, such 'motherclubs' have become one of the most widespread direct marketing avenues for breast-milk substitutes.

Rulings

Nestlé's marketing practices have been the subject of two recent rulings by national regulatory bodies. In 1999 in the Czech Republic, Nestlé was given the highest possible fine for violating national consumer protection legislation because its claim that its complementary food was 'ideal food' for infants from four months of age was deemed to be 'misleading' (Baby Milk Action 1999d; Prague 1 Trade Department 1999).

In the same year, the UK Advertising Standards Authority asked Nestlé to revise its claim that 'Naturally they [Nestlé employees] do not provide free supplies to hospitals for use with healthy infants' because of evidence to the contrary. Nestlé was told that another claim went 'too far', namely: 'Even before the World Health Organization International Code of Marketing of Breast-milk Substitutes was introduced in 1981, Nestlé marketed infant formula ethically and responsibly, and has done so ever since' (ASA 1999).[10]

Avoiding Public Scrutiny

The world's infant food market leader was recently challenged in a more formal arena to prove that marketing practices have changed. In January 1999, the European Parliament recommended the development of 'EU Standards for European Enterprises Operating in Developing Countries' and that regular public hearings under its auspices should be held on industry practices.

The European Parliament Development and Cooperation Committee's First Annual Hearing on Standard Setting by European Enterprises in Developing Countries was held in November 2000. Its broad aim was to identify 'examples of good practice as well as areas for further attention ... as well as [themes] of wider interest in the debate about corporate social responsibility'. Two sectors were chosen for this first hearing: the infant food industry and the clothing industry. Different parties were invited to speak on the 'marketing of infant formula in developing countries according to the WHO rules and the European Council Resolution'. Committee members were also interested in 'the operation and effectiveness of the companies' own voluntary code of conduct'. However, Nestlé officials, who had at first welcomed the opportunity to present the company's views, chose not to attend.[11] The reasons cited for staying away included objections to the presence of representatives from IBFAN and UNICEF (Baby Milk Action 2000a).

If Nestlé disagrees with the interpretation of the Code and subsequent Resolutions used by UNICEF and IBFAN, why wasn't it prepared to discuss this in public? Why did senior management not seize this unique opportunity to present Nestlé's Code compliance mechanisms?

Nestlé might have felt that non-attendance would harm the company's reputation less than having to answer questions about evidence that Nestlé's subsidiary in Pakistan set sales targets for staff and bribed doctors. Company officials may not have wanted to answer questions about alleged death threats to Syed Aamar Raza, a former Nestlé sales representative who publicized internal company documents after a physician friend accused him of contributing to the death of babies (TheNetwork 1999: 8–9). The company did not send a representative of its Pakistan subsidiary either. Instead it sent an external auditor to the European Parliament hearings – who admitted that the audit of Nestlé's subsidiary in Pakistan did reveal Code violations.[12]

Nestlé's apparent avoidance of public discussion of its mechanisms for Code compliance raises questions about its ability to defend its Code compliance mechanisms and marketing practices. Richard Howitt, a Member of the European Parliament who backed this EU initiative, commented that Nestlé had shown 'utter contempt for a properly constituted public hearing'. He said: 'Not to attend reveals a combination of arrogance and distance which has set their cause back' (quoted in Castle 2000).

This was not the only time that Nestlé chose not to attend a properly constituted hearing. The Breastfeeding Promotion Network of India reports that Nestlé used various tactics since 1995 to delay cross-examination on alleged violations of the labelling requirements of the Indian law on marketing of breast-milk substitutes. At first, the company refused to receive the summons. Instead it sent a lawyer to observe the proceedings secretly. When the Court realized that Nestlé's lawyer was in the room it seized the opportunity to serve the summons through him. Between August 1997 and September 2000 Nestlé successfully adjourned 14 proposed court hearings (BPNI 2000; see also Chapter 7).

HIV and the Regulation of the Marketing of Breast-milk Substitutes

HIV and Infant Feeding

Companies have also exploited the discovery that some babies of HIV-positive mothers may contract the virus through breast-feeding. Some companies have drawn attention to the 'risks of breast-feeding' and have presented commercial infant formula as the most suitable way to feed babies of HIV-positive mothers, but have regularly omitted to mention the health, social and financial implications of the use of infant formula. No mention is made of other options for replacement feeding.

When the International Code was adopted in 1981, there was little awareness of HIV infection, and AIDS was not perceived as a public health problem. Since then, the disease has significantly affected the world's health, social and political arenas, particularly in the countries of the South. Nearly two-thirds of the world's 33 million HIV-positive people live in sub-Saharan Africa, which also accounts for 90 per cent of all AIDS deaths.

In the late 1980s, it was discovered that the human immunodeficiency virus (HIV), which is believed to cause AIDS, could be transmitted via breast-milk, although the rate of transmission was not clear.

It was not easy for policy-makers to issue guidance, given the sensitive and complex nature of HIV and infant feeding, and given the many advantages of breast-feeding as compared to artificial feeding. At first, policy-makers were guided by epidemiological considerations. They suggested that in settings where infectious diseases and malnutrition were the primary cause of infant deaths, HIV-infected women should continue to breast-feed. In all other settings, breast-feeding for HIV-infected mothers was to be discouraged.

In 1997, however, international agencies agreed on a central policy position that any HIV-positive woman should have the right to make an informed choice as to how to feed her child and that, whatever her decision, she should be supported in carrying it out (WHO 1998a, 1998b). In the words of a WHO–UNAIDS–UNICEF Technical Consultation on HIV and Infant Feeding:

> HIV-positive mothers should be enabled do make fully informed decisions about the best way to feed their infants in their particular circumstances. Whatever they decide, they should receive educational, psychosocial and material support to carry out their decision as safely as possible, including access to adequate alternatives to breastfeeding if they so choose. (WHO/UNAIDS/UNICEF 1998: 8)

Unclear Data

As for many other health matters, HIV-infected women have to base their decisions on the best available information. Conclusive data on the specific risks of transmission are still not available. Studies to date suggest that approximately 15 per cent of infants breast-fed by HIV-positive mothers (who are not taking any AIDS drugs) may become infected[13] (WHO/UNICEF/UNAIDS 2000).

But these studies did not look carefully at the feeding patterns of the infants. They did not distinguish between exclusive, partial and no breast-feeding. The publication of a study in *The Lancet* in 1999 by Anna Coutsoudis and her colleagues from Durban, South Africa challenged the statistics (Coutsoudis et al. 1999). Coutsoudis's team looked more closely at breast-feeding patterns, distinguishing between exclusive breast-feeding, where infants received only breast-milk, partial breast-feeding, where babies also received water, formula or other liquids or foods in addition to breast-milk, and infants receiving no breast-milk at all (replacement feeding). When the infants were three months old, the study did not find a higher incidence of HIV infection among infants who were exclusively breast-fed than among those who were exclusively formula-fed. HIV incidence was higher, however, in children who were partially breast-fed.

So far, only the Coutsoudis study has looked closely at different feeding patterns, and its findings need to be verified through further research. This may yield a clearer picture of the risk of HIV transmission through various breast-feeding patterns.

The risks of using infant formula, however, are more difficult to quantify because they depend on the particular circumstances. WHO estimates that each year about 1.5 million children die because they are artificially rather than breast-fed. A broad switch to formula feeding would most probably lead to increased infant mortality. Some studies show that, even in optimal conditions, artificially fed infants suffer five times the rate of diarrhoeal diseases that breastfed infants do, and higher rates of respiratory, ear and other infections. One study in conditions of poor hygiene found that the risk of death from diarrhoea was 14 times higher for artificially fed than for breast-fed children (WHO 1998b: 8).

Overall statistical figures, however, are not the same as forecasting the risk for an individual baby of dying from unsafe formula feeding. An HIV-infected mother needs to know that the risks of artificial feeding – whether of commercial or home-prepared formula – for the individual baby depend on a plethora of factors. They include, among others, access to clean water and sufficient fuel, hygiene and sanitation; the mother's or other caregivers' ability to obtain enough infant formula; and access to proper instructions and support in its correct preparation (BFHI News 1998).

Mothers also need to be informed that commercial infant formula is not the only alternative to breast-milk. Replacement feeding options for HIV-infected mothers who decide not to breast-feed include expressing breast-milk and heat-treating it, using breast-milk banks if they are available, wet-nursing, or using formula prepared at home from locally available fresh milk with added micro-nutrients (WHO 1998a).

Exploiting Mothers' Fears

Since the HIV infant feeding debate started, another major concern of policy-makers was that infant food manufacturers might exploit the findings about HIV transmission via breast-feeding to push commercial products for all HIV-positive women. Moreover, such promotion might have a spill-over effect if uninfected mothers and those of unknown HIV-status were encouraged to use breast-milk substitutes as well. There was grave concern that many babies would suffer or die because the risk of breast-milk displacement would be underestimated while that of HIV transmission through breast-feeding would be overestimated.

The statistics on HIV transmission via breast-feeding have to be seen in context. In populations where HIV prevalence is about 20 per cent, even a 15 per cent transmission figure through any kind of breast-feeding means that two or three out of one hundred breast-fed infants may acquire HIV through breast-feeding. The remaining 97 or 98 infants (including infants who might have acquired HIV before or during delivery) will benefit from breast-feeding and are more likely to survive their first year.

The industry was aware of the policy-makers' concern that increased promotion of infant foods could set back years of efforts to reverse the detrimental trend away from breast-feeding. In 1992, the Infant Food Manufacturers' Association (IFM) promised the World Health Organization that it would not exploit the HIV infant feeding dilemma. But at the same time, it told World Health Assembly delegates that mothers should not breast-feed if they were HIV-positive (Baby Milk Action 1997a). Reports indicate that manufacturers now 'educate' women, policy-makers, the media and the general public about the 'risks of breast-feeding', but omit information about the health risks and financial implications of the use of infant formula and about alternative options for replacement feeding as required by the Code.

In 1998, for instance, PRNewswire ran a story about the Pharmaceutical Research & Manufacturers of America (PhRMA) – an industry association that includes all the major US infant food manufacturers – co-sponsoring a *Living with Hope* medical news segment to follow episodes of the popular US TV hospital drama series *Chicago Hope*. According to the PR agency that was instrumental in developing the project, the aim was 'placing PhRMA's message in positive and trusted "health environments"'. PRNewswire reported that the viewers could soon be expected to be 'educated' on 'the risks associated with breast-feeding' (PRNewswire 1998). Soon after, the TV soap opera featured a baby dying because it had been breast-fed.

In 1999, the website of the pharmaceutical and infant food manufacturer Bristol-Myers Squibb claimed that: 'Mother-to-child transmission is a serious problem acknowledged by UNICEF, and the WHO have lessened their strong support for breastfeeding in communities where the risk of HIV transmission through breast-milk is high.' The company's rationale for investing in AIDS-related educational activities was clear:

> education also increases the sales of HIV products by developing the HIV marketplace ... Although education requires longer-term investment, the returns will ultimately materialise ... particularly given that most of this HIV market is untapped. (Bristol-Myers Squibb 1999)

Regulation of Marketing More Important than Ever

Policy-makers know that 'breastfeeding is the ideal way to feed the majority of infants', and many feel that the risks of infant food manufacturers exploiting the HIV pandemic makes implementation of the Code all the more important.[14] Implementation and enforcement of the Code is seen as a critical cornerstone of various policy measures designed to enable HIV-infected mothers to make the most suitable choice between either exclusive breast-feeding or various replacement feeding options, based on the best available information of the known advantages and risks of each feeding option in her particular circumstance.

New policy guidelines have been established to ensure that the nutritional needs of infants whose mothers are HIV-positive are met; they also recommend the strengthening of Code implementation (WHO 1998a; 1998b).[15] As the executive director of WHO's Family and Reproductive Health Programme stated:

> No child should be denied the benefits of breastfeeding based on ignorance or unfounded fears. It is essential that we safeguard the gains that have been made in protecting breastfeeding, ensuring the survival of millions of infants. Governments are urged to take strong measures to prevent 'spill-over' – that is the spread of artificial feeding to infants whose mothers are HIV negative – or who do not know their status and who would benefit from breastfeeding. (Türmen 1998a: 2)

The aim of proper Code implementation is not to discourage women from using commercial foods if they so decide. The aim is to ensure that their infant is fed in the best possible way – not only by ensuring that choices are taken on the basis of unbiased information, but also by ensuring that the labels contain the proper instructions for safe preparation and use of commercial infant food. The HIV infant feeding dilemma has not changed the duties of infant food manufacturers. UNAIDS, WHO and UNICEF stressed in a joint 1997 Policy Statement on HIV and Infant Feeding:

> Manufacturers and distributors of products which fall within the scope of the International Code of Breast-milk Substitutes (1981) should be reminded of their responsibilities under the Code and continue to take the necessary action to ensure that their conduct at every level conforms to the principles and aim of the Code. (UNAIDS/WHO/UNICEF 1997)

Box 6.2 *The Economics of Infant Food*

The regulation of the marketing of breast-milk substitutes is an example of international regulation of a particular practice of a particular industrial sector. The success of regulatory measures and other efforts to influence corporate activities depends on a good knowledge of the particular economic terrain. As business academic Prakash Sethi put it in his chapter on 'Worldwide formula sales, markets, and industry structure':

> The important point to remember is that while internal corporate values condition management's responses to the external environment ... they are also influenced, to no lesser extent, by industry structure and market competition. It is therefore important that we understand the nature of the infant formula industry structure and relative market positions of its major firms. (Sethi 1994: 125–6)

Industry structure can give some indication of the prevalent mode and intensity of competition and of the profitability of the market in question. It can also give some indication of the potential reactions of corporations and their business associations to demands for exertion of restraint regarding a particular practice.

An Oligopolistic Market

It is not easy to obtain reliable data on the infant food industry. Problems include the reluctance of infant food manufacturers to publicize data on worldwide sales and relative market shares, differing definitions of which countries should be considered 'developing countries', and the problem that market statistics often do not clearly distinguish between the infant food categories, i.e. infant formula, follow-on formula and complementary foods, thus posing problems of comparability.[16] Nevertheless, the data that are available do provide some basic insights into the structure and dynamics of the infant food market.

Sethi conservatively estimates that the infant formula market had a turnover of about US$3.9 billion in 1990, of which roughly 30 per cent (US$1.15 billion) was in developing countries (Sethi 1994: 133). In 1997, the *Financial Times* estimated that the worldwide market for breast-milk substitutes amounted to US$6 billion for that year.[17]

The infant formula market displays the 'classic form of an oligopolistic industry in the mature stage of its life cycle' (Sethi 1994: 126). In 1994, around thirty companies produced and sold infant formula on the world market. However, just four companies controlled more than two-thirds of the total market: Nestlé SA, Switzerland, and the three US-based transnational corporations: Ross Laboratories, a division of Abbott Laboratories; Wyeth-Ayerst, a division of American Home Products (AHP);[18] and Mead Johnson, a subsidiary of Bristol-Myers Squibb. Nestlé alone controlled around 40 per cent of the worldwide infant formula market (Sethi 1994: 126, 133).

However, the concrete market distribution may vary with geographical regions and nation states. For example, Nestlé, Milupa of Germany, and the Dutch company Nutricia controlled nearly two-thirds (60 per cent) of the European market in 1994 (Sethi 1994: 135).

Brand Loyalty as the Major Determinant of Economic Success

In technical terms, infant formula is not a complicated industrial product. As Kiran Saluja, chair of the committee of the US National

Association of Women, Infants and Children (WIC) Nutrition Progam Directors put it somewhat polemically: 'basically, formula is cow's milk that you monkey around with a little bit' (quoted in Brick 1999: 12).

Brands do not differ very much from one another. How is it then possible that, according to the market research firm A. C. Nielsen, around 86 per cent of 1999's US$1.9 billion market was dominated by just two brands, Ross Laboratories' Similac and Mead Johnson's Enfamil (quoted in Brick 1999: 12)? And why has Nestlé, the world's market leader, not been able to capture more than 10 per cent of the US market during the period of ten years since it tried to re-enter this market with the acquisition of Carnation Milk in 1988?

A variety of factors make it difficult for newcomers to get a foothold on the infant formula market. Brand loyalty is seen as a major determinant of the economic success of infant formula manufacturers, a loyalty that has often been built over generations of mothers – and health care professionals. As the *New York Times* put it:

> The market leaders have spent decades on building their ties to paediatricians and new parents – and building the mystique of their brands. The formula makers rely mainly on 'ethical marketing,' a concept that includes maintaining Web sites and phone lines to answer parents' questions, sponsoring seminars and conferences for paediatricians and showering doctors and new parents with gifts.

And the concept seems to work:

> Many families are loyal to Similac and Enfamil for generations. And while the companies are careful to chant the ... mantra – that breast-milk is best – they routinely send new mothers home from the hospital with diaper bags filled with cans of formula.[19] (Brick 1999: 13)

Nestlé's difficulty in entering the US market can be explained by another particularity of the infant formula industry structure: the market is basically divided between two groups of industries, the pharmaceutical/health care and the food processing industries

(Sethi 1994: 130). While Nestlé is a food and beverage company, the remaining three major infant food companies are subsidiaries of pharmaceutical companies. As US-based pharmaceutical companies, they have been able to build on long-standing marketing ties with the medical community while Nestlé not only had to establish these ties to begin with but was also at a disadvantage as a food company (Brick 1999: 13).

How much medical endorsement is worth to companies is shown by the intense competition between infant food companies to 'donate' their products to health care institutions. During the 1970s, one company reportedly paid US$ one million to the City of New York for the privilege of providing free formula to all city hospitals. In 1989, Abbott Laboratories and Bristol-Myers Squibb engaged in a bidding war over the exclusive right to donate free formula to Canada's largest maternity ward (Sokol 1997: 79). And an internal Abbott/Ross training manual, which instructed the company sales representatives in 'how to make the physician a low pressure salesman for our products', stated: 'When one considers that for every one hundred infants discharged from hospital on a particular brand, approximately ninety-three infants remain on that brand, the importance of hospital selling becomes obvious.'[20]

A Highly Profitable Market

A Nestlé spokesperson attempted to justify the heavy promotion of infant formula in the United States by claiming: 'Marketing and advertising benefit the market place and consumers by increasing competition, lowering prices and helping educate consumers on product choices' (quoted in Baby Milk Action 1999: 5).

In fact, infant formula manufacturers are not known for their low prices. In a report drawn up in 1998, investigations by the US General Accounting Office (GAO) concluded: 'wholesale prices of infant formula appear to be high in relation to the costs of production indicating the likelihood of high profit margin' (quoted in Brick 1999: 12). In 1994, retail prices of major brands were estimated to amount to as much as five times the cost of manufacture, and gross profit margins were estimated to be as high as 50 per cent (Sethi 1994: 129).[21] Sethi offers the following explanations about the reluctance of infant food corporations to publicize their profit margins:

> Infant formula sales must be so highly profitable that companies are afraid to disclose these figures. Absolute levels of high profits and a higher rate of profits on sales, especially in Third World countries, would make it difficult for the companies to make credible assertions about not using high-pressure sales tactics.
>
> Another supportive argument in favour of the high profit hypothesis is the ferocity and tenacity with which companies have fought their critics and each other to hold on to their markets despite tremendous adverse public opinion and enormous demands on their resources, including management time, to fend off their critics ... Despite tremendous pressure, no major infant formula manufacturer has ever walked away from any of its significant markets. (Sethi 1994: 129–30)

In sum, corporations do seem to use marketing primarily to persuade women to buy their particular infant food brands and to make considerable profit. What tends to be forgotten in economic accounts on market distribution is the fact that infant food manufacturers are competing not only with other companies. Attempts to boost market shares carry the inherent risk of displacing the non-market-based, very best infant nutritional 'product': mothers' breast-milk.

Industry Structure and Spaces for Regulation

Finally, industry structures have to do with influence and power. According to Sethi, 'the presence of a dominant firm influences the types or options available to local governmental authorities for regulating the activities of various firms in a particular industry' (Sethi 1994: 125).

Thus, those intent on regulating the marketing of breast-milk substitutes may benefit from knowing who the major infant food manufacturers in their sphere of authority are. As concerns the power of these corporations, regulators must additionally take into account that infant formula sales often constitute but a fraction of the overall sales of most relevant market leaders. Nestlé Chief

Executive Officer Peter Brabeck-Letmathe recently presented the company as follows:

> Nestlé is the world's leading food and beverage company, with sales of about CHF 72 billion. It has 230,000 employees world-wide and operates 520 factories in 82 countries ... Today Nestlé is about twice the size of its nearest competitor in the food and beverage sector, and combining numbers two and three in the business world would make the new entity roughly our size. (Brabeck-Letmathe 1999a: 1)[22]

Infant formula constitutes only around 2–3 per cent of Nestlé's overall annual turnover. A similar picture applies to the world's other three dominant infant food manufacturers. In 1998, Wyeth's 'baby food' sales were estimated at 3 per cent of AHP's/Monsanto's overall corporate sales, Mead Johnson's baby food sales at 7 per cent of Bristol-Myers Squibb's overall sales, and Abbott Ross/Puleva baby food sales at 10 per cent of Abbott Ross Laboratories' overall sales (Rabobank International 1998: 7).

Regulators must be aware that they are not just dealing with the infant food producers. The relatively small share of infant food in relation to overall sales can have two consequences: the major infant food manufacturers could decide to refrain from aggressive marketing because infants' well being, and a good company reputation, are worth more than profit maximization. Unfortunately, regulators must also be prepared to deal with the possibility that an infant food subsidiary may ask the mother transnational corporation to throw all its weight around to prevent effective implementation of legislation on the marketing of breast-milk substitutes.

Words Versus Deeds

While there have certainly been changes in specific marketing practices over the past 20 years, it is almost impossible for industry outsiders to be sure that any of these changes are due to a greater corporate sense of social responsibility.[23]

Indeed, it is a common and widespread mistake to credit changes in industry practice automatically to increased 'corporate responsibility'.

Changes in corporate practice can be due to many factors: they can reflect a response to outside pressure, be it from social action groups, regulators, ethical shareholders or general public opinion; and they can reflect internal company factors, such as the assessments and personal values of managers, public relations and legal advisers, as well as the views of employees. On the whole, it might be more fruitful to assess changes of corporate practices not in terms of corporate responsibility – a term that suggests a change of heart – but rather in terms of corporations fulfilling their legal and moral obligations.[24]

In a competitive business environment, even the most well-meaning corporate managers have to calculate what amount of short-term profits can be traded for an anticipated increase in long-term profits from, for instance, an enhanced company reputation. Much time is now spent by regulators, policy-makers and citizen action groups on speculating whether improvements in a certain practice are due to a particular corporation's increased commitment to social responsibility. From a strategic point of view, it might be more useful to gauge where the management itself sees the limit set by the company's so-called enlightened self-interest and to strategize how this profit limit can be shifted even further.

What matters for the infants of this world is that regulatory policies are based on a solid assessment of concrete practices. Recent industry independent monitoring reports indicate that infant food manufacturers' marketing methods and the industry's product range have shifted since the International Code was drawn up. Most noteworthy is the increased marketing of products not explicitly covered by the Code, such as follow-on formulas and special foods to mothers of newborns, as well as early marketing of complementary foods, direct contact with mothers in the form of parents' clubs, and more recently, the exploitation of the HIV infant feeding dilemma. The monitoring reports as well as advertising news and rulings indicate that – while the industry does seem to respect certain Code requirements, such as the prohibition of disguising sales personel as 'mothercraft nurses' – what has not changed is that breast-milk substitutes are still promoted in ways that interfere with the practice of breast-feeding. Despite assertions to the contrary, the International Federation of Infant Food Manufacturers (IFM) seems to be either unwilling or unable to ensure that the marketing methods of all its members conform to the letter and spirit of the Code.

These findings confirm general, but often neglected, knowledge about industry self-regulation. Industry associations cannot ensure that all corporations within the same sector follow their rules. Most industry associations encompass just part of the industry sector, not all of it. IFM member companies, for instance, together represent 65–70 per cent of the global infant formula market – not 100 per cent of it (WHO 1998d: 3). Another limitation stems from 'free riders': if just one member company decides not to follow agreed standards, others may feel compelled to lower their standards as well in order to succeed in a competitive business environment. When rules governing corporate conduct conflict with corporate profit making, effective outside regulation is the only means of creating a so-called level playing-field (see also pp. 112–17).

Nestlé, however, could assume global leadership of the infant formula industry in socially responsible marketing if it so desired. The company is among the world's top ten TNCs in terms of foreign assets (UNCTAD 1999: 78). With an annual turnover of about 72 billion Swiss francs (US$40 billion), it is the world's leading food and beverage company – about twice the size of its nearest competitor. Nestlé holds about 40 per cent of the world's infant food market, but infant food constitutes just 2 per cent of the company's overall sales worldwide, while developing country sales of infant food account for less than 1 per cent of total sales.[25] Nestlé is thus in a unique position in that an anticipated loss of sales – at the very least in those parts of the world where infants are most at risk from the unsafe use of breast-milk substitutes – would not have a significant impact on its overall turnover. Reports of Nestlé's continued Code violations seem to indicate, therefore, a lack of will rather than an economic inability to move towards more socially responsible behaviour.

For all these reasons, the European Parliament's 1999 *Report on EU Standards for European Enterprises Operating in Developing Countries* said of the relationship between 'voluntary' industry initiatives and external regulation:

> [Such] approaches are not alternatives, but part of a complementary set of actions … Voluntary regulation can do a great deal to promote better practice, but the worst offences will only ever be prevented through national and international laws and binding rules. Such systems can operate in parallel: binding rules to ensure minimum standards and voluntary initiatives to promote higher standards. (European Parliament 1999: 17)

What is needed from a societal perspective is a coherent web of laws and other regulatory measures that are binding on all TNCs.

Infant food manufacturers that truly want to assume greater social responsibility could demonstrate this in practice by supporting the immediate and universal implementation of effective regulatory measures based on the Code and subsequent Resolutions. This would be the ideal means of ensuring a global 'level playing-field' in which no market competitor could pressure them to lower their standards. The next chapter investigates whether or not corporations have supported the introduction of comprehensive regulatory measures based on the Code.

Notes

1. Zyman 1999: 12–13; original emphasis. Zyman earned the nickname 'Aya-Cola' because of the way in which he directed the company's multi-billion marketing efforts for a total of 13 years.

2. A code used as a precondition for licensing and backed up by an effective check for compliance is completely different from the same code used as a 'marketing tool' to gain a competitive advantage, for instance, by assertion of social responsibility or to avoid legal measures. In both these latter cases, codes are not usually accompanied by any meaningful machinery to monitor compliance or sanction violations.

3. There is evidence that pacifiers (dummies) may interfere with breast-feeding as well. The model law therefore suggests that national laws governing the marketing of breast-milk substitutes should encompass their use (Sokol 1997: 45, 109).

4. This short summary is adapted from the Summary of the Code for Manufacturers (Sokol and Allain 1998: 4). For additional WHA Resolutions about the scope of the Code, see Sokol 1997: 39–40.

5. The pharmaceutical industry has displayed a similar tendency in its promotional practices (Mintzes 1998).

6. For more details, see Sokol 1997: 42–5.

7. For more details on industry marketing of infant food products that undermine breast-feeding but that, according to industry, are not covered by the Code, and for details of the risks of inappropriate marketing of complementary foods, see Sokol 1997: 35, 41–6.

8. *Direct Response* magazine reported: 'Danish local health authorities ... effectively promote breastfeeding and the majority of women breastfeed. As such they are suspicious of communications from companies like Nestlé. Therefore the firm decided to tackle the issue of breastfeeding head on and create a dialogue with health authorities, including midwives and health visitors, mothers-to-be and mothers with small babies. The target audience of the campaign were mothers with children aged from two months to one year.

To recruit new members, Nestlé used ads and inserts in the Danish magazine *Parents and Children*, and carried out quarterly promotional campaigns in supermarkets across the country. More information about baby nutrition and the club was placed in hospitals and maternity clinics. In less than one year, the membership of Nestlé parents club has increased from under 10% to over 75% of Danish parents' (quoted in Baby Milk Action 1997b).

9. OgilvyOne's parent company, OgilvyOne Worldwide, is described by *Business World* as 'one of the leading Direct, Customer Relationship and Interactive marketing networks in the world, with 69 offices in 47 countries, and billings of over $1.6 billion'. OgilvyOne in turn is part of the world's seventh largest advertising and PR company, Ogilvy and Mather. According to *Business World*: 'Dickie Soriano, managing director of OgilvyOne in Manila, said the grand prize was proof that maintaining a more personal and individual relationship with the consumer, "delivers significant, measurable results" for the brand – in this case Nestlé. "When we designed Nestlé's infant nutrition program, we made full use of direct marketing insights and breakthroughs that are now reshaping the way we market brands as well as the relationships between consumers and brands," he added. Included in the Nestlé program are five brands that support the mother from pregnancy until the child is about four. Key to the effectiveness of OgilvyOne's winning program was building a relationship with the customer by communicating with mothers – through various direct mail packs – in all the different stages of motherhood' (*Business World* 1999).

10. Nestlé made three statements in an anti-boycott advertisement in October 1996 in the *Oxford Independent* newspaper. The UK-based IBFAN member, Baby Milk Action, filed a complaint with the Advertising Standards Authority. In May 1999, after a lengthy investigation by the Advertising Standards Authority – which was further delayed by an appeal by Nestlé – the British authority upheld all three complaints. The third complaint which was upheld referred to the statement that: 'The Nestlé Charter concerns Nestlé's commitment to the WHO International Code in developing countries.' The ASA ruled 'when read in context, the claim suggested compliance with the WHO Code over time to a degree that had not been substantiated' (ASA 1999; see also Baby Milk Action 1999a; *Marketing Week* 1999; Wilkinson 1999a, 1999b).

11. Adidas too did not attend (Castle 2000).

12. For a summary and discussion of the audit's findings, see e.g. Yamey 2000b and related rejoinders.

13. Studies are under way to assess the extent to which taking antiretroviral drugs that reduce HIV transmission during pregnancy and delivery may also decrease the risk of HIV transmission through breast-feeding.

14. 'Breastfeeding is the ideal way to feed the majority of infants. Efforts to protect, promote and support breast-feeding by women who are HIV-negative or of unknown HIV status need to be strengthened' (WHO/ UNAIDS/UNICEF 1998: 8).

15. See also the two BFHI Newsletters of September/October 1998 and November 1998 on HIV and infant feeding.

16. For a more detailed discussion of problems of data collection, see Sethi 1994: 126–30. Most of the statistics in this section apply to the infant formula market only.

17. *Financial Times*, 9 January 1997, quoted in Shubber 1998: 51.

18. A number of changes have occurred since. For example, in 1996, Wyeth Nutritionals pulled out of the US infant formula market. According to the *New York Times* the company nevertheless still ranked second on the international infant formula market in 1999 (Brick 1999). Milupa, Nutritia and Cow and Gate merged in 1997 to form Numico.

19. A research report by a stock market analyst described the particular conditions for entering the baby food market in the following words: 'entrants to the baby-food market are hampered by consumer loyalty (passed from mother and doctor to daughter) and legal restrictions on advertising' (Rabobank International 1998: 8).

20. Abbott/Ross in-house publication, cited in ICCR 1982. So-called free and low-cost supplies remain a powerful marketing and corporate PR instrument which helps build brand loyalty through medical endorsement as well as corporate reputation.

21. Numico reportedly claimed that its profit margin on baby food exceeded 50 per cent (quoted in Baby Milk Action 1999: 8).

22. For overall turnover and other data on the world's biggest infant food manufacturers in 1998, see Rabobank International 1998 and Baby Milk Action 1999.

23. UNRISD's Peter Utting makes a similar observation in relation to corporate conduct and sustainable development: 'A review of various corporate surveys that attempt to identify the drivers of corporate responsibility suggest that one of the main factors to respond to environmental and social issues is, in fact, government regulation or the threat of regulation ... Pressures associated with NGO activism, including consumer boycotts and environmental campaigns, the threat of litigation, critical media attention or public opinion may also figure prominently. Other sources of pressure such as so-called ethical investors of shareholders have also emerged in recent years' (Utting 2000: 22).

24. Corporations prefer the notion of responsibility to that of duty and obligation. This word can be better used for image enhancement, and is also useful in replacing the notion of corporate 'accountability' to the public. A public relations professional specializing in the management of corporate reputation writes: 'Corporate citizenship is based on the notion that business corporations have similar legal and moral responsibilities to those of individuals. This is not a question of pure corporate altruism. In a very interdependent society it is sensible for business to get involved with communities for reasons of enlightened self-interest' (Newman 1995: 95–6).

25. These figures are taken from a speech and a letter of Nestlé's current CEO, Peter Brabeck-Letmathe (Brabeck-Letmathe 1999a, 1999b).

CHAPTER 7

. . . .

Corporate Conduct: Acceptance of Outside Regulation?

> In country after country, Nestlé has actively encouraged national adoption of the WHO Code, with strict measures backed up by impartial and effective monitoring. A strong national code obliges all manufacturers to follow the same rules for marketing infant formula, and provides what is known as a 'level playing field'. Nestlé strictly adheres to national codes and all relevant legislation. (Nestlé, *Complying with the WHO Code*)[1]

§ Monitoring reports suggest that infant food manufacturers are either unwilling or unable to ensure that their practices conform to all the provisions of the International Code of Marketing of Breast-milk Substitutes and subsequent WHA Resolutions. Is the industry not complying with just a few particular provisions of the Code? Or is it more fundamentally opposed to external regulation *per se*?

Industry statements today give the impression that infant food corporations fully support the translation of the Code into effective national regulatory measures. At the 1998 World Health Assembly, when Dr Gro Harlem Brundtland replaced Hiroshi Nakajima as WHO director-general, the International Association of Infant Food Manufacturers (IFM) welcomed WHO's 'renewed process to remove obstacles to the implementation of the International Code of Marketing of Breast-milk Substitutes by all countries'. It stated that: 'IFM appreciates WHO's efforts to work with all interested parties in this area and we have pledged our support in this process' (IFM 1998).

Does corporate conduct support the assertion that infant food manufacturers support outside regulation? This chapter examines various industry responses to attempts made by national authorities to implement the Code fully and to devise impartial monitoring mechanisms (or to revise existing national marketing legislation). Recent reports indicate that corporations employ a range of lobbying and legal strategies to prevent the implementation of strong national legislation, and that they exert pressure for their inclusion in committees to draft or monitor national legislation. Such arrangements profoundly blur the distinction between the regulators and the regulated at both legislative and executive levels.

Interference with National Code Implementation

As stated in Chapter 4, the 1981 WHA Resolution urged member states to 'translate the International Code into national legislation, regulations or other suitable measures' in its 'entirety' with the understanding that its provisions were minimum standards for the protection of infants from the ill-effects of the inappropriate marketing of breast-milk substitutes.

Code implementation today requires legislation based not only on the Code but also on all subsequent WHA Resolutions that aim to clarify and update the Code. As with other national consumer protection measures, governments could be expected to set up mechanisms to ensure the prompt detection of violations of legislation as well as to institute sanctions of varying severity, depending on the violation. Causing harm to the life and health of vulnerable populations, in this case infants and young children, is usually taken extremely seriously in consumer protection legislation.

The 1981 WHA Resolution advised governments 'to involve all concerned social and economic sectors and all other concerned parties in the *implementation* of the International Code and the *observance of the provisions* thereof' – WHA Res. 34.22, art. 2(3); emphasis added. Reports received by UN agencies and civil society organizations indicate that the industry does not interpret its role in the implementation process as being one of ensuring their compliance with measures agreed upon by national authorities. Instead, corporations have:

- lobbied for legislation that is weaker than the Code and subsequent Resolutions;
- used trade threats;
- portrayed marketing regulation as a violation of their 'freedom of commercial speech';
- enlisted health professionals to oppose strong legislation;

- challenged legislation in the courts;
- lobbied for full industry participation in law drafting and national monitoring of its marketing practices; and
- lobbied member states to oppose further WHA Resolutions.

Lobbying for Legislation that is Weaker than the Code and Subsequent Resolutions[2]

Manufacturers do not necessarily wait until legislation has been prepared by national governments before they take action. Some companies have taken the proactive approach of presenting an industry version of marketing legislation when national legislation was being considered or prepared.

After the political changes in Central and Eastern Europe over the past decade, for instance, infant food companies have reportedly visited government representatives to offer their advice on how to implement legislation or regulations governing the marketing of infant foods. In Russia, Nestlé provided the authorities with a Russian-language draft law that was much weaker than the International Code and subsequent Resolutions. The draft would have allowed infant food companies to advertise directly to mothers in maternity wards (Baby Milk Action 1997c).

It is also reported that companies informed authorities in several Central and Eastern European countries that the adoption of legislation based on the International Code would prejudice their future membership of the European Union. To qualify as EU members, they were told that they could not adopt legislation stronger than the 1991 European Directive on Infant Formulae and Follow-on Formulae, which does not incorporate all the Code's provisions.

The EU Directive, however, does not prevent EU member states from restricting marketing further in line with the Code if they so wish.[3] The European Court has, for example, upheld Greek legislation that allows only pharmacies to sell processed milk for infants (European Court 1995).

In other countries where governments were establishing legislation based on the Code in its entirety, or even stronger than the Code, corporations have represented the 1981 Code provisions as maximum standards.

Ghana, for instance, was drafting a marketing law in 1988 that encompassed the marketing of so-called follow-on milks and complementary foods because of the adverse effects of the inappropriate marketing of these foods on breast-feeding. Follow-on milks were not explicitly covered by the Code because they existed in only a few countries in 1981.

In the early 1980s, moreover, it was not yet known that the ideal nutrition for infants is exclusive breast-feeding for the first six months followed by sustained breast-feeding for up to two years, a practice that can be negatively affected by too early an introduction of complementary foods. In 1986, the World Health Assembly tried to close this gap in the Code by drawing attention to the fact that 'any food or drink given before complementary feeding is nutritionally required may interfere with the initiation and maintenance of breast-feeding and therefore should neither be promoted nor encouraged for use by infants during this period' and, secondly, that the 'practice of providing infants with … "follow-up milks" is not necessary' – WHA 39.28, art. 3(2).

Nestlé disregarded this Resolution when it wrote in 1988 to 'encourage' the Ghanaian government body to introduce the 'WHO/UNICEF Code of Marketing of Breast-milk Substitutes … *unmodified*' (emphasis added). The letter implied that no country had introduced, or tried to introduce, legislation stronger than the original 1981 Code. The Ghanaians, however, persisted, and after a nine-year struggle a strong law was passed in May 2000.

By the 1990s, most large infant food manufacturers had diversified into marketing follow-on milks and complementary food products. The World Health Assembly urged member states in 1996 to 'ensure that complementary foods are not marketed for or used in ways that undermine exclusive and sustained breast-feeding' – WHA 49.15 art. 3(1). Yet in 1998 Nestlé not only asked the Minister of Health in Uruguay to limit national legislation to the 1981 version of the International Code but also openly questioned the legitimacy of further WHA Resolutions (IBFAN 1998b: 7).

When the authorities in Thailand wanted to renegotiate their voluntary marketing regulation agreement with the manufacturers, the companies simply refused to agree to the proposed inclusion of follow-on milks.[4]

Other countries, however, have specifically included follow-on milks within the scope of national measures to implement the Code. These include Australia, Brazil, Cameroon, members of the European Union, Malaysia, Philippines, Sri Lanka, Tanzania and Zimbabwe (Sokol 2001).

These countries are aware that industry portrayal of the 1981 International Code as a maximum, instead of a minimum, regulatory standard misinterprets the Code's standing. As WHO's former senior legal officer on Code matters, Sami Shubber, points out:

> Member States implementing the Code can go beyond its provisions, and expand them, add to them and so on, according to their social and legislative framework and their overall development objectives. However, they cannot go below the 'minimum requirement' ... So far as expansion of the provisions of the International Code is concerned, it may be necessary because of certain developments in marketing, or the appearance of some new products in the market, since the adoption of the International Code in 1981, e.g. follow-up milks. Expansion of some provisions of the International Code may also be justified in order to clarify the intent of some provisions, and provide for concrete measures thereunder. (Shubber 1998: 204)[5]

Using Trade Threats

But not all countries have been able to protect infant feeding to the extent that they wish. Guatemala, for instance, had to weaken its law after extensive legal and trade pressure from the US company Gerber (which has since become a subsidiary of the Swiss giant Novartis).

Guatemala had adopted a national Law on Marketing of Breast-milk Substitutes in 1983 (and implementing rules in 1987) that prohibited pictures of infants from being displayed on the packaging labels of any manufactured infant foods, including complementary foods. In 1992, Gerber applied to register eight new infant feeding products in the country. Before the Guatemalan Ministry of Health would do so, it asked the company to modify its label in several respects, including removal of its baby picture.

Gerber refused to do so, arguing that the line drawing of a baby's face was its corporate trademark. The Guatemalan Ministry of Health stuck to its position that no baby picture could be allowed on the label. Gerber went on to challenge the Ministry's position in the national courts and lobbied the US government for support. The USA threatened to challenge Guatemala's legislation on the marketing of breast-milk substitutes as a violation of the General Agreement on Tariffs and Trade (GATT) and to withdraw Guatemala's preferential access to the US market for its exports under the Generalized System of Preferences (GSP), which would have resulted in a loss of invaluable income for the country.

The Guatemalan Supreme Court of Justice could find no way out of the dilemma other than to decide in favour of the company. Using a strained interpretation of the national law, it decided in 1995 that the prohibition of infant pictures on labels applied only to locally manufactured complementary foods, not foreign ones (a decision that in fact accorded 'preferential treatment' to a transnational company over nationally based ones). As an importer of infant feeding products, Gerber was allowed to keep its baby picture on its label (for details see Sokol 1997: 127–9).

Similar arguments were used around the same time in Costa Rica, where industry opposed the introduction of the Code on the grounds that a proposed Bill would establish non-tariff barriers to trade in violation of GATT and would interfere with industry's constitutional freedom of speech (Margulies 1997: 419).

The Guatemalan case generated widespread discussion as to whether international 'free trade' agreements were in conflict with the International Code of Marketing of Breast-milk Substitutes. Ellen Sokol, then legal adviser to the International Code Documentation Centre, commented some five years after the Gerber case:

> Nothing in the [Guatemalan] Court's ruling was based on trade agreements. The case shows, however, that raising the spectre of the new World Trade Organization (WTO) can be an effective pressure tool against small countries that want to implement strong health regulations that may also have negative impacts on commercial interests. Such countries can hardly afford to jeopardise trade relations with big economic powers. (Sokol 1997: 129)

The cases of Guatemala and Costa Rica show that the threat of trade retaliation was being used before the establishment in 1995 of the WTO, which has the power to enforce measures in favour of free trade. Although trade threats as well as threats to relocate operations have become important TNC sources of power in an era of globalization, governments do not necessarily have to give in to them.[6]

When Zimbabwe wanted to implement a national law based on the Code and subsequent Resolutions, for instance, Nestlé threatened to withdraw its investment from the country and relocate on the grounds that it would not be economically viable to operate under such legislation. Nestlé UK added: 'This [legislation] would result in job losses for about 200 people and an extremely negative economic impact on local farmers who supply us with milk, wheat, maize and sugar.' In addition, a consortium of infant food manufacturers reportedly lobbied the Zimbabwean Parliament, arguing that the legislation did not support economic growth and development, or trade liberalization and foreign investment. Despite these threats, Zimbabwe went ahead and passed its legislation in May 1998 – and Nestlé's Zimbabwean subsidiary is still operating in the country (Baby Milk Action 1999e; IBFAN 1998b: 6).

Portraying Marketing Regulation as a Violation of 'Freedom of Commercial Speech'

A recurrent and emotionally charged complaint of the infant food and other industries has been that marketing regulations deprive them of their 'freedom of commercial speech' (see Box 7.1). This argument was used when discussions were held on whether to have an International Code of Marketing of Breast-milk Substitutes, deployed again in the mid-1980s to resist WHO's efforts to regulate tobacco, alcohol and pharmaceuticals internationally, and continues to be brought forward whenever there are serious efforts to make the Code effective.[7] The *Report of the Director-General* to the 1992 World Health Assembly reacted as follows to such objections:

> Even when viewed from the perspective of fostering competition, WHO considers that direct advertising to mothers ... is singularly inappropriate because: advertising infant formulas as a substitute for breast-milk competes with normal, healthy breast-feeding, which is not subject to advertising, yet which is the safest and lowest-cost method of nourishing an infant. (WHO 1992: 229)

More recently, allegations that Code implementation interferes with corporate freedom of commercial speech have cropped up in conjunction with the implicit claim that interference with this freedom amounts to killing babies of HIV-infected mothers. During the last decade, a difficult dilemma about infant feeding has been raised by the discovery that some HIV-positive mothers might transmit the virus to their babies through breast-feeding (see Chapter 6). Corporations have exploited this dilemma not only to return to more aggressive marketing but also to argue against strong Code implementation.

In South Africa, the infant food industry formed an agency called the 'Freedom of Commercial Speech Trust', which lobbied to prevent implementation of national legislation governing the marketing of infant foods. The Trust argued that such legislation would interfere with the critical role commercial advertising plays in informing HIV-infected mothers about how bottle-feeding can prevent transmission of the virus to an otherwise healthy infant (IBFAN 1998b: 7; *Pretoria News* 1997). The industry also used the HIV education argument to lobby against strong legislation in Swaziland.

Pauline Kisanga, IBFAN's regional coordinator for English-speaking Africa, commented thus on industry attempts to exploit the HIV-infant feeding dilemma:

> The argument is always about 'information' but advertising is not information. It is ... propaganda. The more complicated and controversial the infant feeding situation is, the more we need a strong Code. The inevitable and necessary arguments and controversies can only be fruitful and help infants, young children, parents, carers and health workers if the commercial interest is kept entirely apart.[8]

Indeed, there is a profound difference between marketing communications and education, a difference that corporate interests have tried to blur. According to propaganda researcher Alex Carey:

> Propaganda [refers to] communication where the form and content is selected with the single-minded purpose of bringing some target audience to adopt attitudes and beliefs chosen in advance by the sponsors of communication ... [In contrast], at least ideally, the purpose [of education] is to encourage critical enquiry and to open minds to arguments for and against any particular conclusion, rather than close them to any conclusion but one. (Carey 1995: 20)

Swaziland's Ministry of Health and Social Welfare listened to the opinions of both infant food manufacturers and IBFAN representatives and came to a conclusion similar to that of Kisanga. It decided to stand firm on the need for a strong regulation and asked infant food companies not to 'educate' the public about HIV and breast-feeding, stating that it regarded it as the government's responsibility to do so (IBFAN 1998b).[9]

Commercial communication does have ethical and, in most industrialized countries, well-recognized legal limits, the most basic being that it should not be misleading. It is not uncommon for additional regulatory requirements to be instituted in areas where disinformation and manipulation of the consumer may have particularly severe adverse effects, illustrated by regulations governing the advertising and marketing of tobacco, alcohol, pharmaceuticals and foodstuffs.

Enlisting Health Professionals to Oppose Strong Legislation

Industry resistance to national legislation has also included attempts to harness the support of health professionals. In Pakistan, infant food manufacturers and distributors are reported to have lobbied since 1992 against the passing of a strong national law (Shubber 1998: 217). In November 1997, Nestlé described draft legislation in a letter to the secretary of health as '*impractical* and *not workable* and therefore bereft of any support from the paediatric association and the industry' (emphasis in the original). The company enlisted the support of certain sections within the Pakistan Paediatric Association, building on long-standing financial ties. Nevertheless, the leaders of the Association eventually voted in support of the law. As of December 2000, however, its adoption is still pending.[10]

In the former Soviet republic of Georgia, companies tried to enlist the support of medical professionals as well. As the process of drafting legislation entered its final stages in 1997, Nestlé approached the Ministry of Health and offered to sponsor and collaborate in a growth-monitoring survey. It also sponsored a tour of medical doctors to the Paediatric Congress of the Russian Federation and awarded monetary awards to two physicians as 'best doctors'. Representatives of Nestlé and the French infant food manufacturer Danone sponsored a Georgian medical congress, while a representative of the German infant food manufacturer Hipp published newspaper articles opposing the draft code in Georgia on the grounds that it would interfere with free trade. Because of public disclosure of these activities, however, and because of the good relationship between the Ministry of Health and Georgian NGOs (many of whose members are high-powered health professionals), the law was passed in 1999 as originally drafted[11] (Nemsadze 2001). The UK IBFAN group, Baby Milk Action, had used its Campaign for Ethical Marketing Action Sheet to support the Georgian law-makers and NGO by prompting campaigners and politicians to demonstrate international concern for the issues at the final meetings to discuss the law.[12]

Challenging Legislation in the Courts

Adopting legislation, however, is not necessarily the end of the matter. In India, consumer groups brought to the attention of the courts breaches of the 1992 Infant Milk Substitutes, Feeding Bottles and Infant Foods (Regulation of Production, Supply and Distribution) Act. Two of the companies cited apologized for the breaches, but Nestlé turned the tables by challenging the national legislation as unconstitutional, arguing that the Act was inconsistent with India's food laws. Its challenge (and the tactics described in Chapter 6) have effectively postponed since 1995 the hearing on Nestlé's alleged breach of the law (Gupta 1999).

Lobbying to Participate in Drafting Legislation and Monitoring Industry Compliance

Regulation requires setting rules and establishing effective means of enforcing them. The most important principle in establishing a 'rule of law' is to ensure that corporations do not exercise undue influence over the regulatory process, that 'the fox is not invited to guard the chicken coop'. As mentioned in Chapter 1, regulatory capture by industry was regarded as a major problem in the USA before the discourse of regulatory reforms turned into one of de-regulation.

Today, as policy-making has largely shifted from public mandatory regulation towards co-regulation with or self-regulation by industry, discussions about 'due process' and 'conflicts of interest' and about whether, when and how public authorities should involve corporations in public regulatory processes are less common.

If a government authority decides to involve industry at any moment in the drafting of a regulation, it is important to ensure that such involvement takes place in a public forum in which industry is not the only party consulted. Key to preventing regulatory capture by industry is a clear specification of the roles of the parties invited to such consultations. When industry is invited to comment, it should be on the understanding that it is the party to be regulated and that the task of the various parties consulted is to assess whether the proposed legislation will protect public interests as far as possible.

The second important ingredient of effective regulation is industry-independent external verification, for binding and non-binding regulation alike (Krut and Gleckman 1998: 95, 99).

The third ingredient of mandatory regulation is sanctions for law violations. The involvement of corporations in monitoring boards, in particular decisions on law enforcement, is a clear conflict of interest in public office.

Some infant food companies have been pushing hard to be an integral part of the legislative and executive bodies intended to regulate the marketing practices of the infant food industry. The industry is reported to have lobbied to be part of the national monitoring committees in Pakistan, Sri Lanka, Swaziland and Zimbabwe.

Nestlé, for instance, wrote to the Sri Lankan government in 1997: 'Article 7.8 [of the Sri Lankan Code] says that manufacturers should establish a monitoring system. It would make more sense to have a government system in which industry participates … as a key stakeholder in the field of infant nutrition and manufacture in Sri Lanka … [Nestlé] should be invited to discuss the Code in depth, prior to finalisation of the said Code' (IBFAN 1998b: 7).[13]

A year later, the company berated the Ministry of Health of Gabon in several letters that it had not been invited to participate in the drafting of the national law and reprimanded the drafting body for its 'apparent lack of desire for a dialogue'. Nestlé complained that it had not received a positive reply to its offers to resolve the 'sterile polemics' and contended that it was the object of a 'systematic witch hunt' rather than being considered a 'good faith' participant.

Government officials may often have felt insecure upon receiving letters expressing a corporation's outrage at an alleged unjust exclusion from the regulatory process. But the state is under no obligation to invite corporations to be party to the drafting process. It is a matter of judgement as to whether, when and how to involve industry in public regulatory processes. The Code states clearly that the responsibility for national Code implementation and monitoring lies with governments:

> Governments should take action to give effect to the principles and aim of the Code, as appropriate to their social and legislative framework, including the adoption of national legislation, regulations and other suitable measures. (Article 11.1)

The Code mentions that governments can call on WHO, UNICEF and other UN agencies for assistance in this task (Article 11.1). It does not say that they should get assistance from industry. Moreover, Article 11.2 of the Code states that:

> *Monitoring the application of the Code lies with governments ... The manu-*
> *facturers and distributors of products within the scope of this Code,* and
> appropriate nongovernmental organizations, professional groups, and
> consumer organizations *should collaborate* with governments to this end.
> (emphasis added)

Manufacturers' collaboration with government monitoring encompasses prompt information disclosure, openness and cooperation when
reported infractions of the Code are being investigated.

As indicated in Chapter 5, the WHA member states that adopted
the Code specified that manufacturers have a responsibility to 'monitor
their marketing practices' and to 'ensure that their conduct at every
level' conforms to the principles and aim of the International Code.
Article 11.3 of the Code thus stresses the moral duty of the infant food
industry to establish company-internal Code compliance mechanisms,
whatever the state of national code implementation.[14] Responsibly
minded corporations could, in addition, commission regular external
Code audits and allow for public verifications of these audits.

The infant food manufacturers' duties in respect to Code compliance are fundamentally different from full industry participation in
the process of national Code implementation. In fact, the delegates at
the 1996 World Health Assembly expressed their concern at the ways
in which industry was trying to influence national implementation
when it urged member states: 'to ensure that monitoring of the
application of the International Code and subsequent relevant resolutions is carried out in a transparent, independent manner, free from
commercial influence' (Res. WHA 49.15).

The industry, however, continues to promote the view that national
monitoring without full industry involvement is not how the Code
should be implemented. IFM President Dr Peter Borasio wrote in
November 1998:

> IFM recognises that sometimes infractions of the International Code
> do take place. However, it is not our intent to 'break and bend' the
> Code to put profits before the health of babies ... A number of coun-
> tries have established *monitoring committees which allow claims of Code
> violations to be reviewed by NGOs, industry and governments together, and
> to decide on remedial action where necessary.* This approach has made a
> clear and *positive contribution* to effective implementation of the Inter-
> national Code, and IFM fully supports this *constructive* method of
> dealing with possible Code violations. (Borasio 1998; emphasis added)

Lobbying Member States to Oppose Further WHA Resolutions

Industry opposition to regulation has sometimes gone beyond simply opposing national laws. In 1996, Nestlé lobbied Venezuela's Ministry of the Family to use its influence to oppose any WHA resolution that might more explicitly include complementary foods in the scope of the International Code. 'Weaning foods were excluded from the scope of the Code because all infants need foods in addition to breast milk after the first 4 to 6 months of life,' it said.[15] 'WHO needs to take the leadership in resolving the controversy over the implementation of the Code, once and for all,' Nestlé continued, 'so that the resources can be concentrated on real priorities, and constructive cooperation between WHO and the infant food industry can be reinforced.' It concluded, 'any attempt to extend the scope of the Code will guarantee that the Code will remain on the WHA agenda for the next 20 years'.

In fact, the Code remains on the agenda of WHO's decision-making forum, the World Health Assembly, for two reasons. The 1981 World Health Assembly decided to ensure that the issue of infant food marketing would very much remain on the global public agenda by requiring WHO's director-general to report on the status of code implementation to consecutive Assemblies every second year (Code art. 11.7). Moreover, many member states still regard infant food manufacturers' marketing and other practices as problematic and still try to address them by passing new Resolutions.

This may be why Nestlé seems keen for the issue to drop off the WHA's agenda. In 1998, the company complained in a fax to Uruguay's national director of health about the 'constant attempts with a clear anti-industry bias to widen the scope of this Code' and referred to an alleged WHO Executive Board decision against new Resolutions:

> At the [1998] WHO Executive Board Meeting it was decided, and rightly so we believe, to take a new approach to infant feeding by prioritizing scientific aspects and avoiding the use of limited time of the Assembly in polemics and propaganda ... As part of this new approach the Executive Board considered it would not be appropriate to take up proposals of resolutions on the WHO Code of Marketing of Breast-milk Substitutes during the Assembly.

Issues for Effective National Code Implementation

Chapters 6 and 7 have explored whether the current conduct of the infant food industry demonstrates a shift on its part towards more social responsibility. Overall, neither marketing practices nor behaviour in national Code implementation seem to demonstrate a significant will or capacity on the part of the infant food industry to regulate itself effectively. Instead, there seems to be a significant gap between statements made at the international level and actual practice on the ground.

There has been no systematic effort by WHO or UNICEF to evaluate and publicize the role of industry in Code implementation (although the agencies are aware of industry interference with Code implementation).[17] Civil society organizations have only recently started to collect and publicize more consistently instances where industry has attempted to undermine national law implementation,[26] but the number of reported instances already gives cause for concern. Current industry statements about national implementation and enforcement processes, in combination with known (let alone unknown) cases of industry pressure for weak marketing regulation, may offer an additional explanation of why so many countries have not fully implemented the Code.

It is unclear to what extent national authorities have adopted weaker regulatory measures and allowed infant food manufacturers to participate in code drafting and monitoring bodies because of industry pressure (or close financial ties with industry), and to what extent they have been confused about the procedures to implement and enforce binding regulation. 'Partial implementation is not tantamount to proper implementation as intended by the drafters of the Code,' as WHO's former legal officer, Sami Shubber, points out. Nor does Shubber see voluntary measures as a proper implementation of the Code. In his opinion, the 1981 WHA intended that the Code be implemented by legally binding instruments. 'Any measure implementing the Code must contain penalties, in order to enforce compliance. Voluntary agreements ... cannot contain such penalties' (Shubber 1998: 206, 211).

How can the weakening of the 'rule of the law' by industry lobbying be prevented? One way is to revive public discussions on how to ensure that those being regulated do not have undue influence on the laws and other measures deemed necessary to protect the public interest. Ensuring 'due process' in law setting and enforcement, and preventing regulatory capture by industry, should be as salient to public debate today as they were in the United States in the 1960s and 1970s. This is particularly imperative in the case of the marketing of breast-milk substitutes. Ultimately, it is the world's babies and young infants who pay for lax Code implementation with their health and lives.

But for those governments that recognize the need to strengthen their regulatory measures, the case studies of industry behaviour in relation to Code implementation hold a positive message, too. In many instances, assistance from WHO, UNICEF and national and inter-national NGOs has helped countries to enact measures that do protect infant health. Such measures have been further bolstered by health professionals who understand the need for strong marketing regu-lations and have raised awareness and support among their peers for the protection of breast-feeding from commercial pressures.[18]

Box 7.1 *'Freedom of Commercial Speech'*

Freedom of speech is a fundamental civil and political right. It is enshrined in the UN's Universal Declaration of Human Rights and in the constitutions of many countries. Arguments advocating freedom of speech – or accusations of interference with it – appeal to the democratic instincts of many citizens and policy-makers. But freedom of speech is not the same as a 'right to unfettered commercial speech', for several reasons.

First, an individual's moral and legal right to free speech is fundamentally different from a free flow of commercial com-munications. Freedom of speech has been accorded a high value in many societies because it is regarded as a crucial safeguard against tyrannies, whether they be tyrannies of states against their citizens or tyrannies of corporations against labour activists. It is considered an inalienable human right 'that pertains to an in-dividual simply by the fact that he or she is a human being' (Cooney 1998: 875).

Corporations, however, are not human beings, even though they have actively constructed an image of themselves as 'cor-porate citizens'. In the USA, corporations acquired through court cases in the late nineteenth century the status of 'natural persons' under the US Constitution and have claimed the freedoms and rights of US citizens ever since (see Chapter 1).[19] They have fought legal battles until 'the Supreme Court has diminished distinctions between the levels of First Amendment protection for political and social expression and for what has been called *commercial speech*' (Baskin et al. 1997: 454; emphasis in the original).

The distinction between citizens and corporations has not only become blurred at the legal level. The anthropomorphized image of corporations as citizens is deliberately used to appeal to emotions usually reserved for people, for human beings.[20] But in discussions about the public regulation of corporations, it is important to remember that corporations are *not* citizens. They are legal entities entitled to carry out profit-making activities as long as they fulfil certain social obligations. Corporate rights are a contractual arrangement with society that can be taken away if corporations do not behave responsibly. As the *Encyclopedia of Applied Ethics* points out, 'The very nature of the company is that it can be dissolved. *Legal personality may bring freedoms ... but they are alienable*' (Wells 1998: 665; emphasis added).

A second major flaw in the freedom of commercial speech argument is one of omission. Corporations and other proponents of this corporate freedom usually do not mention that in the USA, as in many other countries, limits and boundaries are set even on an individual's free speech – and certainly commercial communications. As an important US textbook on public relations points out: 'Free speech is not without limits. Most [US] jurists today interpret the First Amendment to mean that free speech should be balanced against other human values or rights ... The content of all [commercial] public communications – news releases, company newspapers, speeches and advertisements – must meet legal and regulatory requirements' (Baskin et al. 1997: 454).

In the USA, several authorities have regulated various elements of the 'marketing communications mix' for some time.[21] The Federal Trade Commission, for example, regulates advertising and product or service news releases. 'Advertising and news releases are illegal if they deceive or mislead the public in any way ... Business must be able to substantiate all specific product claims.' Other limits are set by the Food and Drug Administration (FDA) which regulates 'both product safety and advertising' (Baskin et al. 1997: 465–6).[22] In the USA, as in most other major industrial countries, the promotion of pharmaceuticals, alcohol and tobacco must comply with additional advertising limits and requirements.[23]

An analogy can be made between the regulation of breast-feeding substitutes and the generally accepted limits to the promotion of pharmaceuticals. Pharmaceuticals, even life-saving ones, can be harmful if they are advertised with the wrong information or if their use is promoted for cases for which they are not needed. A specific problem arises when – because a patient or prescriber has been misinformed about the risk–benefit ratio of the advertised remedy compared to its competitor products – a second-best remedy is chosen instead of the best one.

Commercial infant formulas are nutritionally and immunologically inferior to breast-milk. In the vast majority of cases, they will only be the second-best choice for infant feeding; for some infants they will be fatal choices.

If corporations provide and promote infant formula with misleading information, they could be accused of knowingly withholding knowledge about the potential harms to the consumer (the infant), harms that range from the loss of the multiple advantages of breast-feeding to severe damage to infants, including death. Far from being a minor abuse of a freedom of commercial speech, this could be construed as a corporate crime.[24] There should be no doubt that the international community has a duty to prevent this from happening, given that the 'consumer' – in this instance, the infant – is completely unable to make a choice.[25]

It is a great irony that authorities in the USA – a country that has tried to decrease tobacco use by limiting its marketing since the 1970s and is now forcing its tobacco companies to run corrective advertisements to remedy their prior targeting of teenagers – has actively supported US-based TNCs in lobbying against international regulation of the harmful marketing practices of its infant food, pharmaceutical, tobacco and alcohol companies on the grounds of their supposedly constitutionally guaranteed 'freedom of commercial speech'.[26]

A third point about the freedom of commercial speech discourse relates to the most significant omission, the lack of discussion about the legitimacy of product promotion in a free market. Every marketing textbook stresses that advertising and other promotional activities are intended to 'stimulate demand' (e.g. Baker 1998: 10). Former Harvard Business School lecturer-turned-business critic David Korten points out that 'in classical market economy, the role of business is to respond to demand, not create it'. But none of the proponents of the 'free' market seems to object to the systematic distortion of the supply and demand mechanism by advertising and other promotional activities. Korten analysed the economic and social aspects of advertising and concluded that:

> Advertising, other than purely informative advertising based on verifiable facts, is not in the public interest. Ideally it should be prohibited. At a minimum it should not be deductible as an expense and should be taxed at a rate of at least 50 percent. A portion of the proceeds of such a tax should be used to finance consumer education on healthy, satisfying and sustainable lifestyles. (Korten 1995: 311)

Today, advertising is so entrenched that few policy-makers or citizen activists contemplate advocating a total advertising ban. But the notion of taxing advertising and other marketing activities may be a realistic proposition to finance industry-independent education on healthy infant feeding, for instance. The money raised could also be invested in more effective marketing regulations to ensure that commercial communications do not violate consumers' right to full and accurate information.

Increased taxes on advertising activities may raise significant public resources. In 1998, advertising expenditures were estimated to reach US$437 billion globally, of which nearly half (US$200 billion) was spent in the USA (Elliot 1997; Klein 1999: 11).[27] The advertising and PR budget of Nestlé alone is estimated at US$7.8 billion – more than four times the annual budget of WHO and eight times that of UNICEF (Patti Rundall in Richards 2001: 2)

Notes

1. Nestlé 1998: 6.
2. The following sections are based on reports received by UNICEF

country offices and civil society organizations. All letters quoted were available in original to the author.

3. See also Baby Milk Action 1999b; UNICEF 1998.

4. Ellen Sokol, legal adviser on Code implementation. Personal communication, March 2000.

5. For more details on the rationale for states to interpret the scope of the International Code as comprising follow-on and complementary foods, see Sokol 1997: 39–53.

6. For more information on the issue of the Code and free trade agreements, see Sokol 1997: 127–9. For information on the infant food debate at the Codex Alimentarius, see e.g. Lehners 1998; WEMOS 1997a, 1997b. For discussions on globalization and health policies, see e.g. Koivusalo 1999; Lee 1998.

7. The International Advertising Association (IAA) has also engaged in this crusade for freedom of commercial speech. The association opposed a rumoured 1998 World Health Assembly Resolution on the marketing of complementary foods. 'What is at stake here is the freedom of commercial speech,' protested the New York-based director-general of IAA, Norman Vale. 'The WHA won the battle for [limiting] advertising of infant formula in 1981, and we don't want them to win this one' (quoted in Fannin 1997).

8. Pauline Kisanga, IBFAN regional coordinator for English-speaking Africa, personal communication, March 2000.

9. Ibid.

10. Annelies Allain, director, International Code Documentation Centre, IBFAN Penang, personal communication, December 2000.

11. Personal communication, Ketevan Nemdsadze, National Breast-feeding Coordinator, Claritas, Georgia, 17 January 2001.

12. Mike Brady, campaign and networking coordinator, Baby Milk Action, personal communication, January 2001.

13. Note the company's use of the business ethics term 'stakeholder'. Stakeholder theories were created to emphasize that corporations have to take not only their shareholders but also other societal actors into account (Jackson 1998: 397; Utting 2000: 5). The use here, however, implies that it is ethically unjustifiable to leave the corporation out of the process of drafting a marketing law.

14. Infant food manufacturers have not been noted for setting up effective company internal Code-compliance mechanisms, or for speedy corrections of Code infractions. Thus WHO's executive director of family and reproductive health, Tomris Türmen, called on industry at the 1998 World Health Assembly to be more 'proactive and responsible to monitor its own marketing practices and respond promptly to correct all violations that are reported' (Türman 1998a: 3).

15. Actually the Code restricts the marketing, not the availability, of any particular infant food category.

16. See e.g. Shubber 1998: 216–17.

17. The UK IBFAN group, Baby Milk Action, regularly publishes case studies of industry interference with Code implementation in its monthly *Campaign for Ethical Marketing* Action Sheets and periodical 'Tip of the Iceberg' reports.

18. For additional analysis and proposals see Sokol 2001.

19. See also Korten 1995: 59 and Palmer 1993: 249–50.

20. Unilever's former head of corporate external affairs, Bill Byrnes, advises companies to build up 'reputation, character, and trust' as a mainstay of PR strategies aimed to 'exercise influence effectively' in today's international environment. 'The starting point is reputation ... Reputation contributes to many things but the most important of these is trust ... A corporate relations function will spend much of its time dealing under pressure, with concrete, current issues. The extent to which it succeeds ... will also depend, to a great degree, on the reputation of the company and the quality of relationships which it has developed around the world ... If potential business partners, officials, or ministers have to choose whether to ally or co-operate with your company, they will need to know who they are dealing with. They will always start with some impression of you. *It may not be factual* or concrete. It is likely to concern your standing in industry; whether you are generally seen as responsible, dependable and prudent; if you are thought to be innovative or conservative; and so on. These words are all words which we use to describe people, words which suggest character or personality. *It is significant that we talk about companies the way we speak about people*' (Byrnes 1995: 129, emphasis added).

21. 'Marketing communications mix' is defined by the *Macmillan Dictionary of Marketing and Advertising* as 'a subset of the marketing mix that is available to be deployed in the pursuit of communication objectives ... it comprises advertising, publicity, direct marketing, sales promotion, packaging, sponsorship and personal selling' (Baker 1998: 157).

22. Doubts that infant food corporations fight for the freedom of commercial speech for the sake of the consumer are raised by the following case. The three major US-based infant food manufacturers – Abbott Laboratories, Bristol-Myers Squibb and American Home Products – had agreed with each other to abide by an industry sales code that did not allow formula to be advertised directly to the consumer. In fact, they had no need to do so because, as pharmaceutical manufacturers, they all had good direct contacts with health care professionals. Nestlé re-entered the US market in the mid-1980s when it bought the Carnation company. In 1993, it filed a lawsuit against two of the infant food companies (Abbott and Bristol-Myers Squibb) and the American Academy of Paediatrics, alleging that this voluntary agreement constituted a trade barrier in violation of US anti-trust law. The lawsuit was eventually settled out of court, but the voluntary agreement not to advertise directly to the public collapsed. See Burton 1993; Sokol 1997: 21.

23. In the UK, corporate self-regulation of print media through the Advertising Standards Authority (ASA) and statutory regulation of broadcast and TV media are backed by legal regulation (Baker 1998: 10–12). The fundamental

demand of the country's system of advertising and marketing regulation is that advertising should be 'fair and honest ... and not misleading'. A few excerpts from the 1995 British Code of Advertising and Sales Promotion, produced by the Committee of Advertising Practice (CAP) and overseen by the Advertising Standards Authority (ASA), indicate the generally accepted limits to promotional activities. The first principle of this voluntary code requires that 'all advertisements should be legal, decent, honest and truthful' (art. 2.1). Other key articles are: *decency* – advertisements 'should contain nothing that is likely to cause serious or widespread offence. Particular care should be taken to avoid causing offence on the grounds of race, religion, sex, sexual orientation or disability ... ' (art. 5.1); *honesty* – 'advertisers should not exploit the credulity, lack of knowledge or inexperience of consumers' (art. 6.1);*truthfulness* – 'no advertising should mislead by inaccuracy, ambiguity, exaggeration, omission or otherwise' (art. 7.3); *substantiation* – claims must be 'capable of objective substantiation' through 'documentary evidence' (art. 3.1); *fear and distress* – 'No advertising should cause fear or distress without good reason ... advertisers may use an appeal to fear to discourage ... ill-advised actions; the fear likely to be aroused should not be disproportionate to the risks' (art. 91.1 and art. 9.2); *testimonials* – 'Fictitious endorsements should not be presented as though they were genuine testimonials' (art. 14.4). This advertising code also includes specific rules relating to children, alcoholic drinks, and health and beauty products and therapies. A separate code governs the marketing of cigarettes (Williams 2000: 357–63).

24. A corporate crime is an act committed 'on behalf of the corporation ... The term does not necessarily mean that a criminal law is being violated, the insight offered being the ways in which corporate business can cause major social, financial, and physical harm, yet face few or no legal sanctions ... Examples include price-fixing cartels, long-term fraud, industrial accidents, and pollution' (Marshall 1998: 122). If a country has a corporate criminal law – or a mandatory regulation on marketing of breast-milk substitutes – corporations can be rendered liable for violations of these laws by intent or through negligence. Under the Australian Criminal Code Act of 1995, for example, 'intention, knowledge or recklessness will be attributed to a body corporate whenever it expressly, tacitly, or impliedly authorized or permitted the commission of the offense'. Evidence of 'tacit authorization' or failure to create a 'culture of compliance' are considered offences under this system (as summarized by Wells 1998: 659).

25. In a free market framework, the infant's caretaker is actually the 'buyer', not the consumer. She – primary caretakers are predominantly women – makes the decision on behalf of the ultimate consumer, her child. See Narveson 1998: 623.

26. For further contradictions in the tobacco discourse, see Kuttner 1999: 43.

27. David Korten (1998: 33) points out that this amount is not far off global military spending, which in 1994 amounted to US$778 billion.

. . . .

CHAPTER 8

*Corporate Conduct: Managing International
Issues – Engineering of Consent*

The use of techniques enabling them to come simul-
taneously into contact with millions of people gives Public
Relations practitioners a power that has to be restrained
by the observance of a strict moral code. (International
Code of Ethics of the International Public Relations
Association – PRA – 1968)[1]

The more I thought about it, the more I looked into events
around me, the more certain I became that PR was helping
to screw up the world ... I could see the hand of the PR
man pulling the strings, making things happen, covering
things up. (J. Montgomery, former public relations vice-
president for United Brand, 1978)[2]

The twentieth century has been characterised by three
developments of great political importance: the growth of
democracy, the growth of corporate power, and the
growth of corporate propaganda as a means of protecting
corporate power against democracy. (Alex Carey, expert
on corporate propaganda, 1978)[3]

§ Since the adoption of the International Code in 1981, many infant
food manufacturers have continued to violate the letter and spirit of
the Code and to undermine national Code implementation. They are
also pressing for the public and commercial sectors to cooperate with
each other, urging the public and third sector to go into partnership
with them in the area of infant feeding rather than stirring up controversy over industry marketing practices. Two recent statements are
illustrative:

Nestlé firmly believes that progress in the area of infant nutrition will be made only if all concerned parties work together. The Company places great importance on its close collaboration with UN agencies, governments and NGOs to improve the health and welfare of women and children. It remains unswerving in its commitment to promoting infant health and nutrition, encouraging breast-feeding and the ethical marketing of infant food. (Nestlé 1998)[4]

It has become increasingly clear that private/public sector cooperation is absolutely essential for the improvement of infant and young child health around the world ... Unfortunately ongoing confrontation stands in the way of such vitally needed partnerships. This attitude is typified by ... UNICEF. (International Infant Food Manufacturers – IFM – website, 1999)[5]

Partnerships with the private sector have also been championed since the mid-1990s by the governments of the USA, the UK and more recently Germany. The World Bank now advocates a Comprehensive Development Framework (CDF) – a tripartite system of development policy-making through consensus-oriented discussions between governments, business and civil society – as a new way of policy-making. Much of the new millennium governance discourse touts 'dialogues' and 'partnerships' between big corporations and civil society organizations and/or national governments and/or UN agencies (and other international organizations) as an endeavour that will benefit all.

The major tasks within the 'public–private partnership' framework are to build 'trust' between the parties involved and to identify 'common ground' or 'win–win' situations. Transnational corporations, through their sheer size, have gained an almost natural right to participate in all kinds of fora. The Commission on Global Governance, for example, states that:

The extensive movement in favour of market driven approaches since the end of the 1970s has recast transnational corporations into ... legitimate international actors with a part to play in an emerging system of global governance. (CGG 1995: 26)

Words of caution about the potential risks of the public and commercial sectors being too closely associated with each other, or questions raised about whether TNCs should be so crucially involved in setting rules and making policy, are often dismissed as out-dated. This chapter, however, is just such a word of caution. The growth of TNCs in recent decades has been accompanied by 'international issues management' – a strategic corporate public relations discipline that is more accurately described as 'engineering of consent', the name given to it earlier this century. This chapter argues that any discussion about the usefulness and risks of partnerships with industry or about a legitimate role for transnational corporations in global democratic decision-making has to take this corporate power resource into account.

As with many other socio-political phenomena that now come under the rubric of globalization, corporate 'engineering of consent' is nothing new. Globalization, however, has prompted the fine-tuning of this communication discipline and its more widespread use with the aim of turning international politics more in favour of corporations.

An essential characteristic of corporate public relations (PR) – or corporate propaganda, as it used to be called – is that it is concealed. It is not surprising, therefore, that there is so little awareness of it. As communication scientist Michael Kunczik points out, 'public relations is also the art of camouflage and deception' (Kunczik 1990: 1). The less the ultimate intent or goal of a corporation coincides with that of the targets of its particular PR strategy, the more both intent and source of the PR activities will be obscured.

Disguising PR messages as media articles; encouraging non-corporate middlepersons, unsuspecting or otherwise, to act in the corporate interest; and building up pseudo-grassroots groups to act as a front organization are all part of the day-to-day repertoire of corporate PR laundering.[6]

Corporate PR: A Tool of Power

Corporate public relations was first developed in the USA in the last decades of the nineteenth century (Baskin et al. 1997: 30). According to communication and propaganda theorist Harold D. Laswell, the discovery that 'propaganda … is cheaper than violence, bribery and other possible control techniques' dates back to the early twentieth century (Laswell 1930–35: 524).

Communication scientists see corporate public relations as one of the most important, but least visible, tools of corporate influence. Australian academic Alex Carey concludes that:

The twentieth century has been characterised by three developments of great political importance: the growth of democracy, the growth of corporate power, and the growth of corporate propaganda as a means of protecting corporate power against democracy. (Carey 1995: 18)

Although corporate PR techniques have become increasingly sophisticated over the past one hundred years, the underlying purpose has remained the same. As Baskin, Aronoff and Lattimore, authors of an authoritative PR textbook, point out:

> [Corporate] PR *is a means by which businesses seek to improve their ability to do business.* Effective public relations smoothes and enhances a company's operations and eases and increases its sales. It enables a business to better anticipate and adapt to societal demands and trends. It is the means by which businesses improve their operating environments. (Baskin et al. 1997: 416–17; emphasis added)

It has become easier over the past 30 years or so for corporate PR to work towards its goal of improving the ability of companies to do business because globalization has also involved a trend towards 'increasing concentration of media ownerships in almost all countries … and the growing commercialization of broadcast media in Europe' (Wilcox et al. 1989: 397).

Infant Feeding and Corporate PR
Post-Code-adoption PR

The infant feeding campaign, one of the longest-standing attempts to press for corporate accountability by means of an international code, has significantly influenced the development of PR strategies to undermine efforts to regulate transnational corporations internationally.

For Nestlé, a new phase in corporate communications began with the founding of the International Baby Food Action Network (IBFAN) after the 1979 Joint WHO/UNICEF Meeting on Infant and Young Child Feeding. As mentioned in Chapter 3, Nestlé Vice-President Ernest Saunders expressed his concern over the 'professionalism of the forces involved' and advised his colleagues 'to develop an effective counter-propaganda operation, with a network of appropriate consultants in key centres, knowledgeable in the technicalities of infant nutrition in developing countries, and with the appropriate contacts to get articles placed' (Saunders 1980b).

Five months later, in January 1981, the company appointed an experienced PR executive, Rafael Pagan Jr., as president of the Nestlé Coordination Center for Nutrition (NCCN). Officially the Center coordinated Nestlé's 'nutrition activities' in the USA, but Pagan described the Center as a 'crisis management task force' with an 'early warning system and political threat analysis capability' (Pagan Jr. 1985: 378).

While infant food companies were still lobbying against an international code, the NCCN after the adoption of the Code was laying the ground in case a code was adopted. One of its first public acts was to organize a press conference entitled 'Nestlé completes WHO code implementation process'. The guidelines distributed at the conference instructed company employees in the Code; the 1982 revised version of these guidelines continued to be at variance with the Code even after WHO and UNICEF had pointed out discrepancies[8] (see Chapter 5).

A second task was to create an 'independent social audit committee' called the Nestlé Infant Formula Commission (NIFAC), which was provided with a regular budget by Nestlé and was chaired by a former US secretary of state, Edmund Muskie. The official remit of this committee was to 'monitor' Nestlé's marketing practices (albeit along the weaker Nestlé guidelines rather than according to the Code). Elsewhere, however, NIFAC was described as a 'major factor in Nestlé's gaining the trust of its more moderate and constructive critics' (Pagan Jr. 1985).[9] Nestlé disbanded NIFAC in 1991 after its return from a fact-finding mission in Mexico that concluded that Nestlé had violated the provisions against 'free supplies' of infant formula (Margen et al. 1981).

A Wider Strategy Against International TNC Regulation

Rafael Pagan Jr., the PR executive who advised Nestlé, also developed a comprehensive PR strategy for TNCs in general to fight for corporate 'survival' and to deal 'constructively and effectively' with the 'international regulatory mood' (Pagan Jr. 1982). This strategy included:

- establishing an issues management unit (such as Nestlé's Coordination Center for Nutrition) with a 'responsive, accurate corporate issue and trends warning system and analysis capability';
- 'organizing effective NGOs, and gaining representation for them at every possible UN agency' – by NGOs, Pagan meant international business organizations such as the International Council of Infant

Food Industries (ICIFI) and the International Pharmaceutical Manu-facturers' Association (IPMA).
- working with national and international civil servants 'not to defeat all regulation, but to create regulation that legitimises and channels our rights, opportunities and contributions';
- 'reaching out to hold an ongoing dialogue with the many new publics whose understanding we need to remain in business';
- separating the 'fanatic' activist leaders from those who are 'decent concerned' people, and 'stripping the activists from the moral authority they receive from their alliance with religious organ-isations' (Pagan Jr. 1982).[10]

Awareness of Pagan's international issues management strategy facili-tates better understanding of the ways in which TNCs and their business organizations tried over the subsequent 20 years to influence international public interest debates, particularly at the level of the United Nations.

The following section provides a glimpse into the general nature of issues management strategies, which should be taken into account when decision-making processes about policy intersect with industry interests. Actual corporate PR strategies, however, are constantly changing, even if the goal of reaching a specific aim and objective remains constant.

Issues Management / Engineering of Consent

Issues management is a key PR strategy to foster favourable business climates today – a strategy that was called 'engineering of consent' in the early 1920s. The PR techniques to engineer consent were developed and propagated by Edward Bernays, an influential PR practitioner and theoretician. Bernays described engineering of consent as:

> quite simply, the use of an engineering approach – that is, action based only on thorough knowledge of the situation and the application of scientific principles and tried practices in the task of getting people to support ideas and programmes. Any person or organization depends ultimately on public approval and is therefore faced with the problem of engineering the public's *consent* to a programme or goal. (Bernays 1952: 159; original emphasis)[11]

Issues management is the modern version of engineering of consent. Both are pro-active, systematic propaganda campaigns based on intelligence-gathering and on assessment of the socio-political situation.[12] PR executive Bill Cantor defines issues management as: 'The function of identifying issues that impact on the company and developing programmes to influence desired audiences' (Cantor 1989: 497).

Issues management is used by corporations to 'shape rather than react to public discourse and decision making.' (Baskin et al. 1997: 80–1) Bob Leaf, an executive with major PR company Burson-Marsteller, stressed around the time of the adoption of the International Code:

> Companies can't wait for a thing to become an issue and then react. Because then they are on the defensive. The key of the '80s will be defining the issues before they can have an impact on you so that you can diffuse them, be prepared to have an action plan when something comes up rather than having to act hurriedly under an attack. (quoted in Pfaff 1981)[13]

Baskin and colleagues elaborate further:

> Issues management grew out of the same reality and recognition that led organizations to practice public relations originally. Organizations have been blind-sided for too long by protest groups who gain public support by striking public chords through protest and other tactics. To avoid unpleasant surprises, organizations should scan, monitor and track external forces … These forces should be analyzed in terms of their effects on an organization's image, profit, and ability to act. Based on that analysis, an organization's policy must be developed, strategy planned, and action implemented. (Baskin et al. 1997: 80)

Engineering of consent or issues management strategies usually have three, sometimes overlapping, components:

- intelligence-gathering and an assessment of the socio-political climate in which the particular company is operating;
- attempts to manipulate public debates in a direction favourable to the company; and
- attempts to exclude what the industry perceives as diverging or antagonistic voices from the public debate.

To gain a broader picture of these corporate public relations strategies and techniques, a model framework is described below, based on analysis of actual corporate PR strategies (such as those described in

PR textbooks, issues management industry seminars, leaked industry documents and accounts of activists) and blended with insights from theories on communication and power.[14]

Intelligence-gathering and Assessments

One important PR technique in assessing where a company is at is 'environmental monitoring'. This tracks 'trends in public opinion and events in the sociopolitical environment' that may affect the company's operations. Environmental monitoring is thus an 'early warning system' that helps PR managers to 'locate the smoke and take action before a major fire develops' (Baskin et al. 1997: 80).

Pressure groups and other important organizations are part of this environment that companies constantly strive to assess. Inviting them to participate in 'social audits' is one way of doing so. Other means include infiltrating their organizations, gaining information about them through journalists or private detectives,[15] scanning their newsletters, publications and websites, and embarking on corporate 'philanthropy', 'partnerships' and 'dialogues'.

As a result of such information-gathering, public relations firms have developed data banks on activist and other relevant groups and organizations over the past 10–15 years. While Rafael Pagan was working for Nestlé, he developed dossiers on groups such as the International Baby Food Action Network (IBFAN), the International Organization of Consumers Unions (IOCU) and the Pesticide Action Network (PAN), along with key religious groups and organizations and labour unions (Stauber and Rampton 1995: 53).

Nestlé and many other companies now have sophisticated in-house intelligence systems. The Swiss firm Novartis (which owns the baby food manufacturer Gerber), for example, has a computerized early issue detection system called the Issue Support and Advocacy Network (ISAN). This system alerts the company to any 'global issue' that might entail the 'risk that Novartis's reputation could be damaged'. ISAN also 'helps in the analysis of the information acquisition of key stakeholders, because it contains information about all persons who have ever been in contact with Novartis ... ISAN also includes information on journalists, authorities and politicians and on every question that Novartis has ever been asked in any of their country organizations' (Winter and Steger 1998: 115–16).

Suppression of Public Issues

If, as a result of 'environmental monitoring' and 'social audits', issue managers conclude that a company can no longer ignore a certain issue, they will first attempt to suppress it or at least to prevent it from spreading. At the same time, they will try to influence the public debate by projecting a favourable image of the company.

Secrecy and censorship are routinely employed to keep issues off the public agenda. All kinds of corporate data of public concern and interest are classified as commercially confidential.

Journalists and activists are often silenced through the implied, if not open, threat of libel, confiscation of personal property or legal action, or they censor themselves in anticipation of such an action. Professor Pring of Colorado University coined the term SLAPPs – 'Strategic Lawsuits Against Public Participation' – for this type of silencing. 'SLAPPs sent a clear message,' he said, 'that there is a "price" for speaking out politically' (quoted in Rowell 1998: 303).[16]

Some critics have lost their jobs after their employers have been approached; other reprisals have included imprisonment or threat of physical harm, including death threats. There have been attempts to intimidate corporate critics, journalists, corporate whistle-blowers and high-ranking UN officials with such threats.[17]

Withdrawing financial support can also be used to suppress public debates. Industries have lobbied the US government to withhold its contributions to WHO if the latter continued to meddle with 'free enterprise' through its critical work on regulatory codes and corporate activities. In 1983, for example, WHO was pressured to withhold publication of a study it had commissioned showing a clear link between the marketing practices of the alcohol industry and a rise in alcohol problems in developing countries (Selvaggio 1983). In 1986/87, WHO lost a large chunk of its budget because the USA withheld contributions when WHO was drawing up ethical criteria for drug promotion (see Box 5.2).

Image Management – and Transfer

Whether or not a company manages to suppress a particular issue, most big corporations today invest in a long-standing key PR activity: 'image management' – constructing a good public image for a corporation.[18]

'A strong and positive corporate reputation is the holy grail of every public relations professional,' says Michael Morley, president of Edelman Public Relations New York and deputy chairman of Edelman Public Relations Worldwide. At the Edelman PR company, the 'management of corporate reputation' is defined as 'the orchestration of discreet public relations initiatives designed to protect and promote the most important brand you own – your corporate reputation'. According to Morley: 'corporate reputation – or image, as advertising professionals prefer to term it – is based on how the company conducts *or is perceived as conducting* its business' (Morley 1998: 8; emphasis added). Thus the outward appearance, not the actual practices, of a corporation is what counts.

From a corporate perspective, investment in 'reputation management' holds great potential. 'When corporate reputation is secure, a flow of positive and tangible benefits accrues to the organization. *And it is an important shield in terms of crisis*' (Morley 1998: 8–9; emphasis added).

PR professionals have also helped to build an image of corporations as responsible and concerned 'corporate citizens' while admonishing their employees that only old-fashioned managers would invest corporate money for wholly humanitarian reasons. PR managers know that 'corporate philanthropy' (giving away corporate money for the love of humankind) is a contradiction in terms:

> Some corporate executives seem to think that their corporate philanthropy is an act of benevolent charity. It is not. An act of charity refines and elevates the soul of the giver – but corporations have no souls to be saved or damned ... [W]hen you give away shareholders' money, your philanthropy must serve the longer-term interests of the corporation. Corporate philanthropy should not be, cannot be, disinterested. (Kristol 1977)

And, indeed, research on corporate sponsorship indicates that corporate 'self-interest' prevails (Baskin et al. 1997: 284). Recipients of corporate money and attention, however, are rarely aware that PR practitioners regard sponsorship as a 'hard-nosed business decision undertaken ... with the intention of obtaining a proportionate return to the sponsor of the money invested' (Sedgwick 1985: 397). There has been a noticeable trend within corporate giving towards 'strategic philanthropy':

> Rather than reacting to public issues and public pressures, more firms
> – particularly the larger ones – are taking greater initiative in *channelling
> dollars* and corporate talent *into problem areas that they deem significant
> and in which they wish to make an impact*. (Baskin et al. 1997: 285;
> emphasis added)

Today, images of corporations as socially concerned 'corporate citizens'
are bolstered by corporate 'dialogues', 'sponsorships' and 'partnerships'. Many individuals, groups and organizations that accept industry
funds or enter into 'partnership' arrangements and 'dialogues' with
the industry believe that they will not be used for a company's political
– or marketing[19] – purposes as long as they take care to maintain their
integrity. They believe that being aware of and resisting the risks of
being 'bought' or 'co-opted' by a company or business organization is
sufficient.

Many may still be unaware, however, that in accepting sponsorship
or engaging in 'partnerships' and 'dialogues' with the industry, they
may well be used for *'image transfer'* – the transfer of their good
reputation to the corporate sponsor or initiator of the dialogue.

PR professionals stress that a good public image or reputation is a
key political resource. In the words of Edelman PR Executive Michael
Morley, 'Because businesses today operate in an environment of stress
that often seems close to bursting into crisis, a carefully nurtured
corporate reputation is all the more important' (Morley 1998: 9). For
corporations, their credibility is 'capital', a 'reservoir of goodwill' in
modern societies, which may well translate into a higher legitimacy if
a corporation comes under public scrutiny.[20] If a corporation has taken
care to build a good image, Morley says others may well think that:
'This is a fine, well-managed company with a solid record. There is
probably no truth in the rumours/allegations. Even if there is, they
[the company] will put things right and get back on track without
undue damage' (Morley 1998: 13).

The potential political impact of close association with corporations, and the risk of helping corporations to prevent closer public
scrutiny of and action against its practices, are often underestimated
by civil society organizations and those outside the corporate world.
Helping to boost the positive image of a corporation can profoundly
shift balances of power: while the corporation may gain a greater
'licence to operate', those individuals, groups and organizations that
have not prevented 'image transfer' risk losing their reputation of

being a principled and trustworthy institution, organization, group or individual.

Manipulating Public Debate

If an issue cannot be ignored or hidden from public view, issues managers will usually advise the corporation to engage actively in public debates in order to influence public opinion in the direction the corporation desires. Most often they resort to a mix of four communication strategies: delay; de-politicize; divert; and fudge.

Delay The announcement of voluntary corporate codes, for example, has been a prime means of preventing, or at least delaying, tougher external regulation of corporate activities (UNRISD 1995: 19).[21]

As described earlier, both the infant food and pharmaceutical industry associations drew up codes only when faced with outside regulation. The International Federation of Pharmaceutical Manufacturers Association (IFPMA) managed to delay the adoption of the WHO Ethical Criteria for Medicinal Drug Promotion for several years with the argument that its members must be given the opportunity and time to prove that they could regulate themselves (see Chapter 5).

A few years later, in the early 1990s, dozens of industry associations published or updated environmental guidelines and codes for their membership when faced with calls for effective outside regulation in the wake of the 1992 UN Conference on Environment and Development (UNCED), dubbed the 'Earth Summit'. An UNCTAD-commissioned study of environmental self-regulation by influential industry associations concluded that: 'in contrast to the months of activity in the lead-up to the Earth Summit about how to frame the relationship between industry and environment, the months thereafter have seen comparatively little conceptual movement or progress' (UNCTAD 1996b: 85) – but the environmental code drawn up by the UN Centre on Transnational Corporations and the UN's Code on Transnationals itself had been defeated.

De-politicize A second strategy is to de-politicize debates on societal issues by trying to shift discussions either to less politicized arenas or from political questions to technocratic issues.

When critics lobbied for and obtained public hearings in the USA in the late 1970s on the inappropriate marketing of baby milks in developing countries, Nestlé suggested that discussion about infant formula marketing should be shifted 'back to the sphere of relevant government authorities, health professionals and industry experts' (quoted in Chetley 1986: 57). Its reported aim was to 'depoliticise the controversy' (McComas et al. 1983: 14). The strategy, which was the origin of the 1979 Joint WHO/UNICEF Meeting, failed in this instance. Business strategy expert Prakash Sethi,[22] who analysed Nestlé's statements and actions in the infant food controversy, summarized the result of the debate's move from the USA to the 1979 Joint WHO/UNICEF Meeting on Infant and Young Child Feeding in Geneva:

> Nestlé had hoped to be in a better position to influence the course of events in an international forum such as a WHO conference. However, this would prove not to be the case. Instead, the conference largely accepted the agenda of the industry critics and set WHO towards the inexorable path of enacting a marketing code for infant formula foods. (Sethi 1994: 91)

The industry's role in infant feeding has remained a political and controversial issue ever since.

Divert A further strategy attempts to defuse public controversy by stimulating discussion on issues of secondary importance. This may also give critics the illusion that they are participating in the decision-making process.

Some infant food manufacturers continue to divert attention away from the question of why they have not built up effective Code implementation and compliance mechanisms nearly twenty years after the adoption of the Code by making appeals to help them build more effective national public monitoring systems. This helps them to explain manufacturers' failures in relation to their marketing practices in terms of failures of governments to regulate them.[23]

Others divert attention away from the question of why corporations continue to cause harm to babies through the aggressive promotion of infant foods by blaming mothers in developing countries for incorrect preparation of the commercial products.

Fudge A final strategy is to pretend to support public demands, but then to disseminate a version of the critics' analysis, policy or proposed code of ethics that is slightly but significantly altered. Those unfamiliar with the issue cannot discern easily how the industry version differs from the original.

The baby food industry, for example, proclaims its wholehearted support for the International Code of Marketing of Breast-milk Substitutes – but continues to suggest that the International Code is not intended to be universal in its coverage.

Nestlé stresses in its Charter (Nestlé's own policy on the marketing of infant formula) that it 'DOES ... comply with both the letter and the spirit of World Health Organization's International Code of Breast-milk Substitutes'. The Charter, however, describes Nestlé's compliance only to the 'infant formula policy in developing countries'. An easily overlooked footnote adds 'in developed countries, Nestlé respects national codes, regulations and/or other applicable legislation relating to the marketing of infant formula' (Nestlé 1996; emphasis in the original).

Pointing at footnotes might suggest that critics are overreacting. But analysing propaganda messages entails not only looking at what is said, how and why, but also at what is *not* said. Nestlé's Charter, for instance, does not mention that most existing national laws are weaker than the International Code (not least because of active industry interference). Another easily overlooked aspect of the Charter is that Nestlé commits itself to regulate just one category of breast-milk substitute, namely infant formula, but not other substitutes such as follow-on formula, or special formulas such as hypoallergenic or lactose-free infant foods.

Excluding Diverging Voices

Engineering of consent attempts to ensure that a corporate version of public issues dominates public debate. It also attempts to exclude 'unfavourable' views from the public discourse by neutralizing critics.

During the early days of concerted international pressure for industry accountability, 'red-baiting' – labelling critics as communists or anti-free market – was commonly employed in an attempt to discredit such critics.[24] For example, the statement from Nestlé Brazil's President Oswaldo Ballarin at the 1978 Kennedy hearings, which described the consumer boycott of Nestlé as an attack on the free economic system, appears to have been put together at the highest company level (see Chapter 3). According to business academic Prakash Sethi:

it would appear that Ballarin had originally drafted his own statement which was primarily devoted to the scientific and health care aspects of infant formula feeding in less developed countries. This statement was rejected by the Nestlé people at the company's US headquarters in White Plains, New York. Instead, Ballarin was given a statement and, according to one Nestlé executive, was instructed, over his strong objections, to read it at the hearing. This statement was drafted by Mr Guerrant, president of Nestlé-US and Mr Frank Chiocca, a lawyer with Nestlé-US. The statement was thoroughly reviewed and revised in Nestlé-Switzerland by Paternot and Fookes, the two executives who were heavily involved in the controversy from its very early days. (Sethi 1994: 85–6)

Nestlé was also involved in *Fortune* editor Herman Nickel's article 'The corporation haters', which depicted critics as 'Marxists marching under the banner of Christ' (Nickel 1980) (see Chapter 4).[25] Nestlé's Ernest Saunders described the Nickel article in his 1980 internal memorandum as the most credible 'third party rebuttal of the activist case' and advised:

> There must be maximum exploitation of the opportunities presented by the *Fortune* article and the Ethics and Public Policy Center's willingness to undertake additional activity. Mr Guerrant is somewhat concerned that Nestlé should not be seen as the dominant subscriber to the Ethics and Public Policy Center. Mr Ward [a Washington DC-based lawyer who represented Nestlé in the USA] informs us that there are ways in which this matter can be successfully handled. (Saunders 1980b)

Referring to this and other defamatory articles in the press, WHO Director-General Halfdan Mahler said during the 1981 WHO Executive Board discussions that 'he realized that freedom of expression involved the right to be as far from the truth as possible; that included doing harm to children's health' (quoted in Shubber 1998: 36).

Since the end of the Cold War, discrediting social critics by stereotyping them as 'leftists' has given way to other strategies. Two major approaches are generally employed today.

• *Portraying critics as unworthy of participation* in a 'rational', democratic and professional debate. This includes labelling them as 'anti-industry', 'anti-technology', 'anti-progress', 'irrational', 'emotional' and 'unprofessional' (the latter being a powerful label to use against health professionals and other academics).[26] Now that TNCs are widely regarded as engines of economic growth which need, and

even deserve, an unregulated global market to create wealth supposedly for everyone, it has become easier to assert that anyone
who lobbies for any kind of regulation is responsible for the loss of
jobs and wealth.

• *Divide-and-rule*, which often involves inviting carefully selected
  influential groups and critics to participate in consensus-oriented
  'dialogues' or to engage in 'partnerships' (and using their participation for image transfer) while discrediting groups which do
  not participate as incorrigible 'radicals' who are 'confrontational'
  for the sake of it.[27]

While neutralizing critics through negative labelling, companies often
refrain from answering the content of the criticisms and from changing
their practices substantially.

'Dialogues' or Intelligence-gathering, Image Transfer, Diversion and Division?

Over the past decade, so-called dialogues have emerged as one of
the most sophisticated issues management strategies. Rafael Pagan Jr.
was one of the forerunners of this trend. He urged TNCs in 1982 to
engage in dialogues as an important way to deal with the 'international
regulatory mood' and 'remain in business'. At the Tenth Public Relations World Congress in 1985, Pagan drew attention to more than
thirty different codes of conduct for TNCs or guidelines being considered at the UN level and to the intention of the International
Organization of Consumers Unions (IOCU) 'to create a climate of
support for national and international regulation' (Pagan Jr. 1985: 376).

Pagan anticipated that several industries would be 'certain to be
at the centre of conflict during the next decade'. These included
'pesticides and other agricultural chemicals; oil, natural gas and
petrochemicals; pharmaceuticals; fast and processed foods; alcoholic
beverages; tobacco; nuclear power; armaments and weaponry; news,
media and communications; and banking, insurance and other financial
services'. Pagan warned the audience that 'as the infant formula
conflict proved, the marketing practices of no major industry or
company are exempt from the politics of confrontation' (Pagan Jr.
1985: 376–7).

He criticized corporations for practising an outdated dual strategy
consisting of:

- 'Lobbying – direct behind the scenes negotiations between companies and governments or UN agencies'; and
- 'A public relations orthodoxy that seeks to communicate a decent company image to the general public in order to gain support, or at least consent, for the industry's objectives.'

Pagan advised them to move on to a 'social awareness' concept, a term he preferred to 'issues management':

> If a company opens itself up to dialogue with critics of conscience, seeks support and understanding through openness and dialogue with news media and UN staff members, and acknowledges a broad responsibility for the more remote effects of its marketing practices in the Third World, it can gain respect for its essential decency, legitimacy and usefulness. (Pagan Jr. 1985: 377)

The infant food case study casts doubt on the claim that industry-initiated 'dialogues' were ever meant to be conduits for allowing society to make corporations more accountable. Instead, in many cases, 'dialogues' seem to have been used simply as an additional international issues management tool to engineer consent to socially unacceptable corporate practices.

Marketing lecturer Craig Smith recognizes the dual face of industry-initiated dialogues, stating that dialogues can be used not only to find out what the problems are and to 'comply' with societal demands, but also to fight pressure groups or to manipulate the debate. Smith suggests that, as far as companies are concerned, direct 'dialogue' with pressure groups can be a better tool to assess the extent of the 'threat' posed by critics' demands than 'environmental scanning', and can also be used to co-opt pressure groups (Smith 1990: 273).

Thus dialogues are often anything but open and straightforward discussions about controversial issues. They can be used to gain intelligence, transfer image and divert attention from more pressing issues. Civil society and other organizations should therefore consider carefully whether, when and how to enter into discussions with a company. To contribute to democratic decision-making, such meetings should be conducted and recorded in a way which is transparent to the public.

In 1989, for instance, just after the Nestlé boycott was resumed because the company continued to violate the WHA Resolutions on 'free supplies', the International Association of Infant Food Manufacturers proposed a two-day meeting 'with the participation of WHO and UNICEF' in order 'to resolve the controversy over the free or low-price supplies of infant formula and other breastmilk substitutes in developing countries' (Borasio 1989).

The meeting never took place because most of the organizations invited to attend, such as the World Council of Churches and the International Organization of Consumers Unions, saw no need for it. They said that the industry's interpretation of the Code as permission to continue distributing large amounts of free supplies to maternity wards was clearly contradicted by the 1986 World Health Assembly Resolution, which requested member states to 'ensure that the small amounts of breast-milk substitutes needed for the minority of infants who require them in maternity wards and hospitals are made available through normal procurement channels and not through free or sub-sidised supplies' (Res. WHA 39.28, 1986).

Activists queried why the industry had asked for such a meeting in 1989 – after the boycott had been renewed – but not in 1986 at the time of the WHO Resolution. They regarded the request as another delaying tactic.

Indeed, rather than simply ending their free supplies, the International Association of Infant Food Manufacturers elaborated a statement on how they would work with governments, WHO and UNICEF to end this practice by 1992. Nestlé portrayed these interactions with WHO and UNICEF as follows:

> For the first time, formal international cooperation was initiated between the infant food industry and the leading United Nations agencies concerned with infant health – the World Health Organization (WHO) and UNICEF – in an attempt to resolve the controversy once and for all ... Nestlé will continue to seek solutions, in cooperation with WHO, UNICEF ... health authorities ... health professionals, and research scientists, which will lead to improved infant and child health. (Nestlé 1992, foreword by CEO Helmut Maucher)

In the same statement, Nestlé claimed that it had 'done everything possible to support the spirit and the letter of the International Code, particularly in those countries where there is high illiteracy and infant mortality' and complained that 'these efforts have been hampered by activist groups which have always placed the most negative interpretation on company initiatives and have consistently promoted confrontation rather than cooperation' (Nestlé 1992: 5).

In November 1997, UNICEF suspended discussions with Nestlé because – after years of dialogues – the company would still not agree to the universality of the Code, nor had it stopped distributing free supplies to maternity wards. This did not dissuade the company from using the UN agency for image transfer on its website:

> Nestlé markets infant formula in conformity with the principles and aim of the WHO International Code of Marketing of Breast-milk Substitutes, and *seeks* dialogue and cooperation with the international health community and in particular with the WHO and UNICEF, to identify problems and their solution. (Nestlé 1999a; emphasis added)

'Seeking dialogue' with UNICEF did not involve Nestlé changing its stance on the controversial issues in any way. It meant, among other things, Nestlé complaining in a letter to the UN secretary-general about UNICEF 'clos[ing] the door to any further conversation' and employing professional lobbyist and former US vice-presidential candidate Geraldine Ferraro to press for a reopening of discussions (see Freedman and Stecklow 2000). After being portrayed by the *Wall Street Journal* as being engaged in a senseless 'feud against industry' (*WSJ* 2000), UNICEF received Geraldine Ferraro and a delegation from Nestlé Switzerland on 19 December 2000. (For responses to the allegations of the *Wall Street Journal*, see e.g. Bellamy 2000b and Yamey 2000.)

Shortly thereafter a food business news service spread the following message about this one meeting: '[A]fter a long period of broken communication, outreach efforts by Nestlé have meant that the dialogue between UNICEF and the food giant have been continuing for the last 18 months. The last meeting was held less than six weeks ago' (Harman 2001).

Ruling by Consent? A New Phase of Industry Lobbying

BINGOs, PINGOs and the 'Creators of Wealth'

In sum, in parallel with the international debate about the regulation of the marketing of breast-milk substitutes, infant food manufacturers have contributed to the development of international 'issues management'/engineering of consent PR strategies, a much overlooked corporate tool of power intended to shape public debates.

As mentioned earlier, Rafael Pagan advised transnational corporations to organize 'effective NGOs, and [to gain] representation for them at every possible UN agency' (Pagan Jr. 1982). By NGOs, Pagan meant international business organizations. The infant food industry spared no effort in trying to get the status of a 'non-governmental organization in official relations' for its International Council of Infant Food Industries (ICIFI). In August 1980 it hired Stanislas Flache, former assistant director-general of WHO, to achieve this goal. The day after his retirement from the WHO (in the midst of the International Code drafting), Flache took up the post of ICIFI secretary-general.

The application of most organizations for the status of NGO with the World Health Organization is passed without much debate. In the early 1980s, however, WHO's Executive Board was so concerned about the practices of the members of the infant food association that a decision on ICIFI was deferred three times. The infant food association thus changed its strategy. ICIFI was dissolved, another business organization – the International Association of Infant Food Manufacturers (IFM) – was formed, and another former WHO staff member hired to advise on procedures. IFM applied for NGO status under the umbrella of the International Society of Dietetic Food Industries (ISDI). When ISDI was granted NGO status in 1987, the infant food industry shared this experience with other TNCs in a specific newsletter on 'How companies can gain from NGO status'.[28]

A deciding factor in granting NGO status to ISDI had apparently been the admission of the International Organization of Consumers Unions (IOCU) (one of the co-founders of IBFAN) as an official NGO the year before. The admission of the business association was thus seen as an even-handed gesture (Allain 1991: 27). The International Baby Food Action Network (IBFAN) is just one public advocacy alliance that has been concerned ever since about the political implications of the failure of the United Nations to distinguish clearly between associations representing commercial interests and citizen groups and organizations.

Shifting the Arena

While civil society organizations are still calling on the UN to make an official distinction between the two NGO sub-categories, business interest NGOs (BINGOs) and public interest NGOs (PINGOs), or to create a wholly new subcategory for business so as to allow for more transparent and meaningful debates (see Chapter 2), the industry has moved along and shifted arenas.

Rather than attempting to influence international politics by using the NGO status and image, TNCs are now asking for a privileged status in international decision-making. At the 1996 UNCTAD Global Investment Forum, Nestlé's then executive vice-president, Peter Brabeck-Letmathe, argued that, in setting the global economic framework, 'business and its organizations should not be lumped together with the many single-issue NGOs, but accepted as interlocutors of different stature, as the engineers of wealth' (Brabeck-Letmathe 1996: 3).

In 1997, when Nestlé CEO Helmut Maucher took over as president of the International Chamber of Commerce (ICC), he urged governments to work with business to establish a framework for the global economy. Under the title 'Ruling by consent', he said in a *Financial Times* opinion piece:

> Governments have to understand that business is not just another pressure group but a resource that will help them set the right rules. The International Chamber of Commerce … is the obvious partner from the business side for this intensified dialogue with governments. With its long-established links with the UN system, the WTO and other intergovernmental organisations it is uniquely placed to make the business viewpoint heard in the decision-making bodies that count in today's world.
>
> Under my presidency, the ICC is resolved to take the lead in asserting the business viewpoint more strongly in the Council of Nations … One of our first steps has been to convene a formal dialogue between the ICC and the many important organisations based in Geneva … and to bring together the heads of international companies and the leaders of international organisations so that the business experience is channelled into the decision-making process for the global economy. (Maucher 1997)

A year later, Maucher asserted in the same newspaper that this strategy had already produced visible results: 'We have established the ICC as the preferred dialogue partner for business with the United Nations and other international institutions' (quoted in Williams 1998).[29] Indeed, 1997 marked the beginning of another phase of TNC influence over international decision-making about limits to TNC activities. Rather than lobbying at UN meetings, the industry is now inviting high-ranking UN and government officials to their own business round-tables, in Davos and Geneva, for instance.[30]

Round-table Discussions and Code Implementation

> I can assure you ... that this is not a partnership at any price. Open, transparent dialogue is an obvious prerequisite ... Certainly dialogue and realism must be accompanied by high ethical standards. (Gro Harlem Brundtland, director-general of WHO, 1998)[31]

> The Dutch infant food industry ... is happy with this [WHO dialogue] initiative. We are convinced that the WHO, with this initiative, can be instrumental in ending the ongoing and useless confrontations between the industry and the action groups and will instead call on all parties to solve the real problems in the field of public health in general and of the wellbeing and health of infants, babies, and young children in particular. (Dutch Baby Food and Dietary Food Manufacturers' Association, 1998)[32]

Industry's concerted lobbying efforts to be recognized as privileged partners in global decision-making arenas have coincided with a change of policy approach within WHO. In January 1998, the Executive Board agreed that the global commitment to infant and young child nutrition, in particular breast-feeding, should be revitalized. WHO decided to use 'the good offices of the Organization to initiate, in collaboration with concerned parties, a process for specifying, examining and over-coming the main obstacles to implementing by all countries, both the International Code and subsequent related resolutions' (Türmen 1998b).

Preliminary discussions were held with representatives of consumer groups and the infant food industry in April 1998. In November 1998, the first round-table discussions were held with consumer and breast-feeding groups on their own, and then just with infant food manu-facturers.

The aim of these meetings was to 'discuss the establishment of a consultative mechanism to bring together consumer and community-based NGOs, and the infant food industry, for improved implemen-tation in countries of the International Code and related World Health Assembly Resolutions' (WHO 1998c: 3). This mechanism would be a regular 'WHO forum where NGOs in official relations – representing the infant-food industry and consumers – can engage in good-faith effort to identify, narrow and, if possible, resolve their major out-standing differences' (Brundtland 1998a: 7).

NGOs, however, were not persuaded that this mechanism would

really move Code implementation forward. They argued that the obstacles to Code implementation were not differences in interpretation, but a lack of will on the part of the industry to comply with the Code in letter and spirit, and industry interference with the legislatory and monitoring processes in countries wishing to implement the Code. They also felt that the proper forum for clarifying issues of Code interpretation and implementation should be the World Health Assembly, not a semi-private forum of industry and civil society organizations.[33]

Industry's Reaction to the WHO Initiative

I spend much of my time listening to our customers, public policy makers, opinion leaders, and our 230,000 employees who are in over 100 countries and represent nearly all the cultures of the world. A consistent message I have received is that Nestlé could be more open and communicative in the area of business principles and practices.

We are thus looking for ways to respond to this desire for greater openness and transparency, and the enclosed *Report to the Director-General, World Health Organization* and the *International (WHO) Code Action Report* are two ways in which we are responding. (Peter Brabeck-Letmathe, CEO, Nestlé, October 1999)[35]

We realize ... that some organizations have a different interpretation of the World Health Organization Code of Marketing of Breast-milk Substitutes than we do ... The Director General of the World Health Assembly [*sic*], Gro Harlem Brundtland, has invited both industry and infant formula action groups to join in discussions to resolve once and for all the differences which exist in interpretation of the International Code, so that efforts can be directed to implementing the Code in a practical way in each country.

Nestlé, both directly and through our trade association, has said yes to Dr Brundtland's invitation, but we understand that WHO is still waiting for the campaign groups to accept her invitation, after a year's waiting. We sincerely hope that they will accept Dr Brundtland's invitation, as it is Nestlé's desire that we resolve contentious issues so that we all spend less time debating the Code, and more time actually making it work. (Peter Brabeck-Letmathe, CEO, Nestlé, November 1999)[35]

A chronicle of events following the first meeting with WHO suggests that the infant food industry, in particular market leader Nestlé, has used WHO's dialogue initiative primarily to scale up its issues management activities.

Companies have represented the round-tables with WHO as an initiative to 'end' the long-standing controversy, marking the dawn of a new era in which industry will finally be allowed to contribute to infant health. The question as to why industry has not put its house in order in the two decades since the Code was adopted is represented as unnecessary, or even detrimental, to infant health. Now, the industry firmly claims its place at policy-making tables on matters related to infant and young child feeding.[36]

The assertion that industry has put its house in order has been widely disseminated through a high-powered PR campaign in which Nestlé presented its alleged adherence to the Code in a 180-page *Report to the Director General, World Health Organization* and a new *International (WHO) Code Action Report Magazine*. These were sent not only to the WHO director-general but also to other UN agencies, key policy-makers, members of parliament and journalists.

As UNICEF Executive Director Carol Bellamy pointed out, the *Report* was not in fact proof of Nestlé compliance to the Code and subsequent Resolutions, as Nestle claimed.[37] It was simply a collection of letters from 54 government authorities that had been asked by Nestlé for written confirmation of company compliance with the Code as translated into national legislation[38] (which in many countries does not exist or is weaker than the Code and Resolutions). Many of these countries do not have monitoring mechanisms in place that would allow them to check whether Nestlé or any other company had violated their national legislation or other measures taken to implement the Code. Moreover, nearly half the replies did not affirm that Nestlé complied with national legislation or any other measure – one of them merely acknowledged receipt of Nestlé's letter. The national authorities of at least three countries[39] raised serious concerns about the way their letters were being reproduced, creating the false impression that they were certificates of Code compliance.[40] UNICEF's executive director therefore stressed in a letter to the company:

> I would like to express our reservations to the claim that the *Report* fulfils the company's obligation under Article 11.3 of the Code. As I stated previously, the Code requires that both Governments and Manu-facturers establish distinct and separate monitoring systems. Obtaining certificates of Code compliance where monitoring is not taking place

would not seem to us an appropriate basis for such a claim. (Bellamy 1999b: 1)

Companies have now moved their divide-and-rule strategy into a higher gear. After years of attempting to discredit and isolate the citizen action groups that monitor them and keep the infant food issue on the public agenda, companies are now trying to discredit and delegitimize UNICEF and to divide it from WHO.

In May 1999, for example, at a press conference in the UK, Nestlé's CEO Peter Brabeck-Letmathe attacked UNICEF for its alleged unwillingness to engage in 'dialogues' with the company, but omitted to mention the context for UNICEF's 'unwillingness'.[41] UNICEF in fact has an extensive history of interactions with Nestlé and other infant food manufacturers. In the early 1990s, when UNICEF and WHO urged the companies to stop handing out free supplies to maternity wards and clinics, UNICEF and IFM met every two months to discuss the matter – and yet the industry did not stop providing free supplies.

The meeting Peter Brabeck-Letmathe cited as evidence of UNICEF's unwillingness to engage in dialogues had been arranged by UNICEF on 13 October 1997 to give Nestlé the opportunity to present its efforts at self-regulation and to clarify differences in Code interpretation. Since the Code was adopted, UNICEF has had many direct discussions with Nestlé to stress that the Code applies to all countries, not just developing ones. About two weeks after this October meeting, UNICEF Executive Director Carol Bellamy decided as a last resort to suspend further discussions with Nestlé until the company recognized the universal applicability of the Code. As she explained in a letter to Nestlé:

> We have come to the considered conclusion that there do not appear to be opportunities for cooperation that would be of mutual benefit to our organizations at this time. The outstanding and significant differences in our views on the content and application of the International Code represent a barrier to any such cooperation ... UNICEF remains convinced that the Code applies in all countries. (Bellamy 1997)[42]

Nestlé's new PR magazine subsequently informed its readers that 'WHO ... *alone* has responsibility for Code implementation within the UN system',[43] despite the fact that UNICEF is specifically mentioned in the Code (Article 11.1) as an agency on which governments can call with regard to Code implementation.

Corporate Engineering of Consent and Democratic Global Governance

As pointed out in Chapter 2, the Commission on Global Governance stressed more than fifteen years ago that global governance should be more democratic in the future. The 1999 UNDP *Human Development Report* reconfirmed the need for 'a more coherent and more democratic architecture for global governance in the 21st century' (UNDP 1999: 12). According to former UNDP administrator James Gustave Speth:

> Good governance is participatory, transparent and accountable ... It promotes the rule of law and equal justice under the law. Good governance ensures that political, social and economic priorities are based on broad consensus in society and that the voices of the poorest and most vulnerable are heard in decision making. (UNDP 1998: 1)

But the place of TNCs in the new architecture of global governance is still under-explored. Political and academic discourses are fraught with contradictions on the appropriate role of TNCs, especially in relation to governance understood as setting rules to ensure socially responsible TNC practices. Some documents mention the need for binding regulations on TNCs; others urge rule-setting in partnership with corporations simply because they 'create wealth'.[44]

The rise of TNCs as major economic and political players has been accompanied by the development of international issues management and other PR and lobby strategies. Corporate PR is not simply an exercise in whitewashing previous misdemeanours. Corporate public relations, in particular its strategic issues management/engineering of consent discipline, is now a major tool of power to strengthen and maintain corporations' hegemony in the global arena. Corporate intelligence, techniques to manipulate public debates in the interests of corporations, and neutralization of critical voices through divide-and-rule strategies are now an all-pervasive feature of debates that involve the interests of large corporations.

In the debate about the regulation of the infant food industry's marketing practices, one strategy has been to claim that stirring up controversy does not ensure infant health, but partnerships and co-operation with the infant food industry can do so in the future.

Those who continue to question industry's marketing strategies are derogatively labelled as confrontational. Civil society groups (in particular IBFAN) and UNICEF are the current target of such branding. At the same time, the industry has been using WHO's round-table initiative to enhance its image and to portray the debate as something that needs simply a few more clarifications about Code definitions – a portrayal that needs urgent public rectification from WHO to prevent industry from using its initiative to drive a wedge between WHO and UNICEF.

Regaining Transparency and Space for Democratic Debate

> It is dangerous to assume that the goals of the private sector are somehow synonymous with those of the United Nations, because most emphatically they are not. Business and industry are driven by the profit motive – as they should be and must be, both for their shareholders and their employees. The work of the United Nations, on the other hand, is driven by a set of ethical principles that sustain its mission – principles of the Charter of the United Nations, in the Universal Declaration of Human Rights, in the Convention on the Rights of the Child, and elsewhere in the galaxy of international instruments and treaties that have been promulgated since the UN's founding in 1945 … In coming together with the private sector, the UN must carefully, and constantly, appraise the relationship. (Carol Bellamy, executive director, UNICEF, 1999)[45]

When considering the legitimate role of infant food manufacturers in the regulation of their practices and their participation in policy-making on infant feeding, the existence of corporate PR and corporate lobbying must, as a priority, be taken into account. Their workings must be brought into the open. Without such transparency, there can be no informed democratic decision-making on the appropriate role of the industry.

One way of taking strategic corporate PR into account is to abolish the term 'partnership' for interactions between the public and the commercial sector. This would be an important measure to prevent corporations from using these 'partnerships' to enhance their power and influence, for example, by transferring the good image of religious and civil society organizations or UN agencies to themselves.

It is not interactions *per se* between the public and the commercial sector that are at issue. The infant food industry *does* have a role to play in the infant food arena – one of delivering high-quality, reasonably priced products in a way that does not conflict with the Code and subsequent Resolutions for the minority of infants who need them.

At issue is the need to prevent such interactions from being misused by corporations and their business associations for purposes that conflict with the general and specific mandates of public institutions. One way of doing so is to call these interactions by a specific name:

- sponsorship (for donations in cash and kind);
- negotiations or tender (for instance, for favourable terms for industrially manufactured products); and
- collaboration on a specific project (research collaboration, for example).

Each type of close interaction with industry should be accompanied by unambiguous guidelines and procedures on how such interactions must not interfere with public tasks such as standard setting, policy-making and advocacy for the inclusion of the voices and needs of the vulnerable and marginalized.

Clear criteria for assessing the conduct of corporate counterparts should be established and a UN centre to keep track of corporate practices in relation to public interests and policy-making should be re-established. All UN agencies, moreover, should have their own, publicly accessible, in-house data bank to keep track of the behaviour and actions of corporations with whom they interact closely.[46]

There is also an urgent need for a public debate on whether some of these so-called 'partnerships' between the public and corporate sector do not in fact violate a fundamental – and in practice most embattled – principle of modern democracy: that there should not be a 'one-dollar-one-vote' decision-making system.[47, 48]

Finally, the infant feeding case illustrates why it is important not to shy away from controversial debates simply because corporate PR has worked hard to discredit them. It is essential to bear in mind that controversy is part and parcel of the democratic process. Many UN agencies, governments and NGOs seem to be acceding to the industry portrayal of 'constructive dialogues' and 'partnerships' as being in opposition to 'counter-productive controversy'. If such a stance were to become more widely accepted as the appropriate way to conduct debates about international policy, it would pose a great threat to democracy. As community organizer Saul Alinsky said: 'Conflict is the essential core of a free and open society. If one were to project the democratic way of life in a musical score, its major theme would be the harmony of dissonance' (Alinsky 1971).

Efforts to end the unethical marketing practices of infant food manufacturers show that sometimes conflict has to be continued until there is real change.[49]

Notes

1. IPRA 1968. By January 2001, the International Public Relations Association had members in 72 countries (www.ipranet.org, accessed 15 January 2001).

2. Montgomery 1978. United Brand, formerly United Fruit, hired the services of PR counsellor Edward Bernays to help overthrow the Guatemalan government in the early 1950s. See Kunczik 1990: 196–202 and Schlesinger and Kinzer 1982.

3. Carey 1995 (original essay 1978).

4. Nestlé 1998: 10.

5. IFM briefing document entitled 'Public–private partnerships between health providers and companies including infant food companies are important to improved infant health around the world. Confrontation is counter to the interests of child health'. This website document contrasted the allegedly confrontational attitude of UNICEF with that of WHO and the International Pediatric Association, and concluded: 'Governments should create a favourable climate for constructive partnership, through ongoing dialogue and cooperation with the infant food industry, health professionals, and medical science' (www.ifm.net/briefdoc2.htm, accessed 12 July 1999).

6. For details on concrete concealment techniques used in the infant feeding debate, see Richter 1998: 8.

7. For the politics of corporate PR and lobby, see also Balanyá et al. 2000; Ewen 1996; Greer and Bruno 1996; Rowell 1996; Stauber and Rampton 1995; WHO 2000b.

8. The same guidelines have recently been quoted in the Nestlé International (WHO) *Code Action Report* as proof of Nestlé's long-standing and exemplary efforts to monitor itself. WHO and UNICEF criticisms are not mentioned. Instead, both agencies are cited as 'reviewers' of the 1982 guidelines, an inclusion that has the effect of legitimizing the guidelines. See Nestlé 1999c: 1.

9. NIFAC is still cited today by industry as an example of good PR practice. Novartis's international communications spokesperson Walter von Wartburg (1997) described it as a notable example of 'active agenda setting'. For companies on the defensive, it can be useful 'to refer controversial critical issues to third parties which enjoy public trust'. He contended that this could provide a 'legitimate gain of time' and 'defuse escalated situations'.

10. For a summary of an earlier five-point issues management strategy

whose main aim was to marginalize critics, see Gasche 1975. The strategy was elaborated during a three-day symposium on 'Multinationals in Confrontation: How Can Better Communication Help Meet the Crisis?' organized by the International Advertising Association at the same time as the UN started developing New International Order policies (and two months before the first court hearing against the Swiss Arbeitsgruppe Dritte Welt in relation to the 'Nestlé kills babies' publication). About 250 PR and advertising professionals and corporate top managers from 20 countries met to scrutinize the 'origins of assaults against multinational corporations' and 'to examine ways in which these assaults may be muted' (conference programme, quoted in Gasche 1975: 4).

11. Bernays' PR approach was based on opinion polls, policy analysis and thorough planning. He said that 'it is careful planning more than anything else that distinguishes modern public relations from old-time hit or miss publicity and propaganda' (Bernays 1952). According to communication scientist Kevin Robins and his colleagues, the rise of public relations and other information industries marked a profound shift of political culture: 'Faith in a rational public gives way to the invocation of expertise and to the scientific management of public opinion ... Political rule becomes a matter of social engineering, and the machinery of propaganda and information management becomes all pervasive' (Robins et al. 1987: 10).

12. The reactive version is known as 'crisis management'. For an overview and checklist based on *The Crisis Checklist* of the Public Relations Consultants Association, see Bland 1995. For a depiction of the Nestlé boycott, the Brent Spar oil rig and other public issues as a crisis for corporations, see pp. 90–92 of the chapter 'Crisis and catastrophe communication' in Morley 1998: 79–104.

13. Ten years later, the PR agency sold its services with the words: 'Often corporations face long-term issues, challenges which arise from activist concerns (e.g. South Africa, infant formula) or controversies regarding product hazards ... Burson-Marsteller issue specialists have years of experience helping clients manage such issues. They have gained insight into the key activist groups (religious, consumer, ethnic, environmental) and the tactics and strategies of those who tend to generate and sustain issues. Our counsellors around the world have helped clients counteract [them]' (B-M Brochure 'Public Affairs', circulated in 1991, quoted in Nelson 1993: 57). In 1996 Burson-Marsteller, which started out in 1953 with four staff, had a turnover of US$233 million.

14. The following framework owes much to Claus Mueller's (1973) model of 'constrained communication'; for a model of propaganda analysis, see Jowett and O'Donnell 1986.

15. For example, Nestlé hired a private investigation bureau in Zurich to gather information on the 13 members of the Arbeitsgruppe Dritte Welt and tried to use the material to discredit the members during the 1975 libel trial. See Chapter 2 and Chetley 1986: 46.

16. For an analysis of several high-profile cases of SLAPPs in the USA,

Canada and the UK and questions about their effects upon freedom of speech in modern society, see Donson 2000.

17. Pharmacologist Milton Silverman's life was threatened in the mid-1970s in Mexico during his research for his book *The Drugging of the Americas* (Silverman 1976). This book was one of the first to expose pharmaceutical companies for dumping harmful pharmaceuticals and for their double standards on drug information. Syed Aamar Raza, a former Nestlé Pakistan employee, has alleged that threats were made to kidnap members of his family and that he received death threats when he turned whistleblower in 1997. Raza publicized internal company documents implicating senior management in the boosting of infant food sales by methods that violated the Code. His younger brother alleged that he was fired at at the family home in Pakistan, two days before Aamar Raza was to make a presentation at the British House of Commons at the end of February 2000. Other reported victims of corporate silencing include the Brazilian rubber-tapper leader Chico Mendes, who was murdered in 1989, and indirectly the Ogoni activist Ken Saro-Wiwa, who campaigned against the depredation of Ogoni lands in Nigeria by the Shell oil company, and countless labour activists. See Baby Milk Action 2000b; Bruno 2000: 58; Ghauri 2000; Meintjes 2000: 85, 97; Pallister 2000; TheNetwork 1999: 8–9 Yamey 2000a.

18. For example, the infant food industry has worked hard to create a caring image by financing posters and information leaflets depicting loving mothers breast-feeding their contented, suckling babies – an image that is positive for both political and market purposes. (If companies were not allowed to put their logo on these materials, however, it is doubtful whether they would still be interested in paying for them.)

19. This chapter focuses on corporate PR as a political instrument. The use of PR activities as so-called 'adjunct-marketing' practice is another field of study. Corporations may use many of the current dialogues and partnerships for both political and marketing purposes. UN agencies and other public institutions should be cautious about conflicts of interests in relation to preferential contract awarding of their corporate 'partners'.

20. A UK report of the Prince of Wales Business Leaders Forum on *Business as Partners in Development* uses similar language. It lists enhanced 'reputation and license to operate' and the accumulation of 'ethical capital' as major 'benefits' of public–private partnerships for business. The report predicts: 'The concept of ethical capital, which is closely linked to reputation, is likely to gather credence as a mainstream assessment of a company's worth. In the same way that financial or intellectual "capital" gives a company strength in the marketplace, ethical capital accrued over a long period of time can ensure that a company will avoid costs from overregulation and insurance against legal challenges. The difference between a company with ethical capital and one with ethical deficit – perceived or real – can even determine their "licence to operate" in some emerging markets' (Nelson 1996: 52).

21. UNRISD commented in its report on *The Social Effects of Globalization*: 'One way in which corporations try to fend off official control is by practicing

– or at least vowing to practice – self-regulation through establishing codes of conduct. A more solid basis for ensuring corporate responsibility is some form of international regulation. At present the prospects for this seem slim ... GATT [the General Agreement on Tariffs and Trade] has offered enterprises much greater freedom and has established rules that may penalize governments that try to exert greater control over them. The new World Trade Organization protects the freedom of international trade; it does not protect other freedoms, and so risks exacerbating a fundamental imbalance in global society. International businesses cannot be expected to author their own regulation: this is the job of good governance' (UNRISD 1995: 19).

22. Sethi is also the author of a book on corporate advocacy advertising (Sethi 1987).

23. Nestlé, for example, stated in relation to its failure to meet its public commitment to end free supplies by 1992: 'In 1991, Nestlé and other members of the Association of Infant Food Manufacturers (IFM) agreed with WHO and UNICEF on a co-operative effort. The objective was to secure country-by-country agreements with governments to end free and low-cost supplies to maternity units in developing countries by the end of 1992. Although not yet 100% successful, the results are remarkable. As of February 1994, free supplies from Nestlé were given only in five small developing countries where the government has yet to agree on a change' (Nestlé 1994).

24. For red-baiting of Health Action International by the pharmaceutical industry, see Chetley 1990: 72.

25. The basis for the article was a 'study on the infant formula industry' that Nickel had conducted for the Washington-based Ethics and Public Policy Center – which had received $25,000 from Nestlé. The Center's director, Ernest Lefever, initially denied receiving funds from Nestlé and later stated that he had not received the money specifically for this study. He pointed out that he had also sought and received funds from Bristol-Myers, another infant food company (Sethi 1994: 105, 106). Whatever the truth, it is certain that the Center was encouraged by Nestlé to send reprints of the *Fortune* article (retitled 'Crusade against the corporations') to community leaders using a Nestlé-supplied mailing list.

26. Those who attempt to address industry malpractice in general are often charged of being 'anti-industry' and biased, and of not presenting both sides. Such allegations can be countered with the introductory words of Australian criminologist John Braithwaite to his book *Corporate Crime in the Pharmaceutical Industry*: 'Some ... will think that [this book] is a one-sided account which focuses attention on pharmaceutical industry abuses to the exclusion of all the worthwhile things the industry had achieved for mankind ... Unfortunately, it is the job of criminologists to explore the seamy side of human existence. If a criminologist undertakes a study of mugging and murder, no one expects a "balanced" account which gives due credit to the fact that many muggers are good family men, loving fathers who provide their children with a Christian upbringing, or perhaps generous people who have shown a willingness to help neighbours in trouble. Yet criminologists are expected to

provide such "balance" when they study corporate criminals' (Braithwaite 1984: vii–viii). This statement clarifies the aims of his case study: (1) 'to describe the wide variety of types of corporate crime which occur in one industry', (2) 'to use the pharmaceutical industry's experience to tentatively explore the effectiveness of different types of mechanisms of the control of corporate crime'. Many of the pharmaceutical companies' practices studied by Braithwaite were not illegal according to existing legislation but were potentially fatal, such as the promotion in countries with weaker drug regulatory systems of medicinal drugs that had been withdrawn in a company's home country for safety reasons.

27. ICC, *Business World* April/June 1984, for example, wrote in an article 'Maucher on management': 'Often, said [Nestlé CEO] Maucher, there are in a particular group a handful of fanatics and a majority of reasonable people. So a company's strategy should be to convince those who are reasonable and isolate those who are not.' For the divide-and-rule strategy elaborated by the PR agency Mongoven, Biscoe and Duchin (whose managers used to work with Pagan Jr.'s post-Nestlé consultancy firm Pagan International), see Stauber and Rampton 1995: 66–7.

28. For more details, see Allain 1991: 26–7, 36; Chetley 1986: 81, 148–9.

29. In the same article, he questioned the legitimacy of 'pressure groups' involved in international decision-making (Williams 1998). For the general industry strategy of questioning the legitimacy of pressure groups, see Chapter 9.

30. For more information on European business-lobby round-tables, see Balanyá et al. 2000; CEO 1998.

31. Brundtland 1998a: 7.

32. VNFKD 1998.

33. Interview with Nancy-Jo Peck, scientific adviser to IBFAN/GIFA, June 2000.

34. Brabeck-Letmathe 1999b.

35. Brabeck-Letmathe 1999a. A similar statement was also published in Nestlé 2000: 4.

36. *Guardian* journalist Robert Cowe reported: 'Mr Brabeck said it was time to end the 22-year battle over baby milk. Only technicalities now separated Nestlé from pressure groups and official organisations such as the World Health Organisation' (Cowe 1999).

37. Nestlé CEO Peter Brabeck-Letmathe said in November 1999, 'I gave to the WHO Director General a report about our compliance with the WHO Code. In the report, 54 governments or appointed monitoring bodies provided written, official evidence that Nestlé's policies and practices conform with the WHO Code' (Brabeck-Letmathe 1999a: 4). But another Nestlé communication spells out clearly what the company regards as compliance: 'the criterion used for self-monitoring in the current report is the International Code, as applied and defined by each country. In other words, the criterion is what the government endorses and accepts as the interpretation of the Code in that country' (Nestlé 1999b: 2).

38. For a description of the process, see e.g. the Executive Summary in Nestlé 1999b.

39. The minister of health of the Palestinian National Authority; the head of child health, Ministry of Health, Oman; and the Danish authorities.

40. For further analyses of the Nestlé report, see Baby Milk Action 1999c and IBFAN/GIFA 2000.

41. 'We wanted to start a dialogue. We went to New York for a Meeting. After an hour and a half, Madame Bellamy said she had to make a phone call, and did not return. Six weeks later we got a letter, saying she did not wish to continue the dialogue' (quoted in Koenig 1999).

42. Two months later, Nestlé approached UN Secretary-General Kofi Annan to make a statement on the applicability of the Code. Annan supported Bellamy's view that the Code was universally applicable.

43. Peter Brabeck-Letmathe in an interview with Nestlé's corporate communications professionals (Nestlé 1999d; emphasis added).

44. The accumulation of wealth legitimizes nothing. This activity has no intrinsic ethical value. Questions on the legitimacy of profit-making include: how is this wealth accumulated and how is it distributed?

45. Bellamy 1999a.

46. For concrete comments on the 1999 WHO draft 'Guidelines on interactions with the commercial sector', see IBFAN 1999a.

47. For a discussion on the interrelation between regulation and 'democratic politics, competent administration, and reliable courts', see e.g. Kuttner 1999: 328–62. For more general discussions about possible forms of democracy in a globalizing world, see books on cosmopolitan democracy, such as Archibugi et al. 1998, and the proposals made in Foster and Anand 1999: 499–522.

48. For further literature on public–private partnerships, see Buse and Walt 2000a, 2000b; HAI 2001; SID/WHO/ISS 2000; TRAC 1999; Utting 2000. For concerns about such partnerships within the infant food debate, see Ferriman 2000 and Yamey 2000c, and the rejoinders Bellamy 2000; Krasovec 2000; Nabarro 2000; Naylor 2000; Richter 2000; Rundall and Peck 2000.

49. Denise Lach, who has analysed the role of conflict in the US environmental debate, points out: 'Contrary to the common view that conflict is always a negative force that must be managed to resolution, conflict can be a driving force for social change … Fundamentally, conflict forces us all to clarify and adapt our perspectives in response to changing human interests and environmental conditions' (Lach 1996: 212).

. . . .

CHAPTER 9

Civil Society and the Code

> The collective power of people to shape the future is greater than ever before, and the need to exercise it more compelling. Mobilizing that power to make life in the twenty-first century more democratic, more secure and more sustainable is the foremost challenge of this generation.

> Overall ... civil society organizations and the NGO sector in general are vital and flourishing contributors to the possibilities of effective governance. They must occupy a more central space in the structures of governance than has been the case. (Commission of Global Governance 1995)[1]

§ As shown in Chapters 1 and 2, the regulation of transnational corporations is now often regarded as a task of global governance. Subsequent chapters have analysed the regulation of transnational corporations as a crucial task of global, democratic decision-making and have conceptualized the regulation of corporate practices as contested processes taking place between various actors with differing interests and differing power resources.

This framework provides a clearer picture of the specific roles the various actors have taken over the past two decades and facilitates identification of ways in which checks and balances on the marketing practices of the infant food industry could be made more effective.

While previous chapters explored the role of the infant food industry in the Code debate, this chapter focuses on the role that civil society organizations, in particular the International Baby Food Action Network (IBFAN), have played in shaping the infant food debate for over twenty years.

A brief reflection on civil society discourse is followed by a description of this international network. The chapter attempts to assess the impact of its campaign strategies, reflects on the relationship between corporate watchdog groups and the state, and concludes by asking broader questions about changes in the structure of global decision-making to ensure more effective regulation of transnational corporations.

What are Civil Society Organizations?

Much of the literature on globalization and global governance stresses the rise and contribution of transnational civil society organizations (including NGOs) as a positive development. The 1999 *UNDP Human Development Report: Globalization with a Human Face*, for example, notes:

> One big development in opening opportunities for people to participate in global governance has been the growing strength and influence of NGOs – in both the North and the South. NGOs have been effective advocates for human development, maintaining pressure on national governments, international agencies and corporations to live up to commitments and to protect human rights and standards. Their campaigns have reversed policy – as with their opposition to the Multilateral Agreement on Investment. When developing country governments have found it difficult to stay unified in negotiations, the NGOs have often come forward with alternative approaches. (UNDP 1999: 35–6)[2]

But the assumption that civil society organizations are automatically contributing to a more democratic, socially just and environmentally sustainable world should not be taken for granted. The term 'civil society' in fact has a multitude of meanings.

The concept of civil society dates back to eighteenth-century Scottish Enlightenment thinkers. Other strands of definition derive from later interpretations made by Hegel, Marx, Weber and Gramsci. Many of these definitions do not distinguish between citizen coalitions and business organizations. Moreover, civil society could also be applied to the Ku Klux Klan, the Mafia and religious fundamentalist groups.[3] In addition, over the past decade or so, corporations have been creating PR 'front' organizations and pseudo-grassroots or 'astroturf' groups and networks that outsiders can find difficult to distinguish from genuine activist citizen groups.[4] Corporations have also co-opted societal groups via corporate sponsorships.

Some commentators have stated that the term civil society is analytically so confusing that it is ultimately redundant (Kumar 1994: 130). Social scientist Adam Seligman clarifies its current uses. He distinguishes three ways in which the term 'civil society' is usually employed. The first is the concrete political use of civil society as a political slogan to advance the cause of movements or parties. It is also found in the writings of some Western thinkers who use it to critique certain government policies and as a slogan in the media and policy documents describing the transitions taking place in the Central and Eastern European states.

The second usage is as an analytic social science concept, where it has two broad uses: one is to describe a certain type of institutional or organizational level in political sociology. Here, Seligman questions whether the revival of the concept civil society has anything to add to existing ideas about democracy and citizenship.[5] The other social science use concerns the identification of civil society with analysis of social actors in terms of values, beliefs or symbolic action. For example, much civil society literature stresses the notion of trust as a basis for common action (definitions derived from Gramsci emphasize the notion of reaching hegemony through consensus).

The third usage, which is often confused with the second, refers to civil society as a normative concept, a vision of a desirable social order that would solve the tensions between purely self-interested individualism and a sense of shared communality between particular and universal interests. Seligman questions whether the concept of civil society, either as analytic term or as normative ideal, brings us further in exploring and resolving the contradictions of modern existence (Seligman 1992: 201–6).[6]

There have also been lively and controversial debates in recent years within progressive social movements as to the usefulness of the term civil society. Some groups and writers reject the categorization on the grounds that it has no positive connotation for many non-Western cultures. They stress that Scottish Enlightenment philosophers in the eighteenth century created the term civil society to denote a society that had risen out of a 'barbaric' and 'savage' society – barbaric referring simply to the fact that these societies did not have the concept of private property. They fear that the term might therefore be used to negatively label any society that does not have a concept of private property. The same critics often argue that the civil society discourse was reintroduced as an integral part of neoliberal economic policies and governance discourse by the World Bank and a number of governments. The problem, they argue, is that in this usage citizen groups are not truly welcomed as emancipatory forces but are primarily instrumentalized to fill the vacuums left once the state has been sized down, welfare cut and public services privatized (Samuel 1999).[7] Others argue that the term can be useful for citizen groups, but only if it is defined in a way that explicitly indicates that civil society is 'a means to achieve a better world' (Knight and Hartnell 2000).

In this book, the terms civil society organizations (CSOs) and non-governmental organization (NGO) are used interchangeably as broad terms for citizen organizations. I regard civil society as a term that is theoretically and politically contested and whose analytical meaning is being profoundly challenged as people's alliances transcend national borders.[8]

Because of these difficulties, it seems best to define what one means by the terms civil society and civil society organization as far as possible. I have argued in Chapter 2 that business organizations should be excluded from the term civil society organization. But I would also argue that civil society organizations should not automatically be assumed to be citizen alliances working for the benefit of society as a whole.

It seems more fruitful not to overuse the term civil society organization, but instead to disaggregate it and show the heterogeneity of the groups, organizations and movements that comprise civil society. This should be accompanied by continued critical reflection about the particular group, organization or network's aims and values and the means employed in pursuance of their causes.

This approach does not apply to NGOs and CSOs only. The search for criteria to evaluate the legitimacy and value of actions applies to any societal institution in a particular governance arena, be it a government authority, UN agency, corporation or business organization.

IBFAN: A Transnational Citizen Action Network

Never doubt that a small group of committed citizens can change the world. In fact, it is the only thing that ever has. (Margaret Mead, anthropologist)

In 1979, when the International Baby Food Action Network (IBFAN) was set up, there was no intention of building an organisation, of having a constitution, any head office or a directorship. The people who created the network wanted a new kind of international citizens' coalition, one where each group and each person could do what they were good at and receive help and encouragement from others who share the same principles. In a network, nobody can force anybody to do things but all need to be committed to do the best they can, and together, they grow stronger. (Annelies Allain, co-founder of IBFAN)[9]

History, Aim and Structure

Over the years, a number of networks, groups and church-based organizations have been involved in the Code debate. The longest-standing and most important international network in this area is the International Baby Food Action Network (IBFAN). It is one of the oldest 'single-issue networks' that aims to pressure transnational corporations to change what network members regard as socially detrimental practices.

Networks are a particular organizational form. 'A network can provide enhanced support for a local initiative and a global issue at the same time. It is a flexible method with which to capture a diversity of perspectives and integrate them towards a common goal' (Krut 1997: 48). According to Sylvia Borren, director of projects at the Dutch funding organization Novib, 'networking has often been hailed as the modern way of organizing. The women's movement started early at networking. Open and informal structures, flexible and quick ways of planning and reacting, wide communication networks – many advantages can be recognized. Other movements followed – and today, in a world of increasing globalization, networking has become commonplace' (Borren 1998: 7).

The IBFAN network was founded by six organizations – the Arbeitsgruppe Dritte Welt, Interfaith Centre on Corporate Responsibility (ICCR), Infant Formula Action Coalition (INFACT), International Organization of Consumers Unions (IOCU), Oxfam and War on Want – at the end of the 1979 Joint WHO/UNICEF Meeting on Infant and Young Child Feeding (see Chapter 3). Some 20 years later, it has grown to over 150 groups, organizations and individuals operating in more than ninety countries. Its aim today is 'to improve the health and well-being of mothers and their children through the protection, promotion and support of breastfeeding and optimal complementary feeding practices, by pressing for full and universal implementation of the International Code and subsequent resolutions' (IBFAN 1999b: 2).

Soon after its founding, IBFAN perceived the need for a more formal structure. In 1981, immediately following the World Health Assembly that adopted the International Code, 90 IBFAN activist from 38 countries gathered in Geneva to discuss the future of the network. Ensuring democratic and decentralized, yet efficient, decision-making and information sharing was an enormous challenge.[10]

The structure that was proposed has remained essentially the same ever since. Today, five IBFAN regional offices – Africa, Asia and the Pacific, Europe, Latin America and the Caribbean, and North America – constitute nodes of information coordination in what has been called a fishing-net structure of essentially autonomous and independent organizations.[11] In addition, an IBFAN Coordinating Council (IBCoCo) meets every two years or so to discuss the general policy framework for the network as a whole, while a Convenor's Support Group from within the Coordinating Council deals with urgent issues. There are also several specific working groups and an International Boycott Committee.

To become an IBFAN member, individuals or groups have to work actively for the implementation of the International Code and sub-sequent WHA Resolutions; to communicate with the network; to agree not to accept funding from the infant food and related industries; and to pledge adherence to a set of agreed principles. Today, IBFAN has seven principles expressed in the language of rights:

1. The right of infants everywhere to have the highest level of health.
2. The right of families, and in particular women and children, to have enough nutritious food.
3. The right of women to breastfeed and to make informed choices about infant feeding.
4. The right of women to full support for successful breastfeeding and for sound infant feeding practices.
5. The right of all people to health services which meet basic needs.
6. The right of health workers and consumers to health care systems which are free of commercial pressures.
7. The right of people to organise in international solidarity in order to secure changes which protect and promote basic health.[12]

Changes Over Time

There have been a number of important changes over the past 20 years in the IBFAN network, particularly in the groups comprising the network and its gender composition. Co-founder Annelies Allain notes:

> None of the six groups which collectively started IBFAN were health groups. They worked on development and trade issues, consumer rights and ethical investment concerns. They knew little about babies, nutrition, infection and the like. But they knew about marketing, hunger, poverty and inequality. When they met up with doctors and nurses who could explain the effect of bottle feeding, the causes were quickly lined up. (Allain 1998: 33)[13]

By the 1981 IBFAN meeting, the network had begun to expand and to change. Participants included breast-feeding promotion groups from Sweden, Norway, Kenya and Trinidad (see Chetley 1986: 183). African groups found it important from the outset to link the regulation of the marketing of breast-milk substitutes to support for women in breast-feeding. Today, there are 38 IBFAN groups throughout Africa with this dual focus. Many of them now are deeply concerned about the way the infant food industry is using the HIV/infant feeding dilemma to push its products (see Chapter 6) (BFHI News 1999b: 3).

The link between support for breast-feeding and promotion of the International Code was strengthened further by the adoption of the *Innocenti Declaration* in 1990 and the launch of the Baby-Friendly Hospital Initiative in 1991. Many people who received training as part of these policy initiatives subsequently joined IBFAN or the World Alliance for Breastfeeding Action (WABA) (see Chapter 5).

In the early 1990s, the IBFAN network expanded in Central and Eastern European countries and the former Soviet Union. The profound changes taking place in the economic and political structures of these countries meant that corporate watchdog and other civil action groups were set up at the same time as transnational corporations entered these new markets. A race ensued between them. On the one hand, companies used marketing methods that had been restricted in the rest of the world and lobbied governments for weak marketing regulation. IBFAN, on the other, informed health professionals, government officials and citizens from newly founded consumer and other social action groups about the risks of inappropriate marketing and provided training in Code implementation and monitoring. A decade later, the race is not yet over. Of particular concern was the discovery that infant food manufacturers have used financial crises in the region and wars in Bosnia, Kosovo and Chechnya to promote baby foods under the guise of humanitarian aid and to build a good image of companies donating in their own back yards (IBFAN 1996; BFHI News 1999a: 1, 6).[14]

Many more health professionals from the former communist-ruled states have joined IBFAN than from Western European countries. IBFAN Europe's scientific adviser, Nancy-Jo Peck, believed that this difference in behaviour could be explained by the entrenched financial ties between Western European paediatric and midwifery associations and infant food manufacturers; such ties mean that these health professionals find it difficult to contemplate fulfilling IBFAN's membership criteria of not accepting funds from the infant food industry.[15]

In the early 1980s, when the focus of the network was on campaigning for an international code for infant food TNCs, the ratio between men and women in IBFAN was about 40 to 60. Today, the majority of this corporate watchdog and awareness-raising network are women, possibly because the increased politicization of breast-feeding support groups has led to more women joining in the campaign against harmful marketing practices (personal communication, Annelies Allain, director, International Code Documentation Centre, IBFAN Penang, December 2000). An additional explanation might be that the pay of the employees in some of the coordination offices is relatively low.[16] Whatever the reasons, this composition belies a commonly held view that women are less politically aware or active than men. Women also play an important part in other international single-issue networks such as Health Action International and the Pesticide Action Network.

It may well be, however, that some men who were IBFAN members moved on to other issues as the infant food debate shifted from being one of Third World solidarity towards a woman's right to breast-feed. In the words of Annelies Allain, 'it is easier to campaign over dead babies than over women's rights' (personal communication, December 2000). Yet it would be wrong to understand the issue simply as a 'women's issue' (although all 'women's issues' are ultimately highly political issues). British international relations scholar Peter Willets points out that, at a time when his discipline focused on the East/ West Cold War issue and made a distinction between 'the "high politics" of security, diplomacy and national prestige' and the 'low politics' of economic and social issues,

> No doubt some might regard the baby food issue as unimportant. It would be difficult to find an issue more removed from the nuclear arms race and East/West relations than how babies are fed. It concerns women and children and is not of significance to 'real' men. Yet, in terms of danger to human life, which is one of the standards used to assess the importance of East/West relations, baby foods are also important. Misuse of dried milk has almost certainly resulted in a similar number of deaths to those killed in all the wars since 1945.
>
> Economic and social issues do not belong to some secondary realm of 'low politics'. Baby feeding matters a great deal, it has been a high priority issue for many people and has involved top-level government officials and politicians. There has also been progress derived from the technical and moral strengths of the arguments put by ordinary people working against entrenched economic and political interests. (in Chetley 1986: viii–ix)

IBFAN's Activities

For many ordinary people today, the infant food issue and the Nestlé boycott are closely connected. Yet IBFAN has always run on 'two tracks': direct company campaigns and the promotion of regulation of the industry via the International Code. Both these tracks are regarded as complementary means of protecting babies and infants from the harms of inappropriate marketing of breast-milk substitutes (Allain 1998: 34).

The work of IBFAN groups at national, regional and international levels has encompassed a wide variety of activities. Network members have, for example,

- coordinated company boycotts;
- raised the issue at shareholder meetings;
- organized letter campaigns to support governments in the face of industry resistance to Code implementation;
- raised and maintained public awareness on the need for regulation of marketing of breast-milk substitutes;
- produced public educational material ranging from material for the general public to material for health professionals and the infant food industry;

- researched and published regular Code monitoring reports;
- advocated full Code implementation with governments and regional bodies, such as the EU;
- trained government officials from nearly one hundred countries in Code implementation;
- participated in debates at the World Health Assembly and other relevant meetings (such as those of the FAO's Codex Alimentarius Commission, which has become more significant since the World Trade Organization recognized it as the 'provider of science-based food standards');[17]
- advocated the implementation of UN Conventions, including the Convention on the Rights of the Child; the Convention on the Elimination of All Forms of Discrimination Against Women; and the Conventions of the International Labour Organization, as they relate to the rights of women to breast-feed their child and to have access to accurate information on infant feeding;
- trained health workers for the Baby-Friendly Hospital Initiative (BFHI); and
- networked and cooperated with other civil society organizations, such as Consumers International, the World Alliance for Breast-feeding Action and numerous breast-feeding support groups, as well as with health professionals, government authorities and inter-governmental agencies, in particular UNICEF and WHO.

The Impact of IBFAN

Agenda-setting

For dispersed structures such as transnational citizen action networks to evaluate their impact and usefulness, agenda-setting can be used as one criterion because it is often considered an important function of civil society organizations (Krut 1997: 25).

Indeed, IBFAN and its predecessor groups played an essential part in bringing both the Code and the issue of appropriate infant feeding on to the public agenda and keeping them there. As the late executive director of UNICEF, James Grant, said in the mid-1980s:

it was the voluntary organisations that did the pioneering work ... [to make breast-feeding] an acceptable topic for governmental action. WHO and UNICEF, I regret to say, would never have gotten into this, but for the fact that the field was made an acceptable one for discussion. (quoted in Allain 1986: 8)

Both UNICEF and WHO have commended IBFAN and other NGOs for their role in Code monitoring (Türmen 1998a: 1, 3; UNICEF 1997b).[18] WHO Director-General Gro Harlem Brundtland said at a round-table discussion in 1999 with consumer and community-based NGOs: 'I am quite convinced that, were it not for groups like yours, the International Code of Marketing of Breast-milk Substitutes would:

- never have been developed in the first place;
- if developed, it would probably never have been as strong as it is; or
- applied as widely, and as well, in so many countries' (Brundtland 1998b).

In 1998, IBFAN received the Right Livelihood Award, the 'alternative Nobel Prize', for 'its committed and effective campaigning over nearly 20 years for the rights of mothers to choose to breastfeed their babies, in the full knowledge of the benefits of breastmilk, and free from commercial pressures and misinformation with which companies promote breastmilk substitutes' (Right Livelihood Award 1998).

Influencing Corporate Practice

IBFAN continues to regard company campaigns such as the Nestlé boycott and pressure for effective regulation of the marketing of breast-milk substitutes via the Code as important parts of an interlinked and integrated strategy (Allain 1998: 34). This reflects the experiences of citizen groups that want to change corporate practice, not simply corporate rhetoric.

When the infant food issue was first raised internationally, business leaders themselves put boycotts at the top of their list of 'most effective techniques of the consumer movements to use' (Sentry Insurance Co. 1977). When the late UNICEF director James Grant was asked why infant food companies seemed to be willing to change their policies and practices of distributing free supplies of infant formula, he answered categorically: 'Because of the Boycott' (quoted in CIIR 1993: 30) (see Box 9.1).

Almost all public relations textbooks mention the Nestlé boycott as a prime example from which companies can learn. It was described in 1985 by a PR newsletter as 'the largest consumer boycott ever –

involving more than 700 churches and activist groups worldwide'. Marketing lecturer Craig Smith noted in his assessment of the effectiveness of various types of consumer pressure for corporate accountability:

> The success of the [Nestlé] boycott has been attributed to its economic impact but, more importantly, its damage to the corporate image, its impact on management morale, and the cost of giving management attention to it. Its success was such that it has been proposed as a model or example for other similar campaigns. (Smith 1990: 250)

As pointed out in Chapter 5, relatively few countries have implemented the Code in its entirety, and many lack company-independent monitoring procedures or sanctions that would have any real effect on most transnational corporations. Competitive pressures on baby food manufacturers have not decreased over the past 20 years of economic globalization. Yet corporate marketing practices have improved since the mid-1970s, when the infant feeding issue was brought on to the public agenda. It can be argued that the boycott, together with public monitoring and public disclosure of corporate failure to conform to the Code, has been one of the most effective mechanisms of making corporations change their marketing practices.

Regulatory debates can also be seen as a contest over favourable public opinion. Corporations are sensitive to 'negative publicity' – to naming and shaming – which they can now expect if their violations of internationally agreed norms are made public. Since citizen groups started putting the public spotlight on the infant food industry, the communication arena itself has changed. Two seasoned PR professionals stressed after the 1999 UK Advertising Standards Authority (ASA) ruling against Nestlé:

> The problem that all these companies are facing is that information about their activities is becoming ever more available. If you go back ten to 20 years it was hard to see what the companies were doing. Now the media has made them much more transparent. (quoted in Wilkinson 1999b: 28)[19]

Corporations know that negative publicity may translate into a negative reputation, such as being perpetrators of 'commerciogenic malnutrition' or of being 'baby killers', which may have a host of financial and political consequences, one of the most immediate being increased calls for tighter external regulation.

Box 9.1 Boycotts as a Democratic, Participatory Means to Campaign for Social Justice

Boycotts are a particular means of putting pressure on a company. For political scientist Michele Micheletti, they are an important aspect of 'political consumerism' – a type of political participation where consumers choose their products on the basis of non-economic, political attitudes and values (Micheletti 2000: 3)[20]

Campaigning for changes in the marketing practices of transnational corporations requires considerable amounts of knowledge, skill and time that would overburden many ordinary citizens. Boycotts are an ideal means for them to press for social justice in the marketplace. All they have to do is refrain from buying specific products. Boycotts are educational and participatory. They bring the issue of unethical corporate practices right into the homes of many ordinary citizens. They provide information about the complexity of the structure and operations of transnational corporations, and provide people with an immediate means of expressing their dissatisfaction.

If globalization has involved the spread of neoliberal *laisser-faire* market thinking and Western consumer culture, it has also been accompanied by an expansion of resistance to this culture, expressed by the consumer action and ethical investment movements. Corporations have to be wary of a direct loss of income as a result of boycotts and the indirect impacts of such boycotts on shareholders, corporate stockmarket value, corporate image, and employee loyalty and morale. Marketing lecturer Craig Smith has called for a distinction between a boycott's effectiveness and its success:

> Effectiveness refers to the boycott actually working, and in many boycotts this means economic impact. Success, however, refers to the boycott achieving its objectives ... success is usually conceived as involving acquiescence to a set of demands (Smith 1990: 276)

Social action groups, church and other organizations have been boycotting a number of infant food corporations since they brought the issue of the 'bottle-baby disease' to public attention. Nestlé, for example, has been the target of a consumer boycott since 1977 (except for four years between 1984 and 1988 when action groups believed the company promise that it would stop handing out free supplies).

There are now boycott groups in 20 countries. The International Nestlé Boycott Coordinating Committee (INBC) states that an end to the boycott depends on Nestlé's practices: '[INBC] has a standing agreement to meet with Nestlé collectively to discuss ending the boycott, when the company has anything meaningful to put forward to demonstrate a change in its policy and practice. This has yet to happen' (IBFAN 1999d: 7).[21]

Codes as Means of Raising Public Awareness and Debates

When the usefulness of public 'command-and-control' regulation is compared to that of corporate self-regulation by means of company codes, the accomplishments of external regulation are often assessed by counting the number of countries adopting the particular regulation.[22] As already argued in Chapter 5, this yardstick does not provide a complete picture. The usefulness of an international regulatory code should be assessed not only in terms of the number of countries that have implemented it. Codes also have important functions in terms of being tools to raise and maintain public awareness about particular issues, to help build public pressure on corporations to change those practices that are detrimental to society, and to raise a general debate about standards for corporate conduct.

When the International Code of Marketing of Breast-milk Substitutes was being drawn up, the infant food industry advocated either the use of its own voluntary industry code or the elaboration of broad international principles and more specific codes to be worked out between industry and governments of the various countries (see Chapters 3 and 4). Those drawing up the Code resisted such proposals.

Since the drive towards international regulatory codes went into reverse in the 1980s and early 1990s, governments, UN agencies and many civil society organizations have been moving towards industry self-regulation and so-called co-regulation as a more 'pragmatic' approach at both national and international levels. But keeping the focus of public policy-making and public awareness on the formulation and implementation of a universal code formulated within the public domain has a number of advantages. If policy-makers had yielded to the proposals of the infant food industry – either to let the industry regulate itself or to work out voluntary agreements with national governments – and had not adopted the International Code, the debate would have become fractured and privatized to such an extent that effective international citizen action on transnational practices would have been much more difficult. Without the weight of the World Health Assembly behind the marketing Code, IBFAN and others would have found it harder to campaign for national Code implementation and national authorities could not have called for the support of UN agencies.

The same could be said about current trends within, and pressure on, citizen groups to move towards co-regulatory arrangements with transnational corporations instead of pressing their governments to work on international regulatory codes under the auspices of UN agencies. A 1996 study on the campaigns conducted by European NGOs on transnational corporations, published by the London-based Catholic Institute for International Relations (CIIR), cautioned:

> The system of voluntary codes of conduct needs to be questioned from a long term perspective, since it gives in to the TNCs' strategy that aims to keep control of TNCs out of public/governmental hands. It also presents practical problems: how would thousands of corporate codes of conduct with independent monitoring bodies be followed up? (Vander Stichele and Pennartz 1996: 47)

A proliferation of codes of corporate conduct would certainly increase difficulties not only of monitoring but also of using them as tools to raise public awareness about the practices of corporations operating transnationally. Just the one International Code helped to focus the infant food debate on appropriate universal standards for the marketing of breast-milk substitutes and thus helped to focus policy action, and public vigilance and pressure.

As a recent UNRISD paper, *Business Responsibility for Sustainable Development*, stated:

> Perhaps the most significant concern with some forms of voluntary initiatives and partnerships is that they may serve to weaken key drivers of corporate responsibility, namely governmental and intergovernmental regulations, the role of trade unions and collective bargaining, as well as more critical forms of NGO activism and civil society protest. If one examines the history of corporate environmental and social

responsibility, and some of the major reforms of corporate policies and practices – from the early 1900s when Ford and others in the United States introduced improved working conditions, to the post-World War II years, when social welfare legislation was scaled up in Europe, to the early 1980s when the International Code of Marketing of Breast-milk Substitutes was adopted, to the recent response of Shell to environmental and social issues – one or a combination of these factors has been crucial. (Utting 2000: 34)[23]

These broader societal and political functions of publicly devised regulatory codes are often overlooked. UNCTAD states in an assessment of the international debates during the 1970s and early 1980s:

> The negotiations over codes of conduct, whether ultimately successful or not, were instrumental in defining areas of common understanding over the proper conduct of transnational corporations and in clarifying the standards for their treatment. (UNCTAD 1999a: xxiii)

Corporate Watchdog Groups and the State

> If markets are not perfectly self-correcting, then the only check on their excesses must be extra-market institutions. These reside in values other than market values, and in affiliations that transcend mere hedonism and profit-maximization. To temper the market one must reclaim civil society and government, and make clear that government and civil vitality are allies not adversaries. (Kuttner 1999)[24]

Usurping the Role of Governments?

The infant food industry has reacted to IBFAN monitoring of its practices by claiming that the network is 'usurping the sovereignty of national states'.[25] Similar accusations have been levelled at the civil society organizations that protested against the dominance of corporate interests in global policy-making at the November 1999 WTO meeting in Seattle and subsequent multilateral economic forums.

It is certainly useful to reflect on how citizen groups can best contribute to democratic decision-making in a globalizing world without weakening those states that aim to act in the public interest.[26] But to level a blanket accusation that citizen action undermines nation-states does not help this analysis. As Riva Krut stresses in her study on the influence of civil society organizations in international decision-making:

It is not the function – nor usually the intention – of civil society organizations to usurp the functions of governments. Its role may be to shape and steer public issues and public officers, to monitor the implementation of public policy, to deliver humanitarian relief. Its mission may be to ensure that governance is democratic, accountable, transparent, inclusive, participatory and equitable. In this sense, domestic civil society relies on a strong state which functions best under strong government. Global civil society, in parallel, would rely on strong national government and strong international governance from a reformulated United Nations.' (Krut 1997: 3)[27]

With reference to citizen groups and organizations, UN General-Secretary Kofi Annan has stressed:

We know from experience that neither the United Nations, nor individual States, can by themselves meet the challenges of the 21st century. We know that civil society's participation is essential ... We know this because healthy and democratic societies are ultimately the product, not the creator, of a strong civil society. The same applies to a healthy and democratic international community ... So we need partnerships: partnerships that will allow democratic participation in decision-making; that will encourage Governments to take bold measures or enable them to back down from their mistakes; that will help UN missions operate with integrity. (quoted in Foster and Anand 1999: xiii)

The business discourse about pressure groups usurping the role of governments omits to mention, moreover, that the rise of transnational corporations has been a major challenge to the sovereign decision-making powers of states, a rise that has in turn been an important stimulus to the rise of transnational civil society organizations. In the words of Krut:

The authority and competence of the state ... is also challenged by globalization. As national and international government declines in authority and international economic institutions leap into the space of government, civil society not only has to grapple with what a democratic system of global governance may look like, but has to do so in the absence of active players willing and able to take on the executive roles of governance. Along with the incompetence of the state to deal with global issues, some civil society activists perceive a failure of will. (Krut 1997: 4)

Moreover, industry's claim reflects a narrow view of the setting, monitoring and enforcement of rules in democratic societies. Civil society organizations that strive for the external regulation of transnational corporations are not usurping the role of states but complementing it. So were UN agencies when they strived for international regulation but were warned by TNCs not to behave as 'supranational regulatory bodies'.[28] Limiting harmful corporate activities has never been the exclusive domain of governments. Checks and balances on corporations in Western industrialized states have rarely been established simply because state authorities thought they were needed. In many cases, the need for regulation was first articulated within the public sphere[29] (see Chapter 1).

As far as implementation of the Code at national level is concerned, IBFAN and other civil society groups often had a dual approach towards the state and relevant international agencies: prompting them to take action, and supporting them against industry resistance to regulation.

As far as monitoring industry practices is concerned, meanwhile, IBFAN could not 'usurp' the function of the state in those countries that have not set up appropriate monitoring systems in the first place. Even in the best functioning state system, however, there will always be a place for civil 'watchdog' groups to monitor whether corporations respect ethical principles.

In fact, every individual citizen has the right to watch how corporations conduct their business and to denounce loudly those who harm societal interests. Vigilant, active citizens – a vibrant 'public sphere' – are the very essence of a democratic society. It is all the better if citizens organize to increase their effectiveness in keeping watch over corporate behaviour.

If such organizing sometimes causes frictions not only with corporations but also with public authorities, this should not be regarded as problematic. As US economist Robert Kuttner reminds us in his analysis of the political preconditions for good and effective regulation of the market: 'Strong civic institutions help constitute the state, and also serve as a counterweight against excesses both of state and market.' Kuttner is predominantly concerned about the tendency of big corporations to infringe into areas where they do not belong:

Unless we want our republic to degenerate into a new plutocracy – an oligarchy of the wealthy and fortunate – we face a twin challenge: to keep the market from ruining the polity and to renew the institutions of healthy civic and political life. (Kuttner 1999: 331, 348)

Pressure Groups and Legitimacy

Compared to TNCs and their PR apparatuses, IBFAN groups are tiny. Even the network's regional coordinating offices do not have more than a handful of people working in them. Many IBFAN members work on a voluntary basis. When international relations scholar Peter Willets investigated how small, overworked and under-funded groups had managed to change the practices of powerful economic and political actors, he concluded that one of the pressure groups' greatest assets was their 'ability to mobilize legitimacy' (Willets 1982: 24). And, indeed, legitimacy is an important political power resource.

It is thus not surprising that the infant food industry tends to pay less attention to rebutting the content of the criticisms made against it and more to stripping its critics of their legitimacy and positive reputation. Members of the International Chamber of Commerce, for instance, have not only called for greater industry involvement in shaping the global economy: they have also increased their calls to investigate the role of 'activist pressure groups' in the UN system and to look where their funding comes from.[30]

While it is important not to romanticize CSOs or NGOs, it is also important to consider who is questioning their legitimacy and why. Civil society groups, like other social actors, are a diverse community. Like other actors, they are not perfect: they may get involved in self-serving activities; they may make mistakes. Like any other societal actor, civil society groups have to prove their legitimacy continuously by demonstrating their commitment and contribution to the well-being of the world's people. And just like any other societal group, civil society groups should be assessed according to their deeds, the aims they pursue and the means they employ.

Discussions about the yardsticks by which to judge the actors – be they civil society groups, governments, UN agencies or corporations – involved in global decision-making are still ongoing. Reform of current systems of global governance is still under discussion. Criteria such as 'trust' and 'mutual benefits' are clearly inappropriate for decision-making in the regulatory arena. They should be replaced by 'transparency' and 'societal benefits' or 'public interests'. As for the international regulation of corporations, there is an urgent need to explore how to re-create an institutional structure providing UN member countries and citizen action groups with much-needed insights into the operations and structure of TNCs, and how best to protect and promote public interests in a globalizing world.

According to the UNDP 1999 *Human Development Report*, the task of building more democratic global institutional and procedural arrangements for the twenty-first century encompasses 'putting human concerns and human rights at the centre of international policy and action' and ensuring that the reform is 'driven by concern for people, not for capital' (UNDP 1999: 98).[31]

Civil Society Organizations and the Regulation of Corporations

This chapter has summarized the role played by IBFAN in the regulation of the marketing practices of the infant food industry. It has argued that the international citizen alliance brought the issue into the public arena and influenced corporate practice through awareness-raising and the building up of public pressure. It has contended that IBFAN does not usurp the role of states, and that this network has exercised a legitimate and crucial function in societies as, historically, the expansion of corporations has gone hand-in-hand with struggles to prevent harmful industry practices.

Caution should also be exercised when considering the opposite of the 'usurping the state' discourse, namely, advocacy that states should abdicate their rule-setting and monitoring functions altogether and hand them over to civil society organizations (enforcement through sanctions does not usually figure in this discourse). Much of the current neoliberal governance discourse, for example, implies that, as citizen groups have successfully influenced corporate practices, this task is best left to them and, better still, performed in cooperation with industry.

As argued in Chapter 1, there are areas where co-regulation with industry may be sufficient and useful. But there will always be spheres of the economy that need tight and effective outside regulation. For 20 years, IBFAN has raised the issue of the harmful marketing of breast-milk substitutes and revealed continued violations of the International Code. 'We thought that when the Code was passed the manufacturers and marketing people would do the right thing,' said Nancy-Jo Peck, a member of IBFAN since its inception. 'Unfortunately, little has changed' (BFHI News 1999c: 2).

Most similar issue networks would probably agree that the task of monitoring corporations has often stretched their human resources to the limit. Even less reliance on the state and international agencies than today would in fact run counter to what IBFAN and similar groups have been striving for over two decades: an efficient system of state regulation, backed up by regional and international institutions, in which the role of civil society organizations would be to compensate for the unavoidable limits and shortcomings of such a system.

Establishing efficient systems of regulation of transnational corporations thus entails recognition of the role of so-called radical civil society organizations. It also entails ensuring that such groups have access to the relevant public fora and a more secure funding base than they have currently. More generally, it means further reflection within the international community about global institutional arrangements in which states are effectively backed up by a reformulated and strengthened UN and other institutions such as the International Criminal Court and a revived UN Centre on Transnational Corporations in their efforts to come to grips with those corporations that have grown beyond their national boundaries. This is not a question of economic power. It is, above all, a question of lucid analysis and political will.

It is often said that setting up regulatory systems is beyond the economic means of many states and the UN agencies. If so, why not demand that transnational corporations refrain from further eroding tax systems worldwide?[32] Why not demand that they stop pressuring states – and in particular the UN's main contributor, the USA – to cut UN funds whenever a UN agency engages in international regulatory efforts? Why not demand that governments sit together to strategize how to reverse the massive income redistribution from poor to rich? Why not create a people-oriented Economic Security Council as part of the proposed reform of the UN system? (CGG 1995: 342).

Public institutions should take a fresh look at how to create institutional and decision-making arrangements that truly serve their citizens, with a special emphasis on the needs of the poor, marginalized and vulnerable, arrangements that would ultimately also ensure that public authorities and corporate watchdog groups had the resources to perform their functions properly.

Notes

1. CGG 1995: 1, 34.

2. See also CGG 1995: 32–7, 254–60.

3. For discussions on the issue of the heterogeneity of the NGO and civil society community and questions about their role and legitimacy of involvement in global democratic decision-making, see e.g. CGG 1995: 32–7; Fowler 2000; Krut 1997; UNRISD 2000b: 81–110.

4. For more information on the industry creation of pseudo-grassroots organizations, see e.g. Kuttner 1999: 346; Stauber and Rampton 1995: 77ff.

5. Seligman refers particularly to T. H. Marshall's three forms of citizenship: civil, political and social (Seligman 1992: 204).

6. For more information on Seligman's and other distinctions, see Chris Hann's overview from a political anthropology perspective (Hann 1996).

7. Others argue that the introduction of the notion of civil society in the World Bank and other policy discourses is an opportunity. Robert Archer of the UK NGO Christian Aid, for example, sees it as implicit recognition of the need to set limits to the spread of the undiluted free market model (Archer 1994: 10–13). For a cursory overview in relation to the use of the term within the UN system, see NGLS 1997.

8. The labour and women's movements were already transnational at the beginning of the twentieth century.

9. Allain 1998: 33.

10. For more information on the early period of the network see Chetley 1986: 101–16; see also Allain 1991.

11. In the fishing-net model, 'each knot in the net represents a member group or individual, all of which are linked together and interact without having a centre. Often this develops so that one or more of the knots become motor groups or coordinating groups for the network or for certain activities' (Karl 1998: 23).

12. For IBFAN's five aims and objectives agreed upon at the 1981 Congress, see Chetley 1986: 104. For more information on the network and material relevant to campaigning on the infant food issue, see IBFAN 1999b, 1999c and Linnear 1997. See also Allain 1998, 1999 and BFHI News January/February 1999.

13. At the time, anti-apartheid boycotts against companies and banks that operated in South Africa were at their height.

14. The Ad Hoc Group on Infant Feeding in Emergency commented: 'In emergencies, the adequate supply of appropriate food is obviously of fundamental importance. A common belief is that in emergencies it is infants who are at greatest risk of becoming malnourished – but this is not true of breastfed infants. The ability to breastfeed is robust, even in the face of constraints' (ENN 1999). For optimal infant feeding in emergencies, it makes most sense to focus on the provision of adequate nutrition and support to the mothers of the infants. In cases where alternatives are required, it is imperative that several conditions are met to ensure the infant's survival in potentially crowded circumstances where infection is rife. For more information, see ENN 1999; IBFAN 1996.

15. Interview with Nancy-Jo Peck, scientific adviser to IBFAN/GIFA, June 2000.

16. While many other network members work on a voluntary basis. Ibid.

17. Randell 1995: 40. For a discussion about this change in status and the problems of representation of consumer and developing country perspectives, see Lehners 1998; WEMOS 1998.

18. When UNICEF commended the Interagency Group on Breastfeeding Monitoring (IGBM) on the quality of its 1997 *Cracking the Code* monitoring report, it noted that this report 'vindicated' the regular monitoring activities by IBFAN and proposed that 'IBFAN and other nongovernmental organizations that regularly fulfil the monitoring role assigned by the World Health Assembly to NGOs be given renewed encouragement to continue monitoring compliance with the International Code' (UNICEF 1997b).

20. For more information about boycotts as an important historical means to work for social justice in the United States as a 'weapon of the weak' see also Friedman 1999.

19. Statement by Marjorie Thompson, director of Cause Connection, the 'cause-related marketing arm' of PR firm Saatchi and Saatchi, and Hamish Pringle, former vice-chair of the same company. Their advice was not to react to the ruling but to stress investments in corporate philanthropic projects instead. As Thompson said, 'You are building a surplus account for the times when you have a crisis' (Wilkinson 1999b: 31). This book does not explore the role of another important player in the infant food debate: the mass media and medical journals.

21. For further details of the Nestlé boycott, including why the campaigners see the 1984 suspension of the boycott as a major mistake, see Allain 1991: 30–2; Chetley 1986: 128–99; Smith 1990: 247–50. For details of Nestlé's strategies to break up the boycott – among others by using UNICEF as 'honest broker' – see Sethi 1994: 291–318 and Stauber and Rampton 1995: 51–3.

22. In most assessments of the 'success' of codes, moreover, insufficient attention is paid to the quality and effectiveness of the monitoring and enforcement arrangements.

23. For a summary of broader political concerns about the shift towards so-called multi-stakeholder partnerships from a public policy perspective, see Utting 2000: 22–4. Concerns include: changing the agenda of the public or NGO 'partner' through co-optation; self-censorship and reduced freedom of expression among officials of international agencies; 'institutional capture' of the public agency by corporate interests; weak criteria in the selection of corporate 'partners'; splitting alliances and activist institutions including instigating divisions between UN agencies; weakening the 'key drivers' of corporate responsibility: governmental and intergovernmental regulation, collective bargaining, and NGO activism and civil society protest.

24. Kuttner 1999: 362.

25. The Infant and Dietetic Foods Association, for example, stated in a press release referring to IBFAN's 1998 monitoring report: 'The WHO Code recommends that Governments should give "effect to the principles and aim

of the Code as appropriate to their social and legislative framework, including the adoption of national legislation, regulations or other suitable measures." This means that individual governments can produce their own codes or regulations, which may differ from the WHO Code depending on national circumstances. Indeed many of the countries involved in the IBFAN report have their own codes or regulations to which companies must comply. By continuing to suggest that their subjective interpretation of the WHO Code has greater status and importance than the considered views of the national authorities, IBFAN is usurping the sovereignty of national governments' (IDFA 1998).

26. Business associations are not pressing for a corresponding debate about whether TNCs undermine states.

27. Krut also points out that transnational corporations have become some of the major actors who frame global rules in 'a spirit different from that of the UN Charter' (Krut 1997: 24).

28. This was the term used by the pharmaceutical industry when it lobbied against WHO regulation of its marketing practices in the mid-1980s (Chetley 1990: 87).

29. Economist Robert Kuttner says of the role of citizen participation in rule-setting: 'The issue of how precisely to govern markets arises in liber-tarian, democratic nations like the United States, and deferential, authoritarian ones like Singapore ... Rule-setting and the correction of market excesses are necessarily public issues ... The highly charged question of the proper rules undergirding a capitalist society pervaded political discourse and conflict throughout nineteenth-century America ... Norms that encourage informed civic engagement increase the likelihood of competent, responsive politics and administration, which in turn yields a more efficient mixed economy' (Kuttner 1999: 331).

30. Nestlé CEO Helmut Maucher, for example, now distinguishes between 'activist pressure groups' and 'responsible NGOs'. While heading the International Chamber of Commerce (ICC), he complained at the first Geneva Business Dialogue about 'exaggerations and irrational arguments in environmental politics, due to single issue groups that know nothing and have no responsibilities'. He also asked 'How are they financed and what do they stand for?' (quoted in CEO 1998: 4–5 and in Williams 1998.

31. For additional proposals, see UNDP 1999: 98.

32. The IMF estimates that the amount of funds that have been placed by businesses and rich citizens into tax-free offshore accounts alone amounts to around $8 trillion, which is equivalent to the GDP of the USA. Proposals have been made to deal with the problems of tax evasion by creating a World Tax Organization. Another problem will be dealing with tax competition – the legal economization of taxes where businesses play governments off against each other. Some experts suggest that tax competition in the liberalized economy may in the future drive corporate tax rates to zero. For more details see UNRISD 2000: 31–5.

· ·

CHAPTER 10

International Regulation of TNCs: Issues Raised by the Infant Food Debate

> Governance is not government – it is the framework of rules, institutions and practices that sets limits on the behaviour of individuals, organizations and companies. (UNDP, *Human Development Report 1999: Globalization with a Human Face*)[1]

> How can the international human rights, developmental, environmental, social, gender and labour norms developed through UN forums be implemented through governance which is transparent, accountable and democratic? (John W. Foster, professor of human rights, 1999)[2]

§ This book has analysed the process of formulation, adoption and implementation of the International Code of Marketing of Breast-milk Substitutes from the 1970s up to the present day. The aim of the case study has been to draw out key issues to reveal potentially under-explored ways to rein in more effectively those corporate practices that conflict with people's well-being and other fundamental human rights and social concerns.

The infant food example is relevant to more general issues about the international regulation of TNCs because it is one of the longest-standing efforts to regulate an industry sector internationally. The Code is one of the few international codes adopted under the aegis of the UN at a time when binding international regulation of TNCs was regarded as an important means of making transnational corporations accountable to the countries in which they operated.

The climate for international regulation has significantly changed since then. Today, opinions range from assertions that the policy thrust should be towards working with big business on frameworks of 'good corporate governance' and voluntary 'codes of conduct' to calls for resuming the work to establish a coherent web of mandatory regulatory frameworks for transnational corporations.

While some actors support the shift towards co-regulation with industry and industry self-regulation because they believe industry statements of commitment to corporate responsibility, others advocate co-regulation simply because it is regarded as more pragmatic than pressing for international regulation of transnational corporations. And, indeed, political and economic power balances over the past 30 years have certainly shifted away from such an endeavour in many ways. Is it at all possible to implement public regulatory arrangements that effectively prevent, or at least minimize, harm stemming from activities of transnational corporations? Is there anything else to be considered that might increase the chances of success?

To gain some insights into these questions, this case study has conceptualized debates about the international regulation of transnational corporations as *contested processes* involving specific *actors* with differing *interests* and differing *power resources* in a precise *context*. It has put a particular spotlight on two major actors in the infant food debate: transnational corporations and transnational citizen organizations.[3]

The Regulation of Marketing of Breast-milk Substitutes: Selected Conclusions

1. The international regulation of the marketing of breast-milk substitutes would not have become an issue on the international policy agenda without the involvement of civil society organizations.

2. The formulation and adoption of the International Code of Marketing of Breast-milk Substitutes was characterized by heated controversies. Infant food manufacturers and several industrialized countries, in particular the USA, opposed a tightly worded Code with a strong legal status. Such a Code might have been achieved if those involved had been stricter about industry involvement in the process of Code formulation and if they had not shied away from voting for a stronger legal form – a WHO Regulation instead of a Recommendation.

3. The Code has been implemented in more than one hundred countries – albeit often in ways that fall below commitments made at the time of the Code's adoption in 1981. National implementation of the Code has been hampered by several factors:

- legacies from the process of Code formulation and adoption;
- the continued resistance of infant food manufacturers to strong external regulation (evidenced by their reinterpretation of the Code; interference with national implementation; insistence on being an integral part of law drafting and monitoring committees); and
- a deteriorating climate for industry regulation under a neoliberal economic framework at international and national levels.

4. These obstacles have been overcome at international and national levels in various ways. Countries have been able to implement legislation and other regulatory measures based on the Code or to upgrade existing national measures, in spite of industry resistance. Important factors in this endeavour have been political will and support from UN agencies and civil society groups (and health professionals). In many instances, civil society groups have filled in for international and national authorities or have complemented them.

5. Linking advocacy for regulation of the marketing of breast-milk substitutes to the Convention on the Rights of the Child opened up new avenues for Code implementation. Linking with the United Nations Working Group on transnational corporations and human rights might make the International Code still more effective – especially if there are additional political efforts to make TNCs legally accountable to the International Criminal Court.

6. There is a continued need for effective regulation of the inappropriate marketing of breast-milk substitutes for several reasons:

   a) Knowledge gained over the past 20 years about the benefits of breast-feeding, especially exclusive breast-feeding, indicates that the practice is even more beneficial to children's survival and development than previously thought. It is thus more important than ever to prevent those promotional practices that lead to the displacement of breast-feeding by artificial feeding. Ensuring that infants who could benefit from breast-milk are not deprived of it because of commercial pressures has become even more vital in the context of HIV/AIDS.

   b) The protection, promotion and support of breast-feeding has gained a new dimension since it has been recognized as a human right.

   c) The infant food industry has not demonstrated a significant commitment to changing its marketing practices. On the contrary, reports indicate that it continues to market its products in ways that interfere with exclusive and sustained breast-feeding. Inappropriate marketing practices continue to harm and contribute to the deaths of infants all over the world.

d) Some corporations have been found to exploit the feeding dilemmas faced by HIV-infected women by claiming that marketing regulation interferes with commercial freedom to educate women on infant feeding. But international policy-makers have stated a different opinion. To ensure women's right to unbiased choice between infant feeding options, they have decided that strong Code implementation is all the more important.

7. There are significant gaps between industry statements of its commitment to the Code and what it actually does in practice. This gap is often overlooked or unknown because the infant food industry has built up hidden and deceptive corporate public relations practices to undermine Code implementation and international regulation.

8. 'Dialogues' with industry, from closed discussions in the 1970s with the UN Protein Advisory Group to industry discussions with WHO and UNICEF on free supplies in the early 1990s to the 1999 WHO Round-table Initiative, have had relatively little success in changing corporate practice. Instead, such interactions have been used by corporations in a variety of ways, including attempting to shift the balance of power away from citizen action groups and UNICEF in favour of TNCs by means of divide-and-rule strategies. There is a need for broad-based reflections on how to prevent corporations from using policy negotiations in this way.

9. One of the most effective ways of making infant food manufacturers change their marketing practices has been 'negative publicity' – public exposure of Code violations and naming and shaming the companies involved. Civil society organizations, in particular the International Baby Food Action Network (IBFAN), have played a crucial role in this respect. Consideration should be given as to how this mechanism can be strengthened at all levels and how to support civil society groups in their work.

International Regulation of TNCs: Issues for Further Consideration

Self-regulation Versus Co-regulation Versus External Binding Regulation

The trend towards industry self-regulation and co-regulation needs to be reassessed. This includes an assessment of the degree to which industry statements of increased responsibility correspond to its actions.

Any change in a criticized practice should not automatically be taken as proof of increased corporate responsibility. It may be as much a reaction to outside pressure in a corporation's 'enlightened self-interest'. Changes in industry practice therefore have to be assessed within the broadest possible context.

Effective industry self-regulation is not really possible where industry self-policing interferes with profit maximization. Business associations do not usually cover the totality of an industry sector; corporations that are less socially responsible tend to drag the standard of others down; corporations cannot determine acceptable standards of risks for society because rule- and standard-setting on corporate conduct, practices and products are not only issues of scientific and ethical expert analysis. The ultimate decision, for instance, on the acceptability – or unacceptability – of particular types of marketing practices, the determination of the permissible amount of a pollutant, or a decision to ban a particular chemical or pharmaceutical completely are all political decisions.

Nor can corporations truly police themselves and each other and create what industry calls a 'level playing-field'. Only public regulation can sanction their behaviour in an even-handed way and determine the amount of damages to be awarded to victims of corporate mal-practice or negligence. Self-regulation may be unproblematic when it comes to ensuring a standardized size of shoes, for example. It is insufficient, however, in areas of vital importance to society.

As of today, the task of drawing up and implementing a coherent regulatory web for transnational corporations remains an unfinished agenda of international public policy-making. The foremost duties of corporations in this respect are to abstain from negatively interfering with processes of public rule-setting and enforcement, to establish effective auditing mechanisms along publicly formulated codes and national legislation, and to cooperate in public investigations of potential violations of those rules. Corporations wishing to demonstrate a particular sense of social responsibility can draw up and implement industry codes – but these should be in addition to publicly formulated codes and national legislation, not instead of them.

Clarification of the Process of External Regulation

The example of the infant food industry points to a need for more analysis and discussion on the role of the various actors involved in the process of external regulation. To ensure that regulation is in the best interest of society, the most basic step seems to be aware always of the critical distinction between the party to be regulated and the parties involved in the process of drawing up the regulation and making it effective. There is a need for further reflection on how to ensure that the party to be regulated does not unduly influence the regulation of its practices. This involves clarifying the role of industry in the processes of drawing up regulatory frameworks. It also involves ensuring that monitoring and sanctions are wholly independent of industry.

The prevention of 'regulatory capture' by corporations, however, is ultimately a question of power, of the awareness and civic-mindedness of the relevant public institutions and civil society groups, and of the civic behaviour of corporations themselves.

Regulation and Power

There is still room to pressure corporations to change their practices, despite the increasing economic power of transnational corporations. If child health and and other human rights are to be ensured, it is crucial to explore how the balance of power can be shifted in favour of external regulation.

Such an exploration should include reflection on how governments, even of the poorest countries, can be supported to implement and enforce strong regulatory measures. This may involve increased capacity-building and support from UN agencies. It should also involve reflection on what might be the best possible cooperation between governments, international agencies and national and international public interest networks to ensure the respective regulatory goal.

There is a need to take stock of TNC resources and strategies.

They include:

- economic resources (companies can bribe high-ranking government officials and buy influence through strategic sponsorships);
- threat of relocation if strong regulations are enacted (even though they may not carry out the threat); and
- hidden communication methods (issues management/engineering of consent) and increased lobbying at high policy-making levels.

The power resources of the other actors include:

- the UN community's ability to organize international conferences that set international rules and standards;
- nation-states' legitimacy to make and enforce laws;
- the mandate of governments and intergovernmental agencies to protect, promote and fulfil people's human rights, which legitimizes regulation of corporations; and
- the power of civil society and labour organizations to catalyse public opinion; their freedom to name and shame wrongdoers; their reputation as defenders of public interests.

The study of the infant food debate shows that there is under-explored room to make corporations more socially accountable. Ways of limiting and offsetting the power of TNCs which should be investigated further include:

- relaunching a broad debate about the need for political anti-trust legislation – not just economically motivated legislation to ensure competition – at the international level (that is, countering the trend for TNCs to become economically more powerful than most nations of the world);
- recognizing TNCs' need for social legitimacy (and not giving socially irresponsible corporations more legitimacy than they deserve, thus unduly shifting the balance of power in their favour);
- taking corporate engineering of consent activities into account and exploring ways of offsetting this power resource (for instance, exploring ways to regain maximum transparency and space for democratic decision-making);
- initiating public debate on the social risks of public–commercial sector 'partnerships'; and abstaining from calling interactions with corporations 'partnerships';
- setting and recovering ethical baselines for those types of inter-

actions with corporations where there are clear conflicts of interest between public (or scientific) tasks and profit motives;

- re-establishing a UN Centre on Transnational Corporations to provide public insights into the practices and structures of large corporations;

- finding ways to strengthen civil society 'watchdog' and awareness-raising groups in their task of monitoring industry practices, raising questions about corporate accountability, and keeping industry activities in the critical public eye;

- the use by UN agencies, national authorities and more moderate civil society groups of the mechanism of naming and shaming to influence corporate practice. It is important that this task is not left to a few radical citizen pressure groups, which may not only be overburdened by this task but also risk being marginalized and ultimately silenced.

Regulation and Global Democratic Decision-making

A broad-based debate on the appropriate institutional and political arrangements for ensuring that TNCs do not harm public interests should be encouraged. This would involve: taking stock of proposals calling for a re-evaluation of the role of UN agencies and other key players in the world policy-making arena (such as the World Bank, the International Monetary Fund, the WTO and the G7 states, in particular the USA); and encouraging a broad, public discussion about the criteria along which corporate behaviour should be judged and how such criteria could be rendered effective in making corporations more socially accountable. Transparency and democratic decision-making should be the paramount guiding principles in this process.

It may be necessary to re-evaluate whether the governance discourse is the best discourse to frame discussions on international regulation and other global political decision-making processes. To what degree is the notion of governance – based on the image of a leader steering a ship – really open to bottom-up popular participation? Would it not be more fruitful to discuss matters of international policy-making in terms of cosmopolitan democracy, for instance?

It is important to address several tendencies in the governance discourse dominant today. First, the depiction of rule-setting as a harmonious process between equal partners should be replaced by a more realistic picture of such highly political processes. Second, there should be a clear distinction between business interest and public interest organizations. Third, there is a need to clarify the fact that controversy and healthy distrust are no less valuable, and often more appropriate, than cooperation and trust in relation to the formulation and implementation of regulatory systems. Another crucial measure would be to reassess tendencies to use positively charged terminology such as 'free' market, 'corporate citizens', 'creators of wealth' and 'freedom of commercial speech', and to accept the participation of transnational corporations in 'global governance' as their natural right – while bedevilling the idea and notion of mandatory, public 'command and control' regulation.

If democratic – that is, people-centred and participatory – policy-making is brought to the centre of considerations, then democratic control over transnational corporations becomes more feasible to consider and explore, and the political debate can become refocused from one of corporate responsibility towards one of corporate public accountability.

Notes

1. UNDP 1999: 34.
2. Foster 1999: 461.
3. Additional insights into the concrete processes of regulation at international and national level may be gained by studying more closely the role of governments, UN agencies, health professionals and the media.

Useful Websites

Adbusters: www.adbusters.org/adbusters/

Campaign for Ethical Marketing/Baby Milk Action:
    www.babymilkaction.org

Corporate Europe Observatory (CEO): www.xs.4all.nl/~ceo/observer

HAI 2001: www.haiweb.org/campaign/PPI/seminar200011.doc

Health Action International (HAI): www.haiweb.org

International Association of Infant Food Manufacturers (IFM):
    www.ifm.net

International Baby Food Action Network (IBFAN): www.ibfan.org

International Chamber of Commerce (ICC): www.iccwbo.org

International Lactation Consultant Association (ILCA): www.ilca.org

La Leche League International: www.lalecheleague.org

Nestlé: www.nestle.com

PRWatch: www.prwatch.org

Transnational Resource and Action Centre (TRAC): www.corpwatch.org

Third World Network: www.twnside.org.sg

UNAIDS: www.unaids.org

UNCTAD: www.unctad.org

UNDP: www.undp.org

UNICEF: www.unicef.org

UN Non-Governmental Liaison Service (NGLS): www.ngls.tad.ch

UNRISD: www.unrisd.org

UN partners: www.un/org/partners/

World Alliance of Breastfeeding Action (WABA): www.elogica.com.br/
    waba

Women's Environment and Development Organization (WEDO):
    www.wedo.org

WHO: www.who.int

Bibliography

Alinsky, S. D. (1971) *Rules for Radicals: A Practical Primer for Radicals*, New York: Vintage Books.

Allain, A. (ed.) (1986) *Milk and Murder. Address by Dr. Cicely Williams to the Rotary Club of Singapore in 1939*, Penang: International Organization of Consumers Unions (IOCU).

— (1991) *IBFAN: On the Cutting Edge*, Uppsala: Dag Hammarskjöld Foundation.

— (1998) 'On the cutting edge: the International Baby Food Action Network (IBFAN)', in Women's Feature Service (ed.), pp. 33–7.

— (1999) 'IBFAN: 20 years of monitoring the formula industry', *The Baby-Friendly Hospital Initiative Newsletter*, January/February, pp. 1, 6.

Allende, S. (1972) 'Speech to the United Nations', in H. Radice (ed.), *International Firms and Modern Imperialism*, London: Penguin, pp. 239–40, quoted in Chetley 1986, p. 23.

Apple, R. D. (1980) 'To be used only under the direction of a physician: commercial infant feeding and medical practice 1870–1940', *Bulletin of the History of Medicine* 54 (3): 402, 417, quoted in Palmer 1993, pp. 207–8.

Arbeitsgruppe Dritte Welt (1974) *Nestlé tötet Babys*, Berne: Arbeitsgruppe Dritte Welt (Third World Action Group).

Archer, R. (1994) *Markets and Good Government: The Way Forward for Economic and Social Development?*, Geneva: UN Non-Governmental Liaison Service (NGLS).

Archibugi, D., D. Held and M. Koehler (1998) *Re-imagining Political Community: Studies in Cosmopolitan Democracy*, Stanford, CA: Stanford University Press.

ASA (1999) *ASA Adjudications – May 1999 – Nestlé UK Ltd*, Advertising Standards Authority (ASA), www. asa.org.uk/adj./adj_3586.htm, accessed 13 May 1999.

Baby Milk Action (1997a) 'Breastfeeding and HIV transmission: the need to protect against commercial exploitation', briefing paper, December.

— (1997b) 'Nestlé receives business award for targeting new parents', *Boycott News*, supplement to *Baby Milk Action Update*, 21, October, p. 3.

— (1997c) 'Watch out Russia – Nestlé is coming', *Campaign for Ethical Marketing Action Sheet*, August.

— (1999) 'Bigger than nations: the big 12 companies in the baby food business', *Baby Milk Action Update*, 25, July, pp. 5–8.

— (1999a) 'Advertising standard authority warns Nestlé about claiming to be ethical. And Nestlé's battles against the ASA ruling', *Boycott News*, supplement to *Baby Milk Action Update*, 24, February, p. 2.

— (1999b) 'The Code, the Directives, the UK law', *Baby Milk Action Update*, 24, February, p. 3.

— (1999c) 'Don't judge the book by its cover – the truth behind Nestlé's book "Nestlé Implementation of the WHO Code"', briefing paper, Cambridge: Baby Milk Action.

— (1999d) 'Nestlé fined for breaking Czech law', *Baby Milk Action Update*, 26, p. 4.

— (1999e) 'Responses to April 98 violations: Nestlé threatens "to pull out investment in Zimbabwe"', *Campaign for Ethical Marketing Action Sheet*, March, pp. 2–3.

— (2000a) 'MEPs shocked as Nestlé and Adidas snub public hearing on corporate responsibility', press release, 23 November.

— (2000b) 'Nestlé under investigation by Pakistan anti-corruption body in Raza case', press release, 28 March.

Baker, M. J. (1998) *Macmillan Dictionary of Marketing and Advertising*, London: Macmillan.

Balanyá, B., A. Doherty, O. Hoedeman, A. Ma'anit and E. Wesselius (2000) *Europe Inc.: Regional and Global Restructuring and the Rise of Corporate Power*, London: Pluto Press in Association with Corporate Europe Observatory (CEO).

Ballarin, O. (1978) Statement by Oswaldo Ballarin, president of Nestlé Brazil, quoted in Chetley 1986, p. 53 and Sethi 1994, p. 76.

Barter, I. (1980) Telex from Ian Barter, president of the International Council of Infant Food Industries (ICIFI), to Dr Petros-Barvazian, director, Family Health Division, WHO, 14 February, quoted in Shubber 1998, p. 19.

Baskin, O., C. Aronoff and D. Lattimore (1997) *Public Relations: The Profession and the Practice*, Madison, WI: Brown & Benchmark Publishers.

Baumslag, N. (1995) *Milk, Money and Madness: The Culture and Politics of Breastfeeding*, Westport, CT: Bergin & Garvey, quoted in Sokol 1997, p. 31.

Beck, U. (ed.) (1998) *Perspektiven der Weltgesellschaft*, Frankfurt am Main: Suhrkamp.

Bellamy, C. (1997) Letter from Carol Bellamy, executive director of the United Nations Children's Fund (UNICEF), to Peter Brabeck-Letmathe, executive vice-president, Nestlé SA, 3 November.

— (1999a) Remarks by Carol Bellamy, executive director, United Nations Children's Fund, to Harvard International Development Conference on 'Sharing Responsibilities: Public, Private and Civil Society', 16 April.

— (1999b), Letter from Carol Bellamy, executive director of UNICEF, to Peter Brabeck-Letmathe, chief exececutive officer, Nestlé SA, 31 December.

— (2000) 'UNICEF continues to base its actions and programmes on the best interests of the child', letter to the editor, *British Medical Journal (BMJ)*, 321 (7266), 14 October: 960.

— (2000b) 'UNICEF works to solve Africa dilemma', letter to the *Wall Street Journal*, 14 December.

Bernays, E. L. (1952) *Public Relations*, Norman: University of Oklahoma Press.

Bernstein, M. (1955) *Regulating Business by Independent Commission*, Princeton, NJ: Princeton University Press.

BFHI News (1998a) 'HIV and breastfeeding: assessing the risk proves complicated', *The Baby-Friendly Hospital Initiative Newsletter*, November, p. 1.

— (1998b) 'World Alliance for Breastfeeding Action spurs cooperation', *The Baby-Friendly Hospital Initiative Newsletter*, December, pp. 2–3.

— (1999a) 'Breastfeeding vs. baby food: the race is on in Eastern Europe', *The Baby-Friendly Hospital Initiative Newsletter*, January/February, pp. 1, 6.

— (1999b) 'Breastfeeding group in Africa tailors Code to continent', *The Baby-Friendly Hospital Initiative Newsletter*, January/February, p. 3.

— (1999c) 'Over the years, industry marketing tactics have become subtler, says early IBFAN member', *The Baby-Friendly Hospital Initiative Newsletter*, January/February, pp. 2–3.

— (2000) 'NGOs shake up governments on child rights of implementation', *The Baby-Friendly Hospital Initiative Newsletter*, November, p. 4.

Bienen, D., V. Rittberger and W. Wagner (1998) 'Democracy in the United Nations system: cosmopolitan and communitarian principles', in Archibugi et al. (eds), pp. 287–308.

Bland, M. (1995) 'Strategic crisis management', in Hart (ed.), pp. 276–98.

Blum, R., A. Herxheimer, C. Stenzland and J. Woodcock (eds) (1981), *Pharmaceuticals and Health Policy: International Perspectives on Provision and Control of Medicines*, London: Croom Helm and International Research Group for Drug Legislation and Programmes.

Blundo, G. (2000) 'La corruption entre scandales politiques et pratiques quotidiennes', in G. Blundo (ed.), *Monnayer les pouvoirs: espaces, mécanismes et représentations de la corruption*, Paris/Geneva: Presses Universitaires de France/Nouveaux Cahiers de l'Institut d'Etudes du Développement (IUED), pp. 11–19.

Borasio, P. (1989) Letter from Peter Borasio, president of the International Association of Infant Food Manufacturers (IFM) to Hiroshi Nakajima, director-general, WHO, 31 August.

— (1998) Letter from Peter Borasio, president of the International Association of Infant Food Manufacturers (IFM) to Jacob von Uexkull, Right Livelihood Award Foundation, 4 November.

Borgholtz, P. A. (1988) 'Economic and business aspects of infant formula promotion: implications for health professionals', in Jelliffe and Jelliffe (eds), quoted in Chetley 1996, p. 13.

Borren, S. (1998) 'Networking in the 21st century', in Women's Feature Service (ed.), pp. 7–8.

BPNI (2000) *Note for the Record on Two Court Cases,* New Delhi: Breastfeeding Promotion Network of India (BPNI), September.

Brabeck-Letmathe, P. (1996) 'Intervention in panel 2: towards a multilateral framework of investment?', in *UNCTAD High Level Meeting – Global Investment Forum*, Geneva, p. 3.

— (1999a) 'Beyond corporate image: the search for trust', in *Address by Peter Brabeck-Letmathe, Nestlé CEO, to the University European Affairs Society*, www.nestle.com/all-about/insight/oxford.html, accessed 13 December 1999.

— (1999b) Covering letter for *Nestlé Implementation of the WHO Code: Official Response of Governments – Report to the Director-General, World Health Organization* and *International (WHO) Action Report*, edition 1, 20 October.

Braithwaite, J. (1984) *Corporate Crime in the Pharmaceutical Industry*, London: Routledge & Kegan Paul.

Braithwaite, J. and P. Drahos (2000) *Global Business Regulation*, Cambridge: Cambridge University Press.

Brick, M. (1999) 'Formula fight: a generic vs. the giants', *New York Times*, 26 September, pp. Bu 1, 12–13.

Bristol-Myers Squibb (1999) 'AIDS background', Bristol-Myers Squibb Website, www.bms.com/public/aidba.html, accessed July 1999.

Brundtland, G. H. (1998a) 'Opening remarks by the Director-General', *Round-table Discussions with the International Association of Infant Food Manufacturers (IFM)*, Annex I to the final summary report, Geneva: WHO, 20 November.

— (1998b) 'Opening remarks by the Director-General', *Round-table Discussions with Consumer and Community-based Nongovernmental Organizations*, Annex I to the final summary report, Geneva: WHO, 19 November.

Bruno, K. (2000) 'Corporations, environmental practices and human rights', in CETIM/AAJ/FICAT (eds), pp. 58–61.

Bryant, J. H. (1980) Letter to Dr Halfdan Mahler from Dr John H. Bryant, deputy assistant secretary for international health, US Department of Health, Education and Welfare, 29 March, quoted in Chetley 1986, p. 77.

Buffle, J.-C. (1986) *Dossier N … Comme Nestlé*, Paris: Ed. Alain Moreau.

Buritt, R. L. and P. E. McCreight (1998) 'Environmental compliance by industry', in R. Chadwick (ed.), pp. 47–57.

Burton, T. M. (1993) 'Spilt milk', *Wall Street Journal*, 25 May.

Buse, K. and G. Walt (2000a) 'Global public–private partnerships for health: Part I – a new development in health?', *Bulletin of the World Health Organization – The International Journal of Public Health*, 78 (4), pp. 549–61.

— (2000b) 'Global public–private partnerships: Part II – what are the health issues for global governance?', *Bulletin of the World Health Organization – The International Journal of Public Health*, 78 (5), pp. 699–709.

Business World (1999) 'OgilvyOne wins grand prize for Nestlé loyalty campaign', *Business World*, 30 September, p. 21.

Byrnes, B. (ed.) (1995) *International Corporate Relations*, in Hart (ed.), pp. 125–40.

Cantor, B. edited by C. Burger (1989) *Experts in Action: Inside Public Relations*, New York and London: Longman.

CAP (1981) *The Other Baby Killer*, Penang: Consumers' Association of Penang (CAP).

Carey, A., edited by A. Lohrey (1995) *Taking the Risk out of democracy*, Sydney: University of New South Wales Press.

Castle, S. (2000) 'Adidas boycotts EU ethics hearing', *The Independent*, 23 November.

Cattaui, M. L. (1999) 'UN code of conduct will turn clock back', letter to the editor, *Financial Times*, 21 July.

CEO (1998) 'The Geneva business dialogue: business, WTO and UN – joining hands to regulate the global economy?' *Corporate Europe Observatory (CEO)*, 2, October: 3–6.

— 'The global compact: The UN's new deal with "global corporate citizens"', *Corporate Europe Observer*, 5, October: 2–8.

CETIM/AAJ/FICAT (2000) *Transnational Corporations and Human Rights: Case Studies and Responsibilities*, information and discussion booklet to the attention of the Working Group on Transnational Corporations of the United Nations Sub-Commission on the Promotion and Protection of Human Rights, Geneva: Centre Europe-Tiers Monde, American Association of Jurists and Fundación FICAT (CETIM/AAJ/FICAT).

CGG (Commission on Global Governance) (1995) *Our Global Neighbourhood: The Report of the Commission on Global Governance*, New York: Oxford University Press.

Chadwick, R. (ed.) (1998) *Encyclopedia of Applied Ethics*, San Diego/London/Boston/New York/Sydney/Tokyo/Toronto: Academic Press.

Chapman, J. (1999) 'The response of civil society to the globalisation of the marketing of breastmilk substitutes in Ghana', *Development*, special issue: *Responses to Globalisation – Rethinking Health and Equity*, 43 (4): 103–7.

Chetley, A. (1979) *The Baby Killer Scandal*, London: War on Want.

— (1986) *The Politics of Baby Foods: Successful Challenges to an International Marketing Strategy*, London: Frances Pinter.

— (1990) *A Healthy Business? World Health and the Pharmaceutical Industry*, London: Zed Books.

CIIR (1993) *Baby Milk: Destruction of a World Resource*, London: Catholic Institute for International Relations (CIIR).

Clark, D. (1998) 'Children's rights, children's health: working towards the highest attainable standard', in *Breastfeeding, Women and Work: Human Rights and Creative Solutions. Report of the WABA International Workshop, Quezon City, Philippines: World Alliance for Breastfeeding Action (WABA) & ARUGAAN, 1–5 June 1998*, Penang: WABA, p. 9.

Clement, D. (1988) 'Commerciogenic malnutrition in the 1980s', in Jelliffe and Jelliffe (eds), pp. 348–59.

Commission on Human Rights (1996) *Report of the Secretary-General on the Impact of the Activities and Working Methods of Transnational Corporations on the Full Enjoyment of All Human Rights, in Particular Economic, Social and*

Cultural Rights and the Right to Development, United Nations Commission on Human Rights, Sub-Commission on Prevention of Discrimination and Protection of Minorities (E/CN.4/Sub.2/1996/12), 2 July.

— (1998) *The Relationship Between the Enjoyment of Economic, Social and Cultural Rights and the Right to Development, and the Working Methods and Activities of Transnational Corporations*, Resolution on the Fiftieth Session of the Sub-Commission on Prevention of Discrimination and Protection of Minorities, Geneva, 3–28 August (E/CN.4/Sub.2/RES/1998/8).

— (1999) 'The realization of economic social and cultural rights: the question of transnational corporations', in *Report of the Sessional Working Group on the Working Methods and Activities of Transnational Corporations on its First Session*, United Nations Commission on Human Rights, Sub-Commission on the Promotion and Protection of Human Rights (E/CN.4/Sub.2/1999/9), 12 August.

— (2000a) 'The realization of economic social and cultural rights: the question of transnational corporations', in *Report of the Sessional Working Group on the Working Methods and Activities of Transnational Corporations on its Second Session*, United Nations Commission on Human Rights, Sub-Commission on the Promotion and Protection of Human Rights (E/CN.4/Sub.2/2000/12), 28 August.

— (2000b) *The Realization of Economic Social and Cultural Rights: The Question of Transnational Corporations*, joint written statement by the Centre Europe-Tiers Monde, the American Association of Jurists and Pax Romana, submitted to the UN Commission on Human Rights, Sub-Commission on the Promotion and Protection of Human Rights (E/CN/4./Sub.2/2000/NGO/17), 2 August.

Cooney, W. (1998) 'Rights theory', in Chadwick (ed.), pp. 875–84.

Costello, A. and H. S. Sachdev (1998) 'Protecting breast feeding from breast milk substitutes: the WHO code is widely violated and needs monitoring and supporting', *British Medical Journal*, 316 (11 April): 1103–4.

Coutsoudis, A., K. Pillay, E. Spooner et al.(1999) 'Influence of infant-feeding patterns on early mother-and-child transmission of HIV 1 in Durban, South Africa. A prospective cohort', *The Lancet*, 354: 471–6.

Cowe, R. (1999) 'Nestlé hits back at critics of GM food', *Guardian*, 7 May, p. 27.

Dee, R. (ed.) (1981) *Proceedings of the International Federation of Pharmaceuticals Manufacturers' Associations (IFPMA), 10th Assembly*, quoted in Muller 1982, p. 179 and Chetley 1986, p. 84.

Del Ponte, K. G. (1982) 'Formulating customary international law: an examination of the WHO International Code of Marketing of Breast-milk Substitutes', *Boston College International & Comparative Law Review*, V 2: 377–403.

Dell, S. (1986) 'The United Nations Code of Conduct on Transnational Corporations', in J. Kaufmann (ed.), *Effective Negotiation: Case Studies in Conference Diplomacy*, Dordrecht: UNITAR and Martinus Nijhoff Publishers, pp. 53–74.

Donson, F. (2000) *Legal Intimidation*, London: Free Association Books.

Elliot, S. (1997) 'Advertising: healthy economy shows up in a vital sign: ad spending', *New York Times*, 18 June, p. D4, quoted in Korten 1998, p. 33.

ENN (1999) *Report of the Ad Hoc Group on Infant Feeding in Emergency*, Dublin: Emergency Nutrition Network (ENN).

European Court (1995) *Commission v. Hellenic Republic, case C-391/92 [1995] ECR1 – 1621.*

European Parliament (1999) *Report on EU Standards for European Enterprises Operating in Developing Countries: Towards a European Code of Conduct*, Brussels: European Parliament (EP), Committee on Development and Cooperation, 15 January.

Ewen, S. (1996) *PR! A Social History of Spin*, New York: Basic Books.

Fannin, R. A. (1997) 'IAA fights revived infant-formula threat: WHA proposes stricter role on marketing breast-milk substitutes', *Advertising Age*, 24 November: 40.

Ferriman, A. (2000) 'WHO accused of stifling debate about infant feeding', *British Medical Journal*, 7246 (320), 20 May: 1362.

Fookes, G. A. (1980) Letter to Dr Petros-Barvazian, director, Family Health Division, WHO, 22 January, quoted in Shubber 1998, pp. 18, 19.

Foster, J. W. (1999) 'An environment that enables: civil society, global governance and the struggle for a sustainable just economy', in Foster and Anand (eds), pp. 461–96.

Foster, J. W. and A. Anand (eds) (1999) *Whose World is It Anyway? Civil Society, the United Nations and the Multilateral Future*, Ottawa: United Nations Association in Canada.

Fowler, A. (2000) *Civil Society, NGDOs and Social Development: Changing the Rules of the Game*, Geneva: United Nations Research Institute for Social Development (UNRISD).

Freedman, A. M. and S. Stecklow (2000) 'Wyeth, Nestlé offer free tins to stem spread of AIDS – children's agency balks', *Wall Street Journal*, 5 December.

Friedman, M. (1999) *Consumer Boycotts: Effecting Change Through the Market Place*, New York: Routledge.

Garner, B. A. (ed.) (1999) *Black's Law Dictionary*, St. Paul, MN: West Group.

Gasche, U. (1975) *The Strategies of the Multinationals Against Their Critics: Report on a Symposium*, Zurich: Erklärung von Bern, quoted in Chetley 1986, p. 46; Chetley 1990, p. 73; Richter 1991, pp. 24–5.

George, S. and F. Sabelli (1994) *Faith & Credit: The World Bank's Secular Empire*, Boulder, CO and San Francisco: Westview Press.

Ghauri, A. (2000) 'Going against the formula', *Dialogue – The News on Sunday*, 12 March, p. 27.

Giddens, A. (1990) *The Consequences of Modernity*, Stanford, CA: Stanford University Press.

— (2000) *The Third Way and Its Critics*, Cambridge: Polity Press.

Gleckman, H. and R. Krut (1994) *The Social Benefits of Regulating International Business*, Geneva: UNRISD.

Grant, J. (1982) Letter from James Grant, executive director of UNICEF, to Rafael Pagan Jr. of Nestlé, 10 May, quoted in Chetley 1986, pp. 118–19.

Gravet, H. (1989) Former director with an international marketing firm in Southeast Asia, in a radio interview with Andrew Olle on ABC's 2BL programme *Australia*, quoted in Allain 1991, p. 5.

Greer, J. and Bruno, K. (1996) *Greenwash: The Reality behind Corporate Environmentalism*, Penang: Third World Network.

Gupta, A. (1999) 'Nestlé in India', in *Hungry for Power: The Impact of TNCs on Food Security*, London: UK Food Group.

HAI (2001) 'Public–private "partnerships": addressing public health needs or corporate agendas?', seminar report, Amsterdam: Health Action International (HAI-Europe), www.haiweb.org/campaign/PPI/seminar200011.doc.

Hanks, J. (1999) 'Promoting corporate environmental responsibility: what role for "self-regulatory" and "co-regulatory" instruments?', mimeo, Geneva: UNRISD.

Hann, C. (1996) 'Political society and civil anthropology', in C. Hann and E. Dunn (eds),*Civil Society: Challenging Western Models*, London: Routledge, pp. 1–26.

Hansen, M. (1999) 'Environmental regulation of transnational corporations: needs and prospects', mimeo, Geneva: UNRISD.

Harman, C. (2001) 'Nestlé in the developing world: a formula for trouble?', *Just-food.com Business Knowledge Providers*, 5 February, www.just-food.com/features_print.asp?art=367, accessed 19 February 2001.

Harrod, J. (1988) 'United Nations specialized agencies: from functionalist intervention to international co-operation?', in J. Harrod and N. Schrijver (eds), *The UN under attack*, Aldershot/Brookfield USA/Hong Kong/Singapore/Sydney: Gower Publishing, pp. 130–44.

Hart, N. (ed.) (1995) *Strategic Public Relations*, Basingstoke and London: Macmillan.

Held, D. (1998) 'Democracy and globalisation', in Archibugi et al. (eds), pp. 11–27.

Hildyard, N. (1998) 'The myth of the minimalist state: free market ambiguitites', The Cornerhouse, Briefing Paper 5, March.

Hoogvelt, A. with G. A. Puxty (1987) *Multinational Enterprise: An Encyclopedic Dictionary of Concepts and Terms*, London and Basingstoke: Macmillan.

IBFAN (1996) *Crucial Aspects of Infant Feeding in Emergency and Relief Situations*, Geneva: IBFAN Regional Coordination Office for Europe.

— (1998a) *Breaking the Rules, Stretching the Rules 1998: A Worldwide Report on Violations of the WHO/UNICEF International Code of Marketing of Breastmilk Substitutes*, Penang, Malaysia: International Baby Food Action Network/International Code Documentation Centre (IBFAN/ICDC).

— (1998b) 'Governments under pressure to abandon WHO marketing code', *Third World Resurgence*, 95: 6–7.

— (1999a) *Comments on WHO Guidelines on Interactions with Commercial Enterprises*, www.haiweb.org/news/ibfancomments.html, accessed October 1999.

— (1999b) 'IBFAN INFO', *International Baby Food Action Network Newsletter*, 1 (1), January.

— (1999c) 'IBFAN INFO', *International Baby Food Action Network Newsletter* 1 (2), September.

— (1999d) 'Nestlé boycott news: what is the problem?', *IBFAN INFO*, January, p. 7.

IBFAN/GIFA (2000) *Nestlé Implementation of the WHO Code: Does the Nestlé Report Comply with the International Code? – A Legal Evaluation of the Nestlé Report by a Consultant for the International Baby Food Action Network (IBFAN) and the Geneva Infant Feeding Association (GIFA)*, Geneva: IBFAN/GIFA.

IBFAN/ICDC (1998) *State of the Code by Country: A Survey of Measures Taken by Governments to Implement the Provisions of the International Code of Marketing of Breast-milk Substitutes*, Penang, Malaysia: IBFAN/ICDC (International Code Documentation Centre).

ICCR (1982) 'Confronting the US formula giants', *The Corporate Examiner*, 11 (7–8), New York: Interfaith Center on Corporate Responsibility (ICCR), Infant Formula Program.

ICIFI (1975, amended 1976) *Code of Ethics and Professional Standards for Advertising Product Information and Advisory Services for Breast-milk Substitutes*, Zurich: International Council of Infant Food Industries (ICFI).

IDFA (1998) 'IBFAN report is misconceived and biased says baby food industry', press release, 19 March, London: Infant and Dietetic Foods Association, a member of the Food and Drink Federation.

IFM (1998) *Statement by the Representative of the International Association of Infant Food Manufacturers, Member Association of the International Special Dietary Food Industries, a Nongovernmental Association in Official Relations with WHO [to the 1998 World Health Assembly]*, Geneva: International Association of Infant Food Manufacturers (IFM).

— (1999) *IFM support for the International Code of Marketing of Breast-milk Substitutes*, IFM, Paris, www.ifm.net/commitboklet10.html, accessed 12 July 1999.

IGBM (1997a) 'Cracking the Code: Agencies suspend discussions with infant formula manufacturers', press release, London: Interagency Group on Breastfeeding Monitoring (IGBM).

— (1997b) *Cracking the Code: Monitoring the International Code of Marketing of Breast-milk Substitutes*, London: IGBM.

INBC (1996) 'Nestlé shareholders disregard infant health in the Philippines', press release, Cambridge: International Nestlé Boycott Committee (INBC).

IOMS (1986) *World Health Organization: Heritage Foundation Report on the Politicization of WHO*, New York: International Organization of Monitoring Services (IOMS), quoted in Kanji 1992, p. 60.

IPRA (1968) *The International Code of Ethics*, adopted in Athens on 12 May 1965, modified in Tehran on 17 April 1968: International Public Relations Association (IPRA).

Jackson, J. (1998) 'Business ethics: overview', in Chadwick (ed.), pp. 397–411.

Jelliffe, D. (1971) 'Commerciogenic malnutrition?', *Food Technology*, 55: 55, quoted in Chetley 1986: 40.

Jelliffe, D. B. and E. F. P. Jelliffe (eds) (1988) *Programmes to Promote Breastfeeding*, Oxford: Oxford Medical Publications.

Jowett, G. S. and V. O'Donnell (1986) *Propaganda and Persuasion*, Newbury Park, CA: Sage Publications.

Kanji, N., A. Hardon, J. W. Harnmeijer, M. Mamdani and G. Walt (1992) *Drugs Policy in Developing Countries*, London: Zed Books.

Karl, M. (1998) 'Introduction', in Women's Feature Service (ed.), pp. 17–26.

Kennedy, E. M. (1978) Letter to Halfdan Mahler, director-general, WHO, 20 July, quoted in Shubber 1998, p. 6.

Klein, N. (1999) *No Logo: Taking Aim at the Brand Bullies*, New York: Picador USA.

Kline, J. M. (2000) 'Business codes and conduct in a global political economy', in Williams (ed.), pp. 39–56.

Knight, B. and C. Hartnell (2000) 'Civil society: is it anything more than a metaphor for hope for a better world?', *Alliance*, 5: 16–18.

Koenig, P. (1999) 'Mr Nestlé gets angry: the Swiss giant's boss chose a low-profile press conference for an unscripted attack on food campaigners', *Independent on Sunday*, 9 May.

Koivusalo, M. (1999) *World Trade Organisation and Trade-Creep in Health and Social Policies*, Helsinki and Sheffield: Globalisation and Social Policy Programme (GASPP) based at STAKES (National Research and Development Centre for Welfare and Health), Helsinki and the University of Sheffield.

Korten, D. C. (1995) *When Corporations Rule the World*, West Hartford, CT: Kumarian Press.

— (1998) *The Post-corporate World: Life after Capitalism*, San Francisco and West Hartford, CT: Berrett-Koehler Publishers and Kumarian Press.

Krasovec, K. (2000) 'Why is WHO stifling debate on infant feeding?', electronic letter to the editor, *British Medical Journal*, 12 August.

Krause, A. (1981) 'World Health Agency to weigh code on baby food', *International Herald Tribune*, 4 May, quoted in Chetley 1986, p. 94.

Kristol, I. (1977) 'On corporate philanthropy', *Wall Street Journal*, 21 March.

Krut, R. (1997) *Globalization and Civil Society: NGO Influence in International Decision Making*, Geneva: United Nations Research Institute for Social Development (UNRISD).

Krut, R. and H. Gleckman (1998) *ISO 14001: A Missed Opportunity for Sustainable Global Industrial Development*, London: Earthscan.

Kumar, K. (1994) 'Civil society again: a reply to Christopher Bryant's "Social self-organisation, civility and sociology"', *British Journal of Sociology*, 45 (1): 127–31.

Kunczik, M. (1990) *Die manipulierte Meinung: nationale Image-Politik und internationale Public Relations*, Cologne and Vienna: Böhlau Verlag.

Kuttner, R. (1999) *Everything for Sale: The Virtues and Limits of Markets*, Chicago: University of Chicago Press.

Lach, D. (1996) 'Introduction: environmental conflict', *Sociological Perspectives*, 39 (2): 211–17.

Lancet, The (1982) 'Response by Nestlé to the WHO Code on Breast-milk Substitutes', *The Lancet*, 22 May: 197, quoted in Chetley 1986, p. 118.

Laswell, H. D. (1930–35) 'Propaganda', in *Encyclopedia of Social Sciences*, New York: Macmillan, quoted in Carey 1995, p. 81.

Lee, K. (1998) *Globalisation and Health Policy: A Review of the Literature and Proposed Research and Policy Agenda*, London: London School of Hygiene and Tropical Medicine.

Lefever, E. W. (1981) 'Politics and baby formula in the Third World', *Wall Street Journal*, 14 January, quoted in Chetley 1986, pp. 89, 99.

Lehners, M. (1998) 'World trade agreements and their impact on breastfeeding', in *Codex Discussion Paper: Standard and Lobby*, Amsterdam: WEMOS, pp. 26–34.

Lemaresquier, T. (1980) 'Beyond infant feeding: the case for another relationship between NGOs and the United Nations system', *Development Dialogue*, p. 120, quoted in Chetley 1986, p. 64.

Lewis, S. (1999) 'Malnutrition as a human rights violation: implications for United Nations-supported programmes', keynote speech at the Administrative Committee on Coordination/Subcommittee on Nutrition (ACC/SCN) symposium on 'The Substance and Politics of Human Rights: Approach to Food and Nutrition Policies and Programmes', 12–13 April.

Linnecar, A. (1997) 'The International Baby Food Action Network: defending every child's birthright', *International Journal of Children's Rights*, 5: 473–98.

Lohmann, L. (1990) 'Whose common future?', *The Ecologist*, 20 (3): 82–4.

McComas, M., G. Fookes and G. Taucher (1983) *The Dilemma of Third World Nutrition: Nestlé and the Role of Infant Formula*, Vevey: Nestlé SA, quoted in Chetley 1986, p. 62.

Maak, T. (1998) 'Globalisierung und die Suche nach einer lebensdienlichen Weltökonomie', in Maak, T. and Y. Lunau (eds), *Weltwirtschaftsethik: Globalisierung auf dem Prüfstand der Lebensdienlichkeit. St. Galler Beiträge zur Wirtschaftsethik*, Vol. 20, Bern/Stuttgart/Vienna: Verlag Paul Haupt, pp. 19–44.

Margen, S., V. Melnick, L. Neuhauser and E. Rios Espinosa (1981) *Infant Feeding in Mexico: A Study of Health Facility and Mothers' Practices in Three Regions*, Washington, DC: Nestlé Infant Formula Audit Commission (NIFAC).

Margulies, L. (1997) 'The International Code of Marketing of Breast-milk Substitutes: a model for assuring children's rights under the law', *International Journal of Children's Rights*, 5: 419–38.

Marketing Week (1999) 'Nestlé launches PR offensive over baby milk', *Marketing Week*, 2 December, p. 7.

Marshall, G. (ed.) (1998) *A Dictionary of Sociology*, Oxford: Oxford University Press.

Maucher (1997) 'Ruling by consent: Nestlé chairman, Helmut O. Maucher, urges governments to work with business to establish the framework for the global economy', Guest editorial, *Financial Times*, 11 December, p. 1.

Meintjes, G. (2000) 'An international human rights perspective on corporate codes', in Williams (ed.), pp. 83–99.

Micheletti, M. (2000) 'Shopping and the reinvention of democracy: green consumerism and the accumulation of social capital in Sweden', paper presented at the ECPR joint sessions 2000 workshop 'Voluntary Associations, Social Capital and Interest Mediation: Forging the Link', Copenhagen, Denmark, 14–19 April.

Mintz, M. (1981) 'Baby formula producers challenge UN agencies', *Washington Post*, 18 March, quoted in Shubber 1998, p. 39.

Mintzes, B. (1998) *Blurring the Boundaries: New Trends in Drug Promotion*, Amsterdam: Health Action International (HAI-Europe).

Montgomery, J. (1978) 'The image makers', *Wall Street Journal*, 1 August, quoted in O.W. Baskin and C. E. Aronoff (1988), *Public Relations: The Profession and the Practice*, 2nd edn, Dubuque, IA: Wm. C. Brown Publishers, p. 85.

Morley, M. (1998) *How to Manage Your Global Reputation: A Guide to the Dynamics of International Public Relations*, London: Macmillan.

Mueller, C. (1973) *The Politics of Communication: A Study in the Political Sociology of Language, Socialization, and Legitimation*, New York: Oxford University Press.

Müller, H. R. (ed.) (1975) Statement on BBC TV Programme *Panorama*, 1 December, quoted in Chetley 1986, p. 39.

Muller, M. (1974) *The Baby Killer*, London: War on Want.

Murphy, D. F. and J. Bendell (1999) 'Partners in time? Business, NGOs and sustainable development', UNRISD Discussion Paper DP 109, Geneva: UNRISD.

Nabarro, D. (2000) 'World Health Organization's response', letter to the editor, *British Medical Journal*, 321 (7266), 14 October: 956.

Narveson, J. (1998) 'Consumer rights', in Chadwick (ed.), pp. 623–9.

Naylor, A. (2000) 'Inconsistencies need to be resolved', letter to the editor, *British Medical Journal*, 321 (7266), 14 October: 956.

Nederveen Pieterse, J. (1994) 'Globalisation as hybridisation', *International Sociology*, 9 (2): 161–84.

Nelson, Jane (1996) *Business as Partners in Development: Creating Wealth for Countries, Companies and Communities*, London: Prince of Wales Business Leaders Forum in collaboration with the World Bank and the United Nations Development Programme.

Nelson, Joyce (1993) 'The great global greenwash', *Covert Action Quarterly*, 4: 26–58.

Nestlé (1971) 'Nestlé '71', *Bulletin Nestlé*, 3, Nestlé, Thailand, quoted in Palmer 1993, p. 221.

— (1977) *Infant Formula in Developing Countries: A Perspective*, reprinted in US Senate 1978, pp. 872–3, quoted in Chetley 1986, p. 53.

— (1982) 'Nestlé completes WHO code implementation process', press release, 16 March, quoted in Chetley 1986, p. 117.

— (1992) 'Infant feeding controversy', enclosure to *NMN*, 36, April.

— (1994) *Nestlé and Baby Milk*, Croydon, Surrey: Nestlé UK Ltd.

— (1996) *Nestlé Charter: Nestlé Infant Policy in Developing Countries*, Croydon, Surrey: Nestlé UK Ltd.

— (1998) *Nestlé: Complying with the WHO Code*, Vevey, Switzerland: Nestlé SA.

— (1999a) *Brand Guide/Baby food & Cereals: Growing Worldwide Demand*, www. nestle.com/brands/html/b1.html, accessed 12 July 1999.

— (1999b) 'Nestlé implementation of the WHO Code (International Code of Marketing of Breast-milk Substitutes): official responses of governments', Report to the Director-General, World Health Organization, July.

— (1999c) 'Nestlé initiates new Code monitoring process: 54 countries to date confirm compliance', *Nestlé International (WHO) Code Action Report*, 1, October: 1, 5.

— (1999d) 'Nestlé, monitoring and the WHO Code' *Nestlé International (WHO) Code Action Report*, 1, October: 6.

— (2000) 'Letter from Niels Christiansen, Nestlé Public Affairs to Mike Brady, Baby Milk Action', *International (WHO) Code Action Report*, 3, January: 3–4.

Newman, W. (1995) 'Community relations', in Hart (ed.), pp. 95–105.

NGLS (1997) 'Working with civil society: issues and challenges', informal background note, Geneva: UN Non-Governmental Liaison Service (NGLS).

Nickel, H. (1980) 'The corporation haters', *Fortune*, 16 June, pp. 126–36, quoted in Chetley 1986, pp. 55–6, 60, fn. 40.

OECD (2000a) *The OECD Guidelines for Multinational Enterprises*, Paris: Organization for Economic Co-operation and Development (OECD), www.oecd. org/daf/investment/guidelines, accessed 19 December 2000.

— (2000b) *Regulatory Reform: What is Regulation?*, Paris: OECD, www.oecd.org, accessed 19 December 2000.

OHCHR (2000a) *Business and Human Rights: A Progress Report*, Geneva: Office of the United Nations High Commissioner for Human Rights (OHCHR).

— (2000b) *Business and Human Rights: An Update. Prepared by the OHCHR for the Global Compact Meeting, 26 July 2000*, New York/Geneva: Office of the United Nations High Commissioner for Human Rights.

PAG (1973) 'Promotion of special foods (infant formula and processed protein foods) for vulnerable groups', Protein-Calorie Advisory Group of the United Nations (PAG), PAG Statement No. 23, 18 July 1972 (revised 28 November 1973), quoted in Chetley 1986, p. 41.

Pagan Jr., R. D. (1982) 'Carrying the fight to the critics of multinational capitalism: think and act politically – speech delivered to the Public Affairs Council, New York, 22 April 1982', *Vital Speeches of the Day*, 48 (19).

— (1985) 'The challenge to multinational marketing: a public relations response', in E. Denig and A. van der Meiden (eds), *A Geography of Public Relations Trends: Selected Proceedings of the 10th Public Relations World Congress: 'Between People and Power'*, Amsterdam and Dordrecht: Martinus Nijhoff Publishers, pp. 373–9.

PAHO (1970) 'Guidelines on young child feeding in contemporary Caribbean', Pan American Health Organization (PAHO) Scientific Publication, quoted in Margulies 1997, p. 425.

Pallister, M. (2000) 'David takes on a multinational Goliath over safety of infant milk. Marian Pallister reports about fresh allegations of impropriety by baby food manufacturers', *The Herald*, 16 February.

Palmer, G. (1993) *The Politics of Breastfeeding*, London: Pandora Press.

Patel, S. J. (ed.) (1983) *Pharmaceuticals and Health in the Third World*, Oxford: Pergamon Press.

Peretz, M. (1981) Statement by Michael Peretz, executive vice-president of the International Pharmaceutical Manufacturers' Association (IFPMA), quoted in Muller 1982, p. 112 and Chetley 1990, p. 70.

Pfaff, C. (1981) 'New threats to multinationals', *Advertising Age – Europe*, December: 16, quoted in Chetley 1986, p. 146.

Post, J. E. and E. Baer (1980) 'The International Code of Marketing of Breast-milk Substitutes: consensus, compromise and conflict in the infant formula controversy', *International Commission of Jurists' Review*, December: 52–61.

Prague 1 Trade Department (1999) Letter to Anima/Documentation Center for Breastfeeding Promotion. Doc. number ZIO/K/1888/99St, 24 November.

Pretoria News (1997) 'Breast not always the best', *Pretoria News*, August.

Printer's Ink (1958) 'Powdered milk to African tribesmen: Borden's world-wide marketing mission', *Printer's Ink*, 13 June, pp. 71–2, quoted in Clement 1988, p. 350.

Pritchard, J. (1998) 'Codes of ethics', in Chadwick (ed.), pp. 527–33.

PRNewswire (1998) 'TV news feature bring medical hope to American viewers: Johns Hopkins Hospital supports programme with research and expertise', *PRNewswire*, 28 September.

Rabobank International (1998) *Research Report on Numico by Analyst Iain Wilson*, Amsterdam: Rabobank International, Food, Beverages & Consumer Products Team, 15 September.

Randell, A. (1995) 'Codex Alimentarius: how it all began', *Food, Nutrition and Agriculture*, 13 (14): 35–40.

Reich, M. (1991) *Toxic Politics: Responding to Chemical Disasters*, Ithaca, NY: Cornell University Press.

Richards, D. (2001) *Seeing through the Spin: Public Relations in the Globalised*

Economy – An Education Pack for Teachers and Facilitators, Cambridge: Baby Milk Action.

Richter, J. (1991) 'Public relations, politics and public pressure: recovering the history of corporate propaganda', MA dissertation, The Hague: Institute of Social Studies (ISS).

— (1998) 'Engineering of consent: uncovering corporate PR', Corner-House Briefing Paper No. 6, March.

— (2000) 'A question of standards?', letter to the editor, *British Medical Journal*, 321 (7266), 14 October: 956.

Right Livelihood Award (1998) 'Prizes for peace building, health and putting people before profit', press release, Stockholm, Right Livelihood Award, 7 October.

Robins, K., F. Webster and M. Pickering (1987) 'Propaganda, information and social control', in J. Hawthorn (ed.) *Propaganda, Persuasion, and Polemic*, London: Edward Arnold, pp. 1–18.

Rosenau, J. N. (1998) 'Governance and democracy in a globalizing world', in Archibugi et al. (eds), pp. 28–57.

Rowell, A. (1996) *Green Backlash: Global Subversion of the Environmental Movement*, London: Routledge.

— (1998) 'SLAPPing resistance', *The Ecologist*, 28 (5), September/October: 302–3.

Rundall, P. and N.-J. Peck (2000) 'Compliance to the Code is difficult to judge', letter to the editor, *British Medical Journal*, 321 (7266), 14 October: 960.

SAFEP (1975) 'Does Nestlé kill babies?', mimeo, Swiss Information Groups for Development Policy (SAFEP).

— (1976) 'Nestlé case will not continue: but dispute goes on', Information for the Press No. 5, mimeo, Swiss Information Groups for Development Policy (SAFEP), December 1976, quoted in Chetley 1986, p. 45.

Samuel, J. (1999) 'Civil society and other plastic phrases', *Humanscape*, October.

Saunders, E. W. (1980a) Letter from Ernest Saunders, president, the International Council of Infant Food Industries (ICIFI), to Dr David Tejada, assistant director-general, WHO, 20 March, Zurich, quoted in Shubber 1998, p. 13.

— (1980b) Internal memo to Nestlé's managing director Arthur Furer in August 1980, reproduced with annotations as *Nestlégate: Secret Memo Reveals Corporate Cover-up* (1981), Cambridge: Baby Milk Action Coalition.

— (1981) Letter from Ernest Saunders, president, the International Council of Infant Food Industries (ICIFI), to the members of the WHO Executive Board, 13 January, quoted in Chetley 1986, p. 90 and Shubber 1998, p. 35.

Schlesinger, S. and S. Kinzer (1982) *Bitter Fruit: The Untold Story of the American Coup in Guatemala*, Garden City/New York: Doubleday.

Scholte, J. A. (1999) 'Global civil society: changing the world?', CSGR working paper no. 31/99, University of Warwick, Coventry, UK, May.

Sedgwick (1985) 'Sponsorship – the 4th arm of marketing', in E. Denig and

A. van der Meiden (eds), *A Geography of Public Relations Trends: Selected Proceedings of the 10th Public Relations World Congress – 'Between People and Power'*, Amsterdam: Martinus Nijhoff Publishers, 3–7 June, pp. 396–8.

Seligman, A. (1992) *The Idea of Civil Society*, New York: The Free Press.

Selvaggio, K. (1983) 'WHO bottles up alcohol study on world liquor industry: why did the WHO suddenly drop plans to publish study of world liquor industry – alcohol beverages – dimensions of corporate power', *Multinational Monitor*, 9, quoted in Harrod 1988, p. 139.

Sentry Insurance Co. (1977) *Consumerism at Crossroads: A National Opinion Survey Conducted for Sentry by Louis Harris & Associates, Inc. and Marketing Science Institute*, quoted in Friedman 1999, p. 3.

Sethi, S. P. (1987) *Handbook of Advocacy Advertising: Strategies and Applications*, Cambridge, MA: Ballinger.

— (1994) *Multinational Corporations and the Impact of Public Advocacy on Corporate Strategy: Nestlé and the Infant Formula Controversy*, Boston/Dordrecht/London: Kluwer Academic Publishers.

Shubber, S. (1998) *The International Code of Marketing of Breast-milk Substitutes: An International Measure to Protect and Promote Breast-feeding*, The Hague/London/Boston: Kluwer Law International.

SID/WHO/ISS (2000) *Report on the International Seminar on 'Global Public–Private Partnerships for Health and Equity'*, Rome: Society for International Development (SID), World Health Organization (WHO) and Istituto Superiore di Sanità (ISS) (National Health Council).

Silverman, M. (1976) *The Drugging of the Americas*, Berkeley: University of California Press.

Skogly, S. I. (1996) 'Legal aspects of the protection, promotion, and support of breastfeeding', paper presented at an Informal Expert Group Discussion on the Legal Aspects of the Protection of Breastfeeding, Pawling, New York, 21–26 April.

Smith, C. N. (1990) *Morality and the Market: Consumer Pressure for Corporate Accountability*, London: Routledge.

Sokol, E. (1997) *The Code Handbook: A Guide to Implementing the International Code of Marketing of Breast-milk Substitutes*, Penang: International Code Documentation Centre/International Baby Food Action Network.

— (2000) 'Changes to paper served to stifle debate', letter to the editor, *British Medical Journal*, 321, 14 October: 956.

— (2001) 'Strengthening implementation of the International Code of Marketing of Breast-milk Substitutes', background theme paper, Technical Consultation on Infant and Young Child Feeding, 13–17 March 2000, Geneva: WHO, WHO/NHD/00.9 and WHO/FCH/CAH/00.23.

Sokol, E. and A. Allain (1998) *Complying with the Code? A Manufacturers' and Distributors' Guide to the Code*, Penang, Malaysia: IBFAN in collaboration with Stichting ICDC, The Hague, the Netherlands.

Spröte, W. (1993) 'Negotiations on a United Nations Code of Conduct on Transnational Corporations', *Multinational Business Quarterly*, 4: 331–48.

Stauber, J. and S. Rampton (1995) *Toxic Sludge is Good for You: Lies, Damn Lies and the Public Relations Industry*, Monroe, ME: Common Courage Press.

Stiglitz, J. E. (1998) *More Instruments and Broader Goals: Moving Towards the Post-Washington Consensus*, Helsinki, Finland: United Nations University/World Institute for Development Economics Research (UNU/WIDER).

Taylor, A. (1998) 'Violations of the International Code of Marketing of Breast-milk Substitutes: prevalence in four countries', *British Medical Journal*, 316, 11 April: 1117–22.

TheNetwork (1998) *Feeding Fiasco: Pushing Commercial Infant Foods in Pakistan*, Islamabad: TheNetwork – Association for Rational Use of Medication in Pakistan.

— (1999) *Milking Profits: How Nestlé Puts Sales Ahead of Infant Health*, Islamabad: TheNetwork – Association for Rational Use of Medication in Pakistan.

TRAC (1999) *A Perilous Partnership: The United Nations Development Programme's Flirtation with Corporate Collaboration*, San Francisco: Transnational Resource & Action Centre (TRAC) in collaboration with the Institute of Policy Studies and the Council on International and Public Affairs.

— (2000) *Tangled up in Blue: Corporate Partnerships in the United Nations – Report Written by Kenny Bruno and Joshua Karliner*, San Francisco: Transnational Resource & Action Centre (TRAC).

Transnationals (1992) 'No consensus on code of conduct: fresh approach for global standards for foreign direct investment recommended', *Transnationals*, 4 (3), October: 1–2, 7.

Türmen, T. (1998a) 'Introductory statement by the executive director, family and reproductive health, in Committee A [of the World Health Assembly]', *Provisional Agenda Item 20, Part IX, Infant and Young Child Nutrition*, Geneva: WHO.

— (1998b) *Presentation by the Executive Director, Family and Reproductive Health to the WHO Executive Board 1998*, Geneva: WHO.

— (1999) 'Making globalisation work for better health', *Development. Special issue: Responses to Globalisation – Rethinking Health and Equity*, 43 (4): 8–11.

UN (1995) *Report of the Seminar on the Involvement of Civil Society in the Follow-up to the Social Summit*, United Nations, Mohonk Mountain House, New York, 22–23 June 1995, 12 July.

— (1998) *Basic Facts about the United Nations*, New York: United Nations, Department of Public Information.

— (1999a) *A Compact for the New Century*, www.un.org/partners/business/davos.htm, accessed 17 January 2001.

— (1999b) 'Secretary-General proposes global compact on human rights, labour, environment, in address to World Economic Forum in Davos', press release SG/SM/6881/Rev1. www.un/org/partners/business/davos.htm, accessed 17 January 2001.

UN/ICC (1999) *Business Leaders Advocate a Stronger United Nations and Take up Challenge of Secretary-General's Global Compact*, www.un.org/business/partners/iccun1.htm.

UNCTAD (1996a) *International Investment Instruments: A Compendium*, Vol. I: *Multilateral Instruments*, New York and Geneva: United Nations Conference on Trade and Development (UNCTAD).

— (1996b) *Self-regulation of Environmental Management: An Analysis of Guidelines Set by World Industry Associations for Their Member Firms*, New York/Geneva: UNCTAD.

— (1999) *World Investment Report 1999: Foreign Direct Investment and the Challenge of Development*, New York/Geneva: UNCTAD.

UNDP (1998) *UNDP Today: Promoting Good Governance*, New York: United Nations Development Programme (UNDP).

— (1999) *Human Development Report 1999: Globalization with a Human Face*, Oxford/New York: Oxford University Press.

— (2000) *Human Development Report 2000: Human Rights and Human Development*, Oxford/New York: Oxford University Press.

UNICEF (1983) *Memo to Field Staff*, United Nations Children's Fund (UNICEF), New York, 7 February, quoted in Chetley 1986, p. 137.

— (1989) *Convention on the Rights of the Child*, New York: UNICEF

— (1997a) *Progress Report: Baby-Friendly Hospital Initiative*, New York: UNICEF.

— (1997b) *UNICEF Responds to Report on Violations of Breast-milk Substitute Code*, UNICEF, Communication Section, New York, 14 January.

— (1998) *Implementation of the International Code of Marketing of Breast-milk Substitutes in CEE countries*, Care Workshop, Prague, 16–20 February 1998.

— (2000) 'Tally of BFHI progress', *Update*, New York: UNICEF Nutrition Section, 1 December.

UNRISD (1995) *States of Disarray: The Social Effects of Globalization – An UNRISD Report for the World Summit for Social Development*, Geneva: United Nations Research Institute for Social Development (UNRISD).

— (1997) *Report of the UNRISD International Conference on Globalization and Citizenship*, Geneva, 9–11 December 1996, Geneva: UNRISD.

— (2000a) 'Calling corporations to account', in *Visible Hands: Taking Responsibility for Social Development – An UNRISD Report for Geneva 2000*, Geneva: UNRISD, pp. 75–90.

— (2000b) *Visible Hands: Taking Responsibility for Social Development – An UNRISD Report for Geneva 2000*, Geneva: UNRISD.

US Senate (1978) 'Marketing and promotion of infant formula in the developing countries', report of the US Senate Health and Scientific Research Sub-Committee, Washington, DC: US Government Printing Office.

Utting, P. (2000) *Business Responsibility for Sustainable Development*, Geneva: UNRISD.

van Drimmelen, R. (1998) *Faith in a Global Economy: A Primer for Christians*, Geneva: World Council of Churches.

Vander Stichele, M. and P. Pennartz (1996) *Making It Our Business – European NGO Campaigns on Transnational Corporations*, London: Catholic Institute for International Relations (CIIR).

VNFKD (1998) 'Compliance with the WHO Code', Letter from K. A. de Jong, chair of VNFKD to the Dutch press, The Hague: Vereniging van Nederlandse Fabrikanten van Kinderen- en Dieetvoedingmiddelen (Dutch Baby Food and Dietary Manufacturers' Association), 11 February (trans. Annelies Allain).

von Wartburg, W. P. (1997) 'Umgang mit öffentlicher Kritik: Von der Abwehr zur produktiven Verarbeitung', *Neue Zürcher Zeitung*, 5/6 June, p. 17.

Wall Street Journal (2000) 'Formula for disaster', editorial, *Wall Street Journal*, European edition, 6 December.

War on Want (1975) 'War on Want press statement', reported by BBC programme *Panorama*, 1 December, quoted in Chetley 1986: 49.

— (1980) Internal memo, quoted in Chetley 1986, p. 84.

WEDO (1995) *Transnational Corporations at the UN: Using or Abusing Their Access?*, New York: Women's Environment and Development Organization (WEDO).

Weissbrodt, D. (2000) *Proposed Draft Human Rights Code of Conduct for Companies*, working paper prepared for the Commission on Human Rights, Sub-Commission on the Protection and Promotion of Human Rights, 52nd Session, Item 4 of the Provisional Agenda, Working Group on the Methods and Activities of Transnational Corporations, 18 May.

Wells, C. (1998) 'Corporate responsibility', in Chadwick (ed.), pp. 653–60.

WEMOS (1997a) *The Codex Alimentarius and the World Trade Organization*, Amsterdam: WEMOS.

— (1997b) *There is More to Say about Codex*, Amsterdam: WEMOS.

— 1998) *Codex Discussion Paper: Standard and Lobby*, Amsterdam: WEMOS.

Wennen-van der May, C. A. M. (1969) 'The decline of breastfeeding in Nigeria', *Tropical and Geographical Medicine*, 21: 93–6, quoted in Chetley 1986, p. 40.

WHO (1979) *Joint WHO/UNICEF Meeting on Infant and Young Child Feeding: Statement – Recommendations – List of Participants, 9–12 October*, Geneva: WHO.

— (1981a) 'Excerpts from the introductory statement by the representative of the Executive Board to the Thirty-fourth World Health Assembly on the subject of the Draft International Code of Marketing of Breast-milk Substitutes. Annex 3', in *International Code of Marketing of Breast-milk Substitutes*, Geneva: WHO, pp. 32–6.

— (1981b) *International Code of Marketing of Breast-milk Substitutes*, Geneva: WHO.

— (1992) *Report of the Director-General on Infant and Young Child Nutrition (Progress and Evaluation Report; and Status of Implementation of the International Code of Marketing of Breast-milk Substitutes)*, Geneva: WHO, Doc. WHA45/1992/REC/1, quoted in Shubber 1998, p. 110.

— (1998a) *HIV and Infant Feeding: A Guide for Health Care Managers and Supervisors*, Geneva: WHO, Doc. WHO/FRH/NUT/CHD/98.2.

— (1998b) *HIV and Infant Feeding: Guidelines for Decision-makers*, Geneva: WHO, Doc. WHO/FRH/NUT/CHD/98.1.

— (1998c) *WHO Round Table Discussions with Consumer and Community-based Nongovernmental Organizations*, 19 November, Geneva: WHO.

— (1998d) *WHO Round Table Discussions with the International Association of Infant Food Manufacturers (IFM)*, 20 November, Geneva: WHO.

— (2000a) *Informal Consultation on Health and Human Rights, Geneva, 13–14 December 1999*, Geneva: World Health Organization/Globalization, Cross Sectoral Policies and Human Rights/Department of Health in Sustainable Development (WHO/GCP/HSD), June.

— (2000b) 'Tobacco industry strategies to undermine tobacco control activities at the World Health Organization', *Report of the Committee of Experts on Tobacco Industry Documents*, Geneva: WHO, July.

WHO/UNAIDS/UNICEF (1998) *Technical Consultation on HIV and Infant Feeding: Implementation of Guidelines*, Geneva: WHO/UNAIDS/UNICEF.

WHO/UNICEF (1982) *Infant and Young Child Feeding: Notes on the International Code of Marketing of Breast-milk Substitutes*, Geneva: WHO/UNICEF, quoted in Chetley 1986, p. 119.

— (1993) *Breastfeeding Counselling: A Training Course*, Geneva: WHO/UNICEF.

WHO/UNICEF/UNAIDS (2000) *HIV and Infant Feeding Counselling: A Training Course. Trainer's Guide*, Geneva: WHO/UNICEF/UNAIDS.

Wilcox, D. L., P. Ault and K. Age (1989) *Public Relations: Strategies and Tactics*, New York: Harper & Row.

Wilkinson, A. (1999a) 'ASA rejects Nestlé appeal over baby milk ad', *Marketing Week*, 15 April: 5.

— (1999b) 'Cause or concern: with Nestlé in the spotlight again over its advertising tactics, and the McLibel case back in the courts, companies are facing increasingly stiff ethical demands from consumers. Amanda Wilkinson examines how cause-related marketing and practices can repair reputations', *Marketing Week*, 11 February: 28–31.

Willat, N. (1970) 'How Nestlé adapts products to its markets', *Business Abroad*, June: 31–3, quoted in Palmer 1993, p. 230.

Willets, P. (ed.) (1982) *Pressure Groups in the Global System*, London: Frances Pinter.

— (1998) ' Political globalization and the impact of NGOs upon transnational companies', in J. W. Mitchell (ed.), *Companies in a World of Conflict: NGOs, Sanctions and Corporate Responsibility: Papers from a Workshop Organized in Oslo by the Royal Institute of International Affairs*, London: Royal Institute of International Affairs, Energy and Environmental Programme and Earthscan, pp. 195–226.

— (1999) 'The United Nations and civil society', in Foster and Anand (eds), pp. 247–83.

Williams, F. (1998) 'The voice of business heard around the world: how outgoing President Helmut Maucher got global institutions listening to the once fusty International Chamber of Commerce', *Financial Times*, 29 December.

Williams, F. O. (ed.) (2000) *Global Codes of Conduct: An Idea Whose Time Has Come*, Notre Dame, IN: University of Notre Dame Press.

Winter, M. and U. Steger (1998) *Managing Outside Pressure: Strategies for Preventing Corporate Disasters*, Chichester/New York/Weinheim/Brisbane/Singapore/Toronto: John Wiley & Sons.

Women's Feature Service (ed.) (1998) *Measuring the Immeasurable: Planning, Monitoring and Evaluation of Networks*, New Delhi: Women's Feature Service.

World Bank (1992) *Governance and Development*, Washington, DC: World Bank.

— (1997) *World Development Report 1997: The State in a Changing World*, Washington, DC: World Bank.

WSJ (2000) 'Editorial: formula for disaster', *Wall Street Journal (WSJ)*, European edition, 6 December.

Yamey, G. (2000a) 'Nestlé accused of breaking international code', *British Medical Journal*, 320 (7233), 19 February: 468.

— (2000b) 'Nestlé violates international code, says audit', *British Medical Journal*, 321, 1 July: 8.

— (2000c) 'Unicef accused of forming alliance with baby food industry', *British Medical Journal*, 321 (7254), 14 July: 132.

— (2001) 'The milk of human kindness: how to make a simple morality tale out of a complex public health issue', *British Medical Journal*, 322, 6 January: 57.

Zyman, S. (1999) *The End of Marketing as We Know It*, New York: HarperCollins.

Index

Zed Titles on Transnational Corporations

Zed Books publishes extensively on globalization and modern capitalism. An increasing number of its titles focus specifically on the workings of transnational corporations.

Sharon Beder, *Selling the Work Ethic: From Puritan Pulpit to Corporate PR*

Walden Bello, Nicola Bullard and Kamal Malhotra (eds), *Global Finance: New Thinking on Regulating Speculative Capital Markets*

Ricardo Carrere and Larry Lohmann (eds), *Pulping the South: Industrial Tree Plantations and the World Paper Economy*

John Madeley, *Big Business, Poor Peoples: The Impact of Transnational Corporations on the World's Poor*

Hans-Peter Martin and Harald Schumann, *The Global Trap: Globalization and the Assault on Prosperity and Democracy*

Judith Richter, *The Regulation of Corporations: Business Behaviour, Codes of Conduct and Citizen Action*

Amory Starr, *Naming the Enemy: Anti-Corporate Social Movements Confront Globalization*

Keith Suter, *Curbing Corporate Power: How to Control Giant Corporations*

Peter Utting (ed.), *The Greening of Business in Developing Countries: Rhetoric, Reality and Prospects*

David Woodward, *The Next Crisis? Foreign Debt and Equity Investment in Developing Countries*

For full details of this list and Zed's other subject and general catalogues, please write to: The Marketing Department, Zed Books, 7 Cynthia Street, London N1 9JF, UK or e-mail:

sales@zedbooks.demon.co.uk

Visit our website at: http://www.zedbooks.demon.co.uk